Second to Home

Ryne Sandberg
opens up

Ryne Sandberg
with Barry Rozner

Bonus Books, Inc., Chicago

99   98   97   96   95   5   4   3   2   1

Library of Congress Cataloging-in-Publication Data

Sandberg, Ryne.
    Second to home: Ryne Sandburg opens up / Ryne Sandberg with Barry
Rozner.
        p.   cm.
    ISBN 1-56625-040-4
    1. Sandberg, Ryne.   2. Baseball players—United States—Biography.
3. Chicago Cubs (Baseball team)   I. Rozner, Barry.   II. Title.
GV865.S2A3   1995
796.357'092 B —dc20   95-6434
                                                              CIP

Bonus Books, Inc.
160 East Illinois Street
Chicago, Illinois 60611

Typesetting by Point West, Inc., Carol Stream, Illinois
Printed in the United States of America

To my family,
for your never-ending
love and support.
—Ryne Sandberg

In memory of my mom.
In honor of my dad.
—Barry Rozner

Contents

Acknowledgments

Words are not enough to express my gratitude, but please accept these simple thanks.

To all my friends at Bonus Books, whose sweat made the blood and tears worthwhile. To my *Daily Herald* colleague Dean Spiros, whose experience and wisdom proved invaluable. To Tom Nance for a striking cover photo. To the Cubs' media relations staff, and to Brian Hanley, for your timely tip-ins.

To my parents, Marvin and Gloria, the greatest people I've ever known, to whom I owe everything. To the memory of my sister Andrea, who encouraged me to read more and play less hockey; and to my brother Jay, who encouraged me to read less and play more hockey (he never mentioned the part about keeping my head up in the corners).

To Amy, my wonderful wife and best friend: Happy birthday, happy anniversary and whatever else I missed during the long months I spent locked in my office. She works harder than anyone I know and even if the world doesn't appreciate teachers like it should, I appreciate her every moment of every day.

And finally, to Ryne Sandberg, who'd rather have his teeth drilled without Novocaine than talk about himself; for his patience, honesty and generosity; and for reminding us all that being a decent human being still has its rewards in this world.

—Barry Rozner

Foreword

When I heard the news that Ryne Sandberg had retired, it was probably the most shocking moment in my 50 years of broadcasting baseball.

I just couldn't understand why a guy in his physical condition would walk away in the prime of his career. Ryno had at least five very productive years ahead of him if he'd wanted to stay.

But after reading his story, I understand why Ryno left baseball, and so will you by the time you're finished with this book. You'll see the frustration so clearly that you'll no longer wonder why Ryne Sandberg quit at the young age of 34.

I saw Ryno from the beginning. In fact, Ryno, myself, Dallas Green and Tribune Co. all joined the Cubs at the same time and a lot has happened to all of us since 1982. It's been a very interesting era in Cubs baseball, with a lot of ups and downs.

But during that time, Ryne Sandberg established himself as the greatest second baseman who ever played the game of baseball.

I saw them all. I watched Red Schoendienst, Bill Mazeroski, Bobby Doerr, Jackie Robinson and Joe Morgan, and there's no doubt in my mind that Ryne Sandberg is the best.

He could simply do more than any of the rest of them. If you look at every category, Ryne Sandberg is either No. 1 or No. 2 in every single one of them, and you can't say that about the others.

Ryno could hit for average and he could hit for power. He could field and make the double play better than anyone. He covered so much ground that rarely did he ever even have to dive for a ball. He also had as strong an arm as you'll ever see at second base.

And don't forget his speed. Ryno stole more than 300 bases, and he went from first to third and second to home as good as anyone.

I've often tried to think of a category in which he wasn't first or second among second basemen, but you can't find one. I think the only guy who comes close is Joe Morgan, but Sandberg hit as much as he did and was far superior defensively.

What I personally enjoyed about watching him play was that he was so smart on the field. He's a guy who you never saw make a mental mistake on the baseball field.

They tell a story about Joe DiMaggio and how he never once got thrown out going from first to third. That's how I feel about Ryno. I can never remember him making a mistake like that.

Until I saw Ryne Sandberg, I was sure the greatest player I ever saw was Stan Musial.

I saw 25 years of Musial's career and he was one of greatest stars in the history of the game. But there were weaknesses in his game. As an outfielder, he didn't have a strong arm because he hurt it while he was still a pitcher.

But with Ryne Sandberg, there isn't one single thing connected with baseball that he didn't do exceptionally well.

It's really amazing when you think about it.

I can say this truthfully: I never saw a ball player I admired more than Ryne Sandberg, and to me that puts him on the same level with Stan Musial.

On top of all of that, Ryno is a true gentleman who is just as he appears to be. People come up to me all the time and ask me what Ryne Sandberg is really like, and I say, "He's just what you think he is." He's a good-hearted and affable man who never thought he was too important to speak with anyone. He's a shy guy who minded his own business and asked people to do the same for him.

To me, he seemed like the type of guy who enjoyed playing the game and never cared much for all of the acclaim and the stardom that accompanied his career. Unlike so many others, he disdained the spotlight.

Like Musial, he was a leader, but not by false bravado or yelling. He led by example, with his work habits and his level of consistent excellence. His preparation and dedication was not to be matched by anyone else in the game. In later years, he led with his friendship and by taking young players under his wing. And in 1989, despite tremendous pressure, he put the Cubs on his back and carried them to the playoffs.

The only people who ever said anything bad about him, I think, were the ones who were jealous of him, because there was little or no room for criticism. But when you're at the top as long as Ryno was, people will always find reasons to take shots at you. That's an unfortunate fact of life. In my mind, however, he was nearly perfect on and off the field. He was a true professional in every sense of the word, and a role model for adults and kids alike.

It takes a special man to walk away from $16 million, and it takes a unique individual to leave when he still had so much ability. That's the kind of person he is.

I always considered myself to be nothing more than a fan of baseball, and as a fan I thoroughly enjoyed watching Ryne Sandberg play 13 years for the Chicago Cubs. His time was shorter than a lot of fans had hoped, including myself, but the truth is baseball was lucky to have him at all.

We shouldn't be saying we wish we had more. We should just be saying, "Ryno, thank you for being you."

— Harry Caray, Hall of Fame, 1989
January 1995

Second to home

"If you're not having fun doing what you're doing, no matter what it is, then it's time to do something else. If you respect yourself, like Ryne Sandberg does, then money has nothing to do with it."
—Frank Thomas, Chicago White Sox

I never imagined a day would come that I wouldn't want to play baseball. During the seasons I wished would never end, I couldn't have dreamed there'd be a time I'd want to leave the game I loved so much.

But that's exactly how I felt when I awoke the morning of Saturday, June 11, 1994.

I didn't expect it and I didn't plan it, but when it happened, there wasn't any doubt. I couldn't make myself play baseball another day.

The fire was gone, and shortly thereafter, so was I. Since the day I retired, there's been speculation and rumors about why I walked away. There's been talk of every imaginable personal problem anyone could dream up — and they did dream them up.

You can't believe the rumors I heard. Some of them were sickening, and some of them quite funny. No, I didn't have AIDS. No, I wasn't hired by NASA (I hate flying). No, I wasn't running off to join the circus. And no, I wasn't going to play point guard for the Phoenix Suns. I had just had enough of baseball and I wanted to get back to Arizona to be with my kids. But I guess when you surprise people, they just can't accept it for what it is. They have to invent things. There were reasons I quit that you've never heard before. I'm confident you'll understand these reasons by the time you finish this book, but my marital situation was not one of them.

Millions of people have personal problems, but they don't quit their jobs because of them, and neither did I. I quit because I didn't like my job anymore.

I always took pride in being able to prepare myself for the game no matter what the conditions were around me, or in my life. I played through three deaths in my family during 17 years of pro ball, and only missed a couple of games. I grieved, but in my own way. And one of the ways for me to get back on track was always to play the game.

When I had personal difficulties, I played through them for years when nobody knew, so that was not a factor. The truth is my personal situation had nothing to do with why I announced my retirement from baseball on June 13, 1994, almost exactly 17 years from the day my professional career began.

The reason I retired is simple: I lost the desire that got me ready to play on an everyday basis for so many years. Without it, I didn't think I could perform at the same level I had in the past, and I didn't want to play at a level less than what was expected of me by my teammates, coaches, ownership, and most of all, myself.

Why did I lose the fire? Well, that answer is not at all simple.

My career began with pure joy and ended in pure misery. When I woke up on that Saturday morning, I didn't have the normal feelings that I always had on a game day. The adrenaline wasn't there. The nervousness wasn't there. All my usual feelings on a normal game day were absent.

The competitive feelings that I counted on so heavily in my mental preparation were gone as well. Normally the first thing I would think of when I woke up on a game day was who the opposing pitcher was and how I would bat against him, but those thoughts weren't there.

Amazingly, the only thought I had was of retiring. Suddenly I couldn't stomach the idea of playing another game. Not one more.

It started long before then, but I started hammering the final nail in the coffin in January of '94 when I decided I was going to retire at the end of the 1994 season. It was then that I began to lose my ability to prepare mentally, which was born from a desire to play the game at a high level of excellence.

The true professionals will tell you that once you lose that fire, you're a goner.

I started off 1994 well, and had a good first six weeks or so, but my focus had gotten steadily worse over the weeks before I quit. I'd be driving to the ball park from Lake Point Tower and I'd look out at the people on the beach and see them enjoying themselves in the water and in the sand. Families were fishing and cooking out and boating and playing together.

The drive down Lake Shore Drive used to be a time to prepare for the game and enjoy the view, but in the summer of '94 it stood for all the things I wanted and couldn't have.

On that Saturday, I woke up a little earlier than usual for a day game, about 7:30 a.m. I didn't sleep much Friday night at all. I went to bed expecting to play the next day, with no idea of what was to hit me in the morning, but I tossed and turned all night. I was very uncomfortable.

Once I was up, though, it hit me instantly. I thought about it for just a short time, maybe 15 or 20 minutes, and after I collected my thoughts, I knew I wanted to retire immediately. All I wanted to do was get to the ball park and tell our manager, Tom Trebelhorn, right away what I was thinking.

I showered and got dressed and didn't have a normal breakfast. I always ate a big breakfast before day games, but this day I wasn't thinking about a game or food. I hardly ate a thing.

I was nervous driving to the park. I was also a little bit scared, but even with those feelings there wasn't any hesitation. I wanted to get there early enough to tell Treb before he could post the lineup card. I knew I wouldn't be in the lineup, but he didn't know and I didn't want it to be a scratch, because then people would've asked questions. Besides, it's not proper baseball etiquette to show up and see your name and then get scratched. It's not fair to the manager and not fair to the guy who has to get ready to play in your spot.

I walked into Treb's office about 9:30 and closed the door.

"Can I talk to you for a minute?"

"Sure," he said. "What's on your mind?"

I hesitated for a second before speaking. I was still nervous and scared to say it. I knew I meant it, but I didn't know what the response would be.

"Um," I started quietly, head down. "I think I'm planning on retiring."

Treb just looked at me. He didn't even blink. After a second or two, he kind of shook his head as if to wake himself up and said, "What do you mean?" I think he was wondering when because this would have a bit of an impact on him, too.

"Well, I'm thinking about retiring today."

"Oh," he said, looking more dazed. "Really? Today? What's going on, Ryno? What's this all about?"

I explained that I just couldn't approach the game the way I had the last 17 years. I told him it didn't feel right going out there in the frame of mind I'd been in for the past two months.

"I thought something was bothering you," Treb said. "You haven't been yourself lately."

Treb and I and a couple of coaches had been playing golf together a lot on the off-days, so he'd gotten to know me a little bit better and he was seeing two different guys. There was one Ryne Sandberg on the golf course who was laughing and joking and having a good time, enjoying life, and the other Ryne Sandberg in the clubhouse, who was miserable and depressed.

He thought about these things while we were talking and I guess it started to come together for him and make some sense.

After a minute of silence, Treb nodded, and said, "You know, Ryno, you're really a heck of a guy."

And suddenly, I felt confident again. It made me feel good that he was beginning to understand the situation and respect my decision. Fortunately, he didn't try to talk me out of it.

"What can I do to help?" he asked.

"Well, I don't think I should be in the lineup today. I have some phone calls to make, but beyond that I have no idea what to do next."

"I'll look into it," he said. "Relax today and come see me again first thing tomorrow morning."

I didn't know what the procedure was so I wondered how quickly it could be done. I watched Saturday's game from the bench and went home to make some calls. I hadn't told anyone but Treb. When I woke up on Saturday, I made the decision without talking to anyone, so after the game I talked to my wife, Cindy, and the kids and a couple friends, and then called my agent and good friend, Jimmy Turner, who immediately flew in from St. Louis and spent the next two days by my side.

We stayed in Saturday night and I did a lot of thinking. I felt good because I'd started the process and Treb had been very supportive, but it was tough because I wanted to get it over with.

It took two months of baseball for me to get to a point where I realized I was not the same person, but Treb could see how I'd arrived there.

I'd decided before spring training that I would call it quits after the year, and I told my family that. With my children, Lindsey and Justin, being only six and eight years away from college, I was really worried about missing their childhood.

And the game was also starting to wear on me. The aches and the pains and the traveling and the kids growing so fast all started adding up about January, but I felt obligated to play one more year and I wanted badly to get into the World Series before I retired.

Obviously, that wasn't going to happen in 1994.

On Sunday morning, I went back to see Treb in his office.

"Still feel the same?" Treb asked.

"Definitely. It's what I want. How do I go about doing it?"

"Well," Treb said, "I think we have to go see Larry Himes." Larry Himes was our general manager and about the last guy I wanted to see, but we arranged for a meeting and went up to see him. I told him everything I had told Treb and Larry was surprised, obviously, and didn't really know what to do either.

He didn't show it, but I'm sure he was happy. During our three years together, he did a lot of things I didn't like, and over the last year or two of my career I had been pretty critical of him in the press.

He'd taken over a club that was a player or two away from contending for a title, and completely dismantled it. He ripped it to shreds right before my eyes. I don't know if he ever had a plan, but if he did, I'd like someone to explain it to me.

He got rid of a lot of very good players, who also happened to like being Cubs and wanted to stay in Chicago. When I retired, only Mark Grace and Shawon Dunston were left from the day Himes took over the operation, which was only two and a half years before, and that was a young team only two years removed from a division title.

I saw him treat players like Greg Maddux and Andre Dawson with no respect whatsoever, until they had no choice but to leave, and I saw him trade a lot of players like Paul Assenmacher, who was as decent and loyal a teammate as you could ever hope for. I saw him lose so many quality players, like Rick Sutcliffe, Joe Girardi, Dwight Smith, Bob Scanlan, Chuck McElroy and Doug Dascenzo, and get nothing in return. I saw him fire front-office employees without ever giving them a reason why, and I watched him fire Jimmy Lefebvre as manager after he led us to only our third winning record in the last 22 years. I saw him hurt a lot of people, and I spoke up about it.

Maybe it isn't just the Cubs, but many of the players today don't seem to respect the game or each other anymore. In the clubhouse, I'd hear more talk about money than about who was pitching that day.

It was misery walking into our clubhouse every day, and by the middle of June I couldn't take it anymore.

He didn't say it, but I'm sure Larry was happy to have me gone because of my public comments. He'd also boxed himself into a corner with his payroll because of some bad decisions, and now this would free up some salary for him. The day after my retirement press conference, there was a picture of him in the papers with a big smile on his face, and that picture said a thousand words about how he felt.

Well, that's one thing we had in common: We were both happy I was leaving the game, but that's probably the only thing we ever agreed on.

Larry certainly didn't try to talk me out of it. I guess I didn't know what to expect because I didn't know if he even liked me. We didn't have much of a relationship, but then he didn't seem to have a relationship with anyone on the team except the players he brought in, like Sammy Sosa.

It made for a very tense clubhouse because Himes would walk through and say hello to just one guy, Sammy, and walk right past everyone else. It seemed like he had a grudge against almost the whole team, even though almost the whole team was his. It was strange, to say the least.

I definitely wasn't one of his, and when I signed my last contract with the Cubs, Larry had nothing to do with it. The talks had broken off and the deal was dead until Stan Cook stepped in and kept me with the Cubs.

But now I was retiring and Larry didn't know what to do, so he got Cook, the Cubs' chairman of the board, on the phone. Like Treb, Cook was very supportive. After we talked a while, he summed up everything he thought I meant to the Cubs and thanked me for everything I had done for the franchise.

Right before we ended our conversation, Cook said, "Ryne, it's quite an honorable thing you're doing."

You know, the first thing on everyone's mind was that I was walking away from the $16 million left on my contract, but that was the last thing on my mind. Cook understood that I was doing what I felt was right for me and my family, and I wouldn't hang on just for the money.

Now with his support, too, the nervousness was leaving me and I was feeling pretty good about the way it was going. I was getting the support I was hoping for, and now it was just a matter of when and how to make it official.

I watched the game from the bench again on Sunday, but it was uncomfortable because I knew people would start to wonder why I was skipping two days in a row. I felt like maybe the cameras were on me a little bit more, and thought the announcers might be trying to figure out why I was sitting out again.

I might get a day off once a month during a normal season, but never two in a row. Except for 1994 when I retired, 1987 when I missed a month with a severely sprained ankle, and 1993 when I missed a month with a broken hand, I averaged 156 games a season during my 13-year career with the Cubs.

So I was uncomfortable Sunday, since I wasn't hurt and the Cubs didn't make any announcements. I was in a slump and Treb did a good job of keeping everyone off the trail by saying I was watching for a day or two to get a different perspective. That was true, anyway.

After the game, I tried to get out of the clubhouse as soon as possible without running into anyone, and that made me uncomfortable, too, because that wasn't my style.

We set up the press conference for noon Monday, but I was anxious. I would've liked to have had it on Sunday and gotten it over with. I just wanted noon to come as soon as possible.

I spent Sunday night thinking about what I would say, and that was easy because it was all on my mind. Still, it was another long, sleepless night.

My wife, Cindy, flew in on the red-eye from Phoenix, and we got a few minutes sleep early Monday morning when I got a wake-up call at 6:30 from Cubs broadcaster Ron Santo.

"Ryno, is it true?" Santo said. "It can't be true. You can't do it."

"It's true," I said. "I'm retiring."

Ron tried to talk me out of it, but he didn't know all the things that were going through my mind. It was pretty funny, though, because I was totally out of it at 6:30 and I was trying to explain to Ron why I was leaving baseball after 17 years. But finally he accepted it and said he'd see me at the press conference.

Five minutes later, the phone started ringing and all of Chicago called for the next five hours. So much for sleeping. Now it was just more waiting.

We listened to the radio a little and watched some TV and people were speculating like crazy. Some of it was pretty pathetic, but like I said, people can't seem to accept the truth when it's so simple.

After pacing for a couple hours, I showered, put my suit on and set out for Wrigley Field for the last time as an active player. It was 11:45 a.m.

I wanted to get everything off my back and off my chest, put the rumors to rest and fly home to see the kids, but the morning seemed to take forever.

While pulling into the players' parking lot at Wrigley Field, I realized it was almost over and I started to get nervous again.

Cindy and I walked slowly down the concourse to the Stadium Club, but after we got up the stairs, I got a little shaky and had to go into the bathroom and compose myself.

As you're probably well aware, I never liked speaking engagements much, and making matters worse, I was getting emotional, something I rarely let happen in public. On the field, I rarely lost control of my emotions. I felt it was disrespectful to the other team, and that I had to stay in control to perform at my highest level. But when I walked out into the crowd at the press conference, I was a little bit overwhelmed by the number of people and the cameras and the lights. I think it was live on all the radio and TV stations in Chicago, and ESPN and maybe CNN, too. I was surprised at all the people because I didn't think it was that big of a deal.

It seemed like everyone I had known in the Chicago media over 13 years was there, and all the familiar faces made me feel better.

"It looks like everyone's here," I said with a laugh. "Thanks for coming."

That drew some chuckles and I relaxed a little. I simply said what had been on my mind all weekend. I thought I did OK, but I was emotional and I choked up a couple times.

It was hard to believe that the day had come. Every player wonders when his last game will be, and it dawned on me in the middle of that press conference that it was over for me. As ready as I was to leave, it was a little hard for me to believe I'd never put on a Cubs uniform again.

Truthfully, I never thought a day would come that I wouldn't want to play baseball. For 17 years I woke up every morning with goals and dreams and, most importantly, adrenaline. Now it was gone. Just like that.

It was a tough press conference, but I was relieved to finally be done with it and I felt great. I did separate interviews with almost everyone there and it took about three hours.

I was totally drained, but I felt reborn.

We walked back through the concourse underneath Wrigley Field, and it was very quiet. Very peaceful. I went into the clubhouse and shook hands with a few of the guys, who were getting ready to fly to San Diego. Outside the park, I stopped to sign some autographs, like I did after every game at Wrigley Field.

And as I drove back to Lake Point Tower I watched the people on the boats again. But now, I thought to myself, I can be one of them.

I loved the game of baseball and had some of the greatest times of my life in the game, which really was my life for 17 years. I'm so grateful that I was able to play in the great city of Chicago and for the best fans in the world at the best ball park.

I'm fortunate to have had some great teammates, coaches, managers and friends in my 13 years with the Cubs, and I'm grateful to Tribune Co. and the Cubs organization for all they did for me. The ending may not have been happy, but the beginning and middle was awesome, and for that I thank everyone who helped me along the way. I can tell you honestly I never imagined that my career would end this way, but then again, when I left Spokane, Washington, 17 years before, I never expected to play 13 years in the majors.

2 **I did it my way**

"I think with Ryno, what you see is what you get. He goes about his business and doesn't bother anybody. He talks to you when you talk to him. He's also the best bleeping baseball player I've ever seen. What else do you need to say?"
—*All-Star first baseman Mark Grace*

Some say that my retirement was a condemnation of baseball in general, and more specifically, the Cubs as an organization.

That's true to some extent. Certainly there's no getting around the fact that baseball changed significantly from the time I signed out of high school to the time I retired. The Cubs also changed dramatically from the day I arrived in 1982 to the day I left in 1994.

I feel like I missed my baseball generation by a decade or two. I would've loved playing in the days of Pete Rose and Willie Mays and Mickey Mantle. I would've loved those Cubs teams of the late '60s with Ron Santo and Ernie Banks and Billy Williams. Players from that era loved the game and gave everything they had to the game. They played for their teammates and because they were proud of their uniforms. And teams often were kept together for a decade or more.

When I first joined the Cubs in 1982, and for my first eight or 10 years in the big leagues, there was still a lot of that feeling, but by the time I retired there was little, if any, remaining.

In the end I was caught between two generations: The one I came up with, which still cared about the game; and the one I left behind, which hardly cared at all.

In the '90s, I saw too many guys having fun after losses if they got a few hits or did something good for themselves. That didn't appeal to me at all.

There's a lack of respect today for the game and for each other. When I was a young player, we respected the veterans and were intimidated by them. As a veteran, I didn't feel that the young players had that same respect for the older guys or the game in general.

My approach was always that I felt fortunate to have been given the opportunity to play professional baseball, with the chance that I might someday make it to the majors. And when I was given the chance to play in the majors I took advantage of it. I put in a lot of hard work and struggled a lot and was completely dedicated to the game for 17 years; maybe even dedicated to a fault. I missed out on a lot of leisure and personal time because of my dedication, but I don't know any other way I could've done it.

My work habits got better as the years went on and I got to the point where I felt I had to go to spring training earlier each season.

Most young players today won't come in early or go for that extra work unless a coach tells them to. That's odd, too, because so many of them can't execute the fundamentals. Part of the problem is that there are too many teams and some players are rushed up to the big leagues before they're ready, but another part of it is the lack of desire to practice.

When I was coming up I knew what I had to work on because I could feel it. Players went to coaches and asked for extra work. I don't see that work ethic today. I'm afraid that they think it's easy because they've already made it to the majors.

And today they don't talk about baseball the way we did. They talk about their years of service and arbitration status, not who's pitching tomorrow. Even on the bench between innings I'd hear them talk about contracts or spending money.

I'd come in off the field in Montreal at the end of an inning and I wouldn't hear the young guys talking about the game. They'd be talking about what suits they saw on St. Catherine Street that day. In New York, it wasn't whether Doc Gooden had his best stuff that day. It was the sales at Bloomie's and Macy's.

That's something about the game that hasn't changed for the better.

I played for the love of the game and the enjoyment that came with winning. If that sounds funny, then you don't understand the era I came from. You can laugh if you want, but it's true. We played because we loved the game. It just so happens that with success in baseball comes money. The fact is the game pays well and I feel lucky to have been in a situation where I could make money and support my family. I was just lucky my whole career when it came to contracts. It was a great opportunity and I'll be eternally appreciative to baseball and to the Cubs for always looking after me and my family.

I love Wrigley Field for so many different reasons. I can certainly relate to the importance of tradition and I respect its substance and consistency.

As a player, my consistency is one of the things I'm most proud of. That's why the expectations that followed the signing of big contracts never bothered me. That goes with the territory and my expectations would go up like the fans' expectations did. But the bottom line is I knew what I could do and I just concentrated on playing good baseball.

When it was time to talk contract, my only concern was stability for my family and myself. Knowing where I'd be for a long period of time was more important to me than the value of the deal.

A couple of years after all the contracts I signed, I ended up making less than my so-called "market value," but I never cared about that. That was frequently a topic of discussion, but you never heard me complain about being underpaid and you never heard me say the word "re-negotiate." Throughout my career people said I was underpaid. Until, of course, I signed my last contract and then everyone said I was overpaid.

But if I really cared about the money, I wouldn't have walked away from $16 million and I'd still be playing baseball today. The dollars were never the most important part of a contract to me, maybe because of the way I was brought up.

I grew up in a lower income family. We weren't poor, but we weren't middle class, either. Before every school year, I'd get one pair of tennis shoes and a pair of dress shoes. Even if we grew during the year, that was all we'd get. It's something I always remembered, so when money was discussed, I turned that over to the business people. All I worried about was the length of the deal, and in that regard I was always very happy.

Another way I could've made bundles of money during my career was by doing endorsements, but I was really picky about that and kept it to a minimum. I did some things I thought would be easy and fun, and not take a lot of time away from my family or workout time.

I had a short relationship with Chevrolet after the '84 season, and that was easy because it was shot during spring training and I didn't really lose much personal time. For the most part, though, I stayed away from endorsements and people always thought that to be strange.

I'll admit, what people will pay you for a little work on a commercial is a staggering amount of money, and the hourly rate just for showing up somewhere is incredible. A big name can get $20,000 or $30,000 for a personal appearance or card show, but my time with my family was worth more to me than money during my career.

The way I pictured my career was like this: I wanted to work at baseball on my own time in the off-season, and then during the season play the game, put everything I had into it and go home after the game.

At home I could guard my privacy carefully, and Cindy and I did that as much as we could. I just wanted to be with my family, and I didn't think that just because of who we were we had to live some outrageous life that I've seen some players live.

I was very comfortable at home or in our neighborhoods, playing Whiffle ball with my kids and their friends. I'd speak at my kids' schools and I was referred to more as "Lindsey and Justin's dad," than I was as "Ryne the baseball player." That's the way it's supposed to be.

I just wanted my kids to live as normal a life as possible, and I tried hard to make that happen.

I'm basically a shy person and never enjoyed being in the spotlight, but it doesn't mean I hesitated to go to a movie or go to the store or go walking downtown, because I did do those things.

I didn't lock myself in the house because if I'd never been seen, it would've made life more difficult when I did leave the house. I made sure I was always visible and approachable, and the people in Chicago and Phoenix got used to that.

The fans in Chicago are very knowledgeable when it comes to their athletes. They read and learn about them and care about how they treat them. So when I was walking downtown I'd get a lot of handshakes and waves and horns honking, or maybe a few autographs, but never a crowd that got out of control.

I feel bad for Michael Jordan because of his total lack of privacy. If he walked down Michigan Avenue or just stopped to put gas in his car, the police would have to be out there directing traffic. That's a rough way to live.

I never had that problem. If I was doing an appearance for charity or something, I could just walk right in past everyone and do my thing. I'd sign a few autographs and shake a few hands and when I left, I'd walk right back through the crowd. I felt like I could blend in. I never had a limo or an entourage, and I certainly never caused a scene by the way I acted or dressed, because I was always very casual.

I got some good advice after the 1984 season from Larry Bowa and John Vukovich. Larry was a veteran player of 15 big-league seasons, and Vuk was a coach who always tried to look out for me and cared about me.

After I won the MVP, they said, "You had a great year, but be careful. Don't change. Don't change anything about yourself. Stay the same."

They'd seen players have success and gain some popularity and then change who they were — rarely for the better. It was good advice and it stuck with me.

I never wanted my private life to become a part of my public life, and at least until I retired I was able to do that. But a dramatic change occurred during my career in the relationship between the media and players.

There was a time, not so long ago, when the media covered the games and wrote about what occurred on the playing field, but it isn't that way any longer. A man's private life isn't just his private life anymore and that's a shame. It was disappointing when court records of my divorce became a public discussion and a media event. The same reporters I had gotten along with so well and had always been so honest and truthful with, didn't believe what I had said at my retirement press conference.

Suddenly, according to some, I hadn't retired because I missed my kids and had lost my desire to play. They decided I retired because of my marital situation.

Certain writers speculated and tossed out hearsay. There was one article in a Chicago paper that talked about a possible reconciliation, which was totally wrong, and the writer questioned my reasons for retiring. He didn't call me and ask me about it. He just tossed out phrases like "sources said" and "friends say," and it infuriated me. I had always been honest with the media, but the payback from a select few was the speculation that I hadn't retired for the reasons I said. And some gossip columnists dreamed up some of the sickest rumors you could ever imagine.

Those things hurt me. I honestly don't understand how a human being could print lies about another person and sleep at night. And what do they really gain from it?

It hurt me, and it surprised me. Throughout my career, I got along with and enjoyed working with most of the media people. I'm aware of the fact that 99.99 percent of them treated me exceptionally well. For that, I am also grateful, and I still hold them in the highest regard. But I guess no matter what the business, you'll find a few who'll always look for the negative even when there isn't any, and I won't blame an entire industry for the sick actions of a few.

The truth is, when I retired I missed my family terribly. That, combined with my utter disgust with the Cubs organization at the time, robbed me of a desire to prepare mentally and perform physically.

All of those things go hand in hand.

My wife, Cindy, and I had gone through some rocky times throughout the previous year, and that certainly didn't help my frame of mind. We were just like a lot of other married couples in America.

But to the best of my knowledge at the time I retired, everything was fine. When I left the Cubs on June 13, 1994, Cindy and I were together. I had no idea that would change.

But it had nothing to do with my retirement. I don't know how to make that any clearer.

We split up about 10 days after I returned to Phoenix, but I didn't know that was in the cards. It also didn't change, in any way, what I had done and why I did it. I still had no desire to play baseball, and I still wanted to be home with my children. I wanted to get on with my life. That's what I've done.

Nothing that I said at the press conference or in the weeks and months following my retirement has changed.

I wanted to be home with my kids and that's exactly what's happened. I get to see them as much as I want and several nights a week I cook them dinner and tuck them in bed at night. I'm doing fine with them.

I'm just another statistic now, but I think Cindy and I have done as good a job as two people can do in this situation. We remain friends, communicate daily, and are trying to help each other as much as possible.

Cindy's house is very close to mine, and we plan to keep it that way so the kids won't have to learn new schools or make new friends or change their after-school activities. The kids are doing well and we're all coping as well as can be expected. It doesn't mean it's not difficult. We were married 15 years and for a long time very much in love. I'm sorry that it's over, but it's a part of life that we have to accept and deal with now.

I left baseball for a lot of reasons, but my divorce was not one of them. I didn't even know it was going to happen. If that's too simple for some people to accept, that's too bad. It's the truth.

Besides, look around your office or your neighborhood and you'll see that 50 percent of the people have gone through the same thing. There were players on the Cubs when I quit who had been divorced or were going through it. You don't see people quitting their jobs because of it — and neither did I.

All I ever wanted was to play baseball. I didn't ask for any of the things that went along with it, like the money or the fame or the glory. I just wanted to play and have fun. I loved being a professional and I loved associating with people who were professional. I'm not talking about pro athletes necessarily, but anyone who took their jobs seriously, whether it was the umpires or ushers or journalists or anyone who worked hard and acted professionally. That's what gave me a rush.

I loved playing hard on teams that played hard and against teams that played hard. That's what the whole deal was for me. It's what I lived for.

I thought I could give back to the fans by showing up and playing hard every day. I think the fans accepted that. The fans never asked me to be someone I wasn't.

I tried never to bother anyone and minded my own business. The game, the way it was taught to me, was simple and pure: You gave your best to the game and it gave back to you in the form of pride and pleasure.

From the day I broke into pro ball to the day I retired, it was often said that there weren't a lot of people who knew me very well. I guess that's basically true. It doesn't mean that I'm not blessed with many friends. I'm very fortunate in that regard.

But it's true that I've always kept things to myself. I've kept my private life private and not even my closest teammates ever really knew what was going on in my head, because I preferred to handle things on my own. Everybody deals with things in their own way, and that was my way. Some of it might go back to when I was a kid, and my dad used to tell me: "Keep your mouth shut and keep your eyes and ears open. You might learn something."

I was always aware of what was going on around me, like in the clubhouse or any room full of people. I liked to watch the room because you can learn a lot about people that way. But sometimes if you talk too much, you get distracted and might miss something. I know a lot of people thought I was quiet, but it didn't mean that I didn't know what was happening.

The important thing is to go with what works for you, and being reserved was what worked for me. I didn't plan it that way, but that was me. I don't think I hurt anyone by being that way, but I guess people always hoped for a little more.

I couldn't be like Rick Sutcliffe, for example. He was a true leader, well-spoken, who knew how to handle the media. And I couldn't be like Mark Grace, who looks and sounds great every time he's interviewed.

Sometimes the press criticized me for not being more of a leader in the clubhouse or more vocal or more exuberant, but I never understood that. What was I supposed to do, throw chairs around the room? Over the years, I saw guys do things that weren't natural for them, and they lost track of what they were supposed to do on the field. I felt like I had enough to do just worrying about myself, making sure I took care of myself and did my job, and I would've been uncomfortable forcing my help on someone else.

In some ways I did become more of a leader as I got older, but it was a natural progression. I didn't have to change my personality. As a veteran, younger players looked up to me and asked me questions and I was happy to help. If a player asked me to keep an eye on him for a week and see what he was doing right or wrong, I'd watch and give him my opinion. And I was never as quiet as the public perceived me to be anyway, but I was quiet around new people, in new situations, or when I was preparing for a game.

I always had butterflies before games, even at the end of my career. When young players would ask me about being nervous, I tried to explain to them that it was OK and actually a good thing. That's when the adrenaline was flowing and the nerves were working and I knew I was ready to go. When I didn't have those feelings the day I decided to retire, I knew something was wrong because it had never happened before.

It wasn't something I showed on the outside. My demeanor was very consistent, so my teammates or the fans might not have known how nervous I really was, but I was always exactly the same before every game I ever played.

That goes back to high school sports and grade school piano recitals. In fact, there was one piano recital just before Christmas every year and for the month of December I'd be a miserable, nervous wreck. But once the day arrived, I'd do a good job and be proud of what I did.

And I was always nervous before games — not like those piano recitals — but I liked to keep to myself and get mentally prepared for that day's game.

I didn't go around kicking tables and chairs, but when I got on the field, I didn't kick too many grounders, either.

Leadership comes in a lot of different ways. Like me, Andre Dawson hardly ever said a word, but he sacrificed his body and played hard every day. He was the epitomy of leadership. I saw guys get very emotional when they watched what Andre went through to prepare for a game, suffering with his knee problems. He was an inspiration just by being himself, so throwing chairs and yelling isn't necessarily the answer. I was criticized for not doing more, but I'll guarantee you if I had done more, there would've been guys criticizing me for being a clubhouse lawyer.

They would've said, "He thinks because he's an All-Star or makes all that money he can tell everyone what to do." You can't please everyone, so the best thing you can do is be yourself. That's what my parents instilled in me and that's what I did.

It also doesn't mean I didn't get mad, because I've thrown my share of bats and helmets and coffee cups. It just didn't happen

too often. Usually I kept it locked up inside me. Poor Tom Trebelhorn was the recipient of one of those outbursts. He was our
manager in the spring of '94 when we finished a week of split
squad games with a weekend series in Las Vegas. At that point I
had played nine innings about five days in a row and that's a little
unusual for spring training, since you don't want to peak a month
before you start a 162-game schedule.

My back was killing me, my legs were sore, it was March 13
and I was ready to break camp. There was only one problem:
There were three weeks of spring training left.

I came off the field after one game muttering something
about it being the middle of July and then destroyed a whole shelf
full of coffee cups and tossed a couple helmets.

I did occasionally get mad at myself, but I rarely showed it on
the field because I didn't think it was right. It's really a matter of
self respect and respecting your opponents and coaches and teammates.

Since I retired, friends of mine in the game have told me that
there were teammates who were jealous of me and tried to find
things wrong with my game near the end of my career. All I can
say is that I gave everything I could to the game, the best way I
knew how, and when I couldn't give at a level appropriate for me
anymore, I walked away.

This won't exactly shock some people, but I wasn't the best guest
speaker you could possibly hire. I had a little success and I guess I
was supposed to be able to go to banquets and talk about it, but I
didn't have the advantage of a college education like a lot of people did. I got used to the media after a while because I was forced
into doing it every day, but to go speak in front of 5,000 people,
that just wasn't my idea of a good time.

But with my friends and in the locker room and on the field
and on the bench, I was a different guy.

I was a closet practical joker, but nobody ever suspected me so
it usually got blamed on Sutcliffe, who everyone thought was the
biggest prankster. I was the last guy they suspected, so I could get
closer to my victims without being detected.

I used to crawl up behind trainer Tony Garofalo in his office and yell "look out" or something to scare the daylights out of him. I got him so often and made him so jumpy that he was afraid to turn his back when I was around. I preferred, actually, to instigate and give someone an idea. I'd say, "Hey, this is a perfect time to get that guy," and the guy I told would say, "You're right." Then I'd sit 10 feet away and watch while someone else got in trouble. But I was pretty quick myself with shaving cream in a guy's socks or nailing his shoes to the floor or giving him the hot foot. Anything to have a little fun. I used to raid a player's locker and put whatever I could find in the freezer. Sometimes it'd be his glove or his shoes or his hat. I got Shawon Dunston a lot with that and he always suspected me, but he never had any proof.

I liked to have fun when it was the right time and place. I mean, playing baseball was fun and it was a kids' game, and I felt like a kid sometimes.

To me, that's what baseball was all about.

From Montana to Mesa

"Ryne Sandberg could've been one of the great three-sport stars in college history. Not many guys can make that transition from football to basketball, and then basketball to baseball. But he had the perfect body for it."
—Washington State baseball coach BoBo Brayton

I was born Ryne Dee Sandberg on Sept. 18, 1959, in the beautiful town of Spokane, Washington. The youngest of four children (three boys), I was named after Yankees pitcher Ryne Duren (the "Dee" is an abbreviation for Duren).

My parents, Derwent and Elizabeth, had seen the reliever pitch for the Yankees in the World Series the year before and liked the name because it was different. After Duren saved a game, they saw his name in the headlines and couldn't resist the temptation.

They were average sports fans and didn't go to many games, but they saw that one on TV, wrote down the name and it stuck with them until they gave it to me.

It's worked pretty well for me, and I guess for Duren, too. The first time I met him was in a Phillies minor league camp when I was about 18 years old. He was there to talk about alcoholism and what it did to his career. I'd heard his name for so long and knew he was a baseball player, but I couldn't believe it when he was right there in front of me.

I went to him afterward and told him how I'd been named after him. We spoke for a minute and that was the end of it until I met him again in the late '80s. But this time he came up to me. He said it was kind of funny how the tables had turned.

I still have the ball he signed that read: "To Ryne Sandberg from the first Ryne, Ryne Duren."

I think he was kind of saying that the name has been good for both of us since I made it to the majors.

Six of us lived on my dad's income as a mortician. My oldest brother was Lane, who passed away in 1992, and then it's my brother Del, my sister Maryl and me.

My mom was also a full-time registered nurse for most of my years growing up, and I'm sure that paid for some of our baseball, football and basketball shoes.

But we didn't think about what we didn't have. We just took what we had and made something out of it.

Del and I made up a game using a plastic golf ball we found and a skinny old fungo bat. We'd pitch to each other for hours at a time, day after day in the front yard. It was tough to hit because the ball would break about three feet on a curve and rise on a fastball. We had a great time and it didn't cost a penny. (The neighbors who got the golf balls through their windows might disagree.) But that helped me learn how to hit.

Another thing we had was each other. We had a lot good times together on family vacations, fishing and camping, and that was as much fun as you could have as a kid.

I learned most of my baseball early from my brother Del — who, naturally, was named after Phillies outfielder Del Ennis. He played a big role in my pursuit of a major league career.

Del was five years older than me and I kind of followed in his footsteps. I hung around with him, playing street games with him and his buddies. They were a lot older, but the competition was good for me and that's probably the biggest reason I advanced so quickly in so many different sports. If I wasn't with Del, then I'd find some way to practice on my own. I used to throw a golf ball against the stairs leading up to the house. It was a sort of solitaire pinners, and it was great for practicing agility and reflexes because I never knew where the ball was going.

Fortunately, I had a lot to work with. I was given a good athletic body with good size, good foot-speed and overall natural ability.

I also worked hard from the time I was in about third grade, playing sports 12 months a year.

My parents weren't great athletes. My dad bowled a little and my mom played field hockey as a youngster, but the fact that I had the competition with my brother and his friends made a difference.

Del was a heck of a baseball player and was looked at by a lot of scouts in high school, but he ended up going to a junior college and then played second base for Washington State, which went on to a College World Series while he was there.

But Del felt like scouts never took him seriously once he went to college, and that was on my mind when I was getting college offers to play three sports all over the country in the summer of 1978.

I was an All-America quarterback at North Central High School in Spokane and made the *Parade* magazine team in 1978. But I was also all-state in baseball and all-city in basketball.

I made some recruiting trips for football to Washington State, Washington, Nebraska, Oklahoma and Arizona State, but Washington State was only an hour south of Spokane, and that looked like the place to be.

They all wanted me to be a quarterback and play baseball, too, while somehow finding time to study. Some schools even talked about three sports.

During that last winter when I was still playing basketball, I was taking college trips, trying to make it back for games and practices, while attempting to study, too. Plus, I was leaving home for the first time ever on these trips, flying in planes for the first time, and needless to say, I was just a tad shy.

I was feeling the pressure big time, but I developed an ability to play without letting all the outside influences get to me. When I was on the field or court, I shut it out and performed well. That's something I got to be pretty good at. I used my time on the court to get away from things and enjoy myself.

But I wanted to pick a college, because the mail was nonstop and the phone was ringing off the hook and I couldn't take it anymore.

I needed relief, so I signed a letter of intent to play football and baseball at Washington State, and I also talked to George Raveling, who was the basketball coach at that time. Everyone in town expected me to play all three sports. The baseball coach, BoBo Brayton, and the football coach, Jim Walden, would call frequently to talk and all of Spokane was yapping about it: North Central star going to Washington State. You know, hometown boy makes good.

But I was a senior in high school and this was already one of the biggest decisions of my life. I was trying to decide which sport to focus on and what classes to take and I felt like the pressure of the world was on me.

I signed the letter of intent a couple of days before the June 8, 1978, baseball draft. I hadn't graduated high school yet and I was getting ready for American Legion ball, but I was already registering for my classes at Washington State and even had a roommate.

Meanwhile, the baseball scouts were still all over the place and wanted to know my intentions. The Phillies had a scout, Bill Harper, who'd been watching me for two years, and they were hot after me. There were 14 other teams calling, too, but I scared them all off and I told everyone I was going to college.

The Phillies were going to take me in the third round, but wound up waiting until the 20th round after I signed with Washington State. They took a shot, but I don't know why because I told everyone where I was headed.

Once I was drafted, though, all the pressure was back again. Already, even at age 18, I was developing a distaste for the business side of sports. I just wanted to play. I didn't want these other parts of the deal and I didn't like the decision-making process.

I started talking with Del again, and he felt that if I really wanted to play baseball professionally and have a legitimate shot at making it to the majors, I should probably sign with the Phillies right away.

I didn't have a lot of ambition to go to college and study and try to play a sport at the same time, but to play football I'd have to go to college. With baseball, there was another option: turning pro.

Back in those days, baseball teams wanted young players out of high school. That's when you got the most attention as a baseball player. Once you got to college, your chances were slimmer of getting to the minors. And in the minors, at least you'd get a lot of coaching and teaching and an opportunity to improve.

Del had gone to college and didn't get that chance, so he had me leaning toward turning pro and signing with the Phillies.

The pressure was unreal, because everyone wanted me to go to Washington State, from my parents to everyone in Spokane to the whole state of Washington. For a city of 350,000 people, Spokane is a pretty close-knit community, and the expectations were very high.

But eight days after the draft, on June 16, 1978, I called the Phillies in to make an offer — and I accepted it. I shocked everyone, including the Phillies.

If it were today, I would've done it differently and gone to Washington State. Today, a college player can still get drafted and work his way up, and you also get started on that college degree. My only regret is that I never got a degree.

I don't recommend that anyone pass up a chance to go to college because even though it worked out for me, 99.99 percent of the players never make it to the majors, and you're better off in college with a degree to fall back on. My choice to sign with the Phillies not only meant I wouldn't go to college, but it also meant I'd be leaving the house I lived in my first 18 years. What I didn't know is that I'd never really make it back.

I spent the next 17 years in professional baseball, which turned out to be half my life when I retired at age 34.

The day I signed with the Phillies I had an American Legion game that afternoon and went to sit on the bench with the guys and watch the game. I told them what I did and they couldn't believe it, but they wished me luck and sent me on my way.

It wasn't unlike a game in June some 17 years later, almost to the exact day, when I sat on the bench at Wrigley Field the day before I announced my retirement. No one could believe that, either.

I left immediately for Helena, Montana, which for me was like going into the army. In reality, it was where the Phillies had their Rookie League team for players that had just been drafted or signed as free agents.

Only 10 days earlier I'd been sure I was going to Washington State in Pullman, only 60 miles from home. Now I was going to Helena with no place to live, no car and no idea where I was going, and I'd never been away from home in my life, except for a couple of recruiting trips. All I had was the address of the ball park and a couple of phone numbers.

I ended up finding a garage to live in, which was about all I could afford on a $500-a-month salary. I had no bathroom or kitchen or lights or anything. I used the facilities in the house when the guy living there was out of town, and I borrowed a desk and lamp and wrote a lot of letters to my parents.

I was lonely and homesick and living in a garage. Welcome to minor league baseball.

Before a ball player ever makes it to the top, he earns very little for four or five years in the minors, sometimes while supporting a family. And only 1 in 200 ever makes it to the big leagues.

I was given a $24,000 bonus when I signed with the Phillies, and that's what I lived off of for a couple years in the minors. It's something I never forgot, and it's probably part of the reason why I've always been pretty conservative when it comes to finances.

So the garage in Helena was my home for my first summer in pro ball, and I walked two miles each way to the park every day.

There was only one place to eat breakfast in town and all the guys would go there. One morning I sat with a kid from the Dominican Republic who couldn't speak much English, and I helped him order from the menu. I had taken two years of Spanish in high school and that came in handy a lot during my pro career.

Oh, the kid I helped order an omelette? His name was George Bell, and we became pretty good friends that year and had a lot of fun together. The thing I remember most about George was having to run out onto the field all the time after he charged the mound. George started a lot of fights that year, and we learned important lessons on how to handle ourselves in bench-clearing brawls.

George went on to become a three-time All-Star, MVP and one of the best clutch hitters I've ever seen. That year, however, Ryne Sandberg and George Bell were just two scared kids a long way from home and an even longer way from major league baseball.

I had a pretty good year at Helena, hitting .311, but my talent was very raw. I had played shortstop in high school but I didn't know the basic techniques, like the crow-hop (a quick, two-step movement to get your feet under you in preparation for a throw). I just threw it flat-footed with a quick release.

In the spring of 1979 I went through my first spring training in Florida, and made the move from Rookie ball to Class-A.

I met Dallas Green for the first time that spring. He was the Phillies' farm director and it was his staff, specifically scout Bill Harper, that drafted and signed me. I spent my summer in a place called Spartanburg — as in South Carolina — and that might as well have been the other side of the world for all I knew.

As was often the case during my years in the minors, I was lonely and scared. So when my high school sweetheart, Cindy White, came to visit me in Spartanburg, I wouldn't let her go back to Spokane.

We didn't like being apart and this time we'd been a whole country apart. We lived together for about three or four weeks and I wasn't really comfortable with that, so we got married two weeks later and didn't even tell our parents until afterward.

The wedding took a day to plan and it was a real big production. It took about 15 minutes at the justice of the peace. The

manager, Bill Dancy, was there with about five of the guys and
their wives. That was it, but that's how you do it when you're in A-
ball. You get married at 11 a.m. and play a game that night.

We found a cheap apartment to live in and immediately started dipping into our college funds. It was all we had to live off of,
but it was nice to have someone to be with and someone to share
the experience with.

The spring of 1980 was a tough one for me. I expected to move up
to a higher class of A-ball and played all camp with the high Class-
A team and all my old teammates from the year before at Spartanburg. But the last week of spring training they moved me up to
Double-A, which was in Reading, Pennsylvania. It was uncomfortable for me because I didn't know anyone.

Plus, once you get to Double-A it's a much different level of
baseball. It's pretty good baseball and it's serious, so it took some
time to adjust and I got off to a slow start. It took me two or three
weeks before I got it going, and that April was the first time a
coach told me I'd never make it to the big leagues. It wasn't the
last time I'd hear it, either.

Despite those discouraging words, I made the All-Star team
and moved up to Triple-A Oklahoma City for the 1981 season.

In between the '80 and '81 seasons, I went to play winter ball for
the first time in Maracaibo, Venezuela, and it was more bad news.

I couldn't make the darn starting lineup! I went down there
and sat on the bench and took ground balls for two months.
Manny Trillo was the second baseman and Todd Cruz was the
shortstop, and I was a utility guy in winter ball! That's like being
the water boy in high school. Nothing against being a water boy,
because I never looked down on anyone. But I'm supposed to have
a major league future, and I can't even make the winter ball lineup?
It wasn't good. I didn't know what my future would be after that.

I went to Triple-A and Oklahoma City in 1981, which represented another nice step up. I had a good year, and that earned
me a September call-up with the Phillies. And though I only batted six times, I did get my first major league hit at, of all places,

Wrigley Field. I singled off the Cubs' Mike Krukow on Sept. 27, and little did I know that it would be the only hit of my major league career that didn't come as a member of the Cubs.

But winter ball in Venezuela was the same old story.

"Manny Trillo's coming here in three weeks," one of the coaches told me when I arrived. "You can play second base until then, and then we'll see if we can get you in a game after that."

They didn't.

Trillo showed up and I sat on the bench the rest of the time. It was another wasted winter ball season and I was really concerned about my future.

Those guys were out of my league. If I couldn't play in winter ball and they were that far ahead of me, I had no business thinking about the major leagues. That's not even in the same world.

At times, Maracaibo didn't seem like the same world, either. Every day I left my living quarters, the Hotel Presidente, I wondered if I'd make it back that night safely.

The people take their baseball very seriously down there, and about once a week our bus was attacked after leaving a visiting park. Sometimes they tried to tip it over, and on other nights it was just your basic stoning and rock throwing.

The buses themselves were scary, as were the drivers. One night we were returning from a game in pouring rain. Near the end of a six-hour drive, at about 4 a.m., we came upon a nasty car wreck and didn't even know it.

We always took the back roads with no lights and everyone drives very fast, so when we got to the wreck the driver didn't see it until the bus was just a few feet away. I'm not sure the driver was even awake.

All of a sudden someone yelled, "Look out." The driver hit the brakes and the bus slid into a cement overpass head on. It's a good thing we were all laying down and sleeping because we hit the seats in front of us and no one was seriously hurt. The bus was totaled and that could've been it for all of us right there.

Another bus had to come get us and that took the rest of the night, and then we just went to the park and played a game. "OK, we're here. Let's play." Like that.

It was always a good feeling to be at the ball park, too. The ushers either carried machine guns or machetes and when the players looked up at the stands from the field, we could see the American wives section totally surrounded by guards with machine guns.

One time in the middle of a game, someone set a bonfire in the middle of the left-field bleachers. It just burned until it was out of gas. No one said a word and the game never stopped.

That was winter ball — and I had a good view of it all from the bench.

After Cindy and I got back to Florida from Venezuela in early 1982, we took off from Florida, where we'd left our car before winter ball. We were driving across the country in late January on our way back to Washington, when we stopped in Phoenix to visit some relatives.

One day we took a drive for no particular reason and went over to Mesa, where the Cubs' spring training facility is. We heard it was there, so we stopped to take a look at HoHoKam Park. I have no idea why we felt the need to see it that day, but it was something we wanted to do. We got out of the car and took a look around and I checked out the field.

The very next day was January 27, 1982, and that morning I got the call that I'd been traded to the Cubs with Larry Bowa for shortstop Ivan DeJesus.

I should say, Larry Bowa was traded for DeJesus, because I was just a throw-in. I was a throw-in that Dallas Green insisted on having. It was his first major deal since becoming general manager of the Cubs a couple months earlier.

We all came in at the same time: Me, Tribune Co. and Dallas Green. It was to begin a whole new era in Cubs baseball, not that I knew anything about the previous 105 years of Cubs baseball.

Tribune Co. had bought the Cubs from the Wrigley family in the summer of 1981, and Dallas left the Phillies to come in and run the show at the end of the 1981 baseball season after three years as manager in Philadelphia.

Now I was a part of it, and I wasn't happy about it. I had been a Phillie my whole career. I was disappointed because my goal was to play for the Phillies' big-league club. That's how Dallas and everyone in the minor-league system brought up the young players. There was a pride and a tradition and there was only one goal.

But I had been traded for the first time in my life and I knew nothing about the Cubs. Being from Spokane, which is on the east edge of Washington, 300 miles from Seattle, and never being around major league baseball, I didn't know much about any team but the Phillies.

Before I played for the Phillies in September of 1981, I had only been to two major league games in my life. Both were on family vacations to Boston and Minnesota. The third game I ever saw I played in. Now I was going to the Cubs and I didn't even know who they were.

When I was in the Phillies' system, I had figured that Larry Bowa was near the end of his career as the Phillies' shortstop and thought maybe I'd step up and be their next shortstop. I'd had a good solid year at Triple-A and had some coaches tell me that I was right there, ready to step in at the major league level.

But I was always a year ahead of Julio Franco in the Phillies' system and he'd done more offensively than I did in the minors. I was a good, solid minor league player and better defensively than Franco but I guess I didn't really stand out. I didn't lead the league in homers and I didn't set records and that's what they must've looked at.

I didn't have many backers in the Phillies' system, either. Most of them rated Franco far ahead of me, except for Larry Rojas, who was my manager at Helena and later a roving, minor-league infield instructor. He always stuck up for me at organizational meetings, but he was basically alone in his evaluation.

The Phillies wanted DeJesus, who was 29 years old. He played a few years for them, but a year after they traded me, they traded Franco and they haven't really had a shortstop since. In 1982, I'd been down at winter ball where I hardly played and I guess they thought throwing me in the trade was no big deal. Actually, I was surprised they traded Larry Bowa. He was one of the best in the game at the time.

Now I was with the Cubs and Larry Bowa was still the short-stop ahead of me. I was with a new team in a new city, didn't know anyone on the team and didn't have a position to play.

There was nothing I could do except look for a place to live in Mesa and get ready for spring training.

We never did finish the drive back to Washington and Phoenix became our permanent home.

For now I was just a Cub — and I was scared.

A man without a position

> "The way he started, a lot of guys would've folded up the tent, packed it in and been sent down. But not Ryno. You could see his physical tools, but the mental toughness is something no one knew about."
> —16-year veteran Larry Bowa

Since the day I signed my first pro contract with the Phillies, I dreamed about being in major league camp. Well, now it had happened, but it wasn't with the team I had dreamed about.

I wasn't in Clearwater, Florida, with the Phillies. I was in Mesa, Arizona, with the Cubs and I didn't know which end was up. It was just a month ago that I couldn't make a winter ball team, and now I was in my first major league camp with a bunch of strangers.

Making the team was hardly on my mind in 1982, considering the fact that they didn't have a position for me. Nobody, not even manager Lee Elia, knew where I would play.

I spent some time at shortstop, third, second and center, but a month into spring training I was a man without a position — or a clue, for that matter.

Larry Bowa was the shortstop, Ken Reitz was at

third, Bump Wills at second, and the outfielders were Steve Henderson in left and Tye Waller in center. Leon Durham was still in right field because Bill Buckner was the All-Star first baseman.

I figured I had no chance to make the team. I was playing two innings here and three innings there and two innings everywhere.

My brother-in-law, Don White, came out to watch me play a spring training game and he began the day behind the wall in center field, yelling at me from behind the bushes.

From there he had a good view when a ball hit off the Green Monster in center, banged off the metal and hit me in the chest. While I kicked it and stepped all over it, guys circled the bases like it was a track meet.

"Hey, you gotta catch that ball," Don yelled after he stopped laughing. "What are you doing out here?"

Not much, so two innings later I was at second base, picking up Bump Wills, and there was Don behind first base yelling at me from over there. Next I went to shortstop and Don moved over near the third base dugout. I finished up at third base and there was Don waiting for me in the left field stands when I was chasing a foul ball. He came to watch me play and he was all over the ball park, getting as much exercise as I did.

I had three different gloves in my locker and didn't know what to think. I definitely wasn't thinking about making the team. How could I? I couldn't make the winter ball team at any position.

I was uncomfortable, too. I was around Bill Buckner and Larry Bowa, two big-time All-Stars. I had read about Larry Bowa for four years coming up through the Phillies' system and now I was on the field with him. I used to see Buckner play for the Dodgers' Spokane club when I was a kid. I was afraid to take ground balls and I was afraid to go in the locker room because I didn't feel right. I was a mess. With a week left in spring training, Lee Elia called me into his office. I thought, here we go, I'm off to Iowa — wherever Iowa might be.

"We just released Ken Reitz," Elia said. "You're our Opening Day third baseman. You're gonna play there every day from now on."

I just looked at him. I couldn't believe it. I'm thinking, I'm going to be the Opening Day third baseman at Riverfront Stadium in Cincinnati. It blew me away.

But that was the plan, so they put me on a crash course.

They had me out there every day early and every day late taking ground balls. At the same time, everything I hit was a double or a triple, and the veterans were telling me, "Save some of those hits. This is only spring training and they don't count for anything."

They didn't know how right they were.

The day after I made the club, I walked into the clubhouse and found a big No. 23 Cubs jersey hanging in my locker. I thought, whoa, this is a high number. I was thinking more like 14, which was my baseball number in high school, or 19, which was my football number.

I must've been feeling an unusual burst of confidence because I'd made the team, so I went to Yosh Kawano, the clubhouse boss who'd already been there about 50 years.

I said, "Yosh, can I get something lower, like 14 or 19?"

Yosh just looked at me as if I ought to be committed. Then, he spoke to me real slowly.

"Well," Yosh said without even looking up, continuing to darn a sock. "No. 1, Ernie Banks wore No. 14 and it's retired. No. 2, you'll wear 23."

"Oh, OK," I mumbled and walked away, tail between my legs.

Yosh didn't play that, a rookie trying to pick his own number. Yosh was older than Moses and he made the decisions around there. He'd let me know what I would wear. Some guys were convinced Yosh ran the entire Cubs operation from the 40-year-old manual typewriter he still uses today.

A few days later, we broke camp and flew straight from Phoenix to Cincinnati. I didn't know what the rules were for anything, so I brought two bags with me.

One was a suitcase, which I left in the clubhouse because the guys told me it'd be waiting for me at the hotel if I left it in there.

The other was a carry-on, hang-up bag, which nobody else had brought on the plane but me.

I was feeling a little better because I made the team and the guys were talking to me and trying to make me feel more at home, even though I was scared to death of Opening Day. When we got to Cincinnati, everyone walked off the plane, talking to each other, and I followed them to the bus. We went through some one-way, revolving security doors, and that's when it hit me.

My hang-up bag!

I turned around and went flying into the revolving doors, but they locked up as soon as I got inside, and I was trapped in the glass. Alarms went off all over the place and I was stuck in there.

It was my worst nightmare come true. I could see the headlines already: "Rookie Cub arrested for breaking into airport."

There was no one around at all because the airport was empty and the guys were all on the bus. No one saw me, and I was stuck in that thing.

I was panicking like crazy but I used everything ounce of energy I had to force the doors open, and went tearing back to the plane. When I finally got my bag and came back out those doors, the bus was just sitting there, and the engine was off.

Now I was in trouble.

I'd held up the team bus. All the veteran players were on it and I had to walk past the manager and all the coaches. All the guys in the back were yelling at me.

"Let's go, rookie," they're hollering. "Whatsa matter with you, rookie."

And now I was uncomfortable again. I had just started to feel good and now they were hootin' at me and yelling all the rookie stuff and I was really uncomfortable.

This was the night before Opening Day. It was to be the first of many sleepless nights in 1982.

The thing I couldn't get out of my mind was how three months earlier there was no spot for me in Maracaibo and now I was the Chicago Cubs' Opening Day third baseman.

That strange thought occurred to me as I made the long walk from the clubhouse to the field at Riverfront Stadium. I had to go through a damp, dark tunnel that smells worse than the clubhouse. It wasn't what I expected.

But when I walked up the stairs and onto the carpet, it was exactly what I expected — and I was in awe. There was Johnny Bench and Dave Concepcion and I went a little numb. I could've very easily stopped and gotten their whole starting lineup to sign a baseball for me. That's what I wanted to do. Those were guys I'd watched on TV forever.

As if my butterflies weren't enough, in my first game I was facing Mario Soto, who was just the strikeout leader the year before and probably the best pitcher in the league. He had a great fastball and a nasty changeup.

I batted seventh and went 0-for-3, but we were snowed out after 6 innings and got the 3-2 victory. The new second baseman, Bump Wills, homered to lead off the season, and nobody did that again until Tuffy Rhodes led off the '94 season with a dinger.

I made a couple of nice plays at third and felt pretty good about it. I mean, at least I didn't really embarrass myself. I didn't get a hit, but it was only the first game. I didn't know how good a hitter I was, but I always believed I could hit. I had hit at every level I'd ever been at, so how much different could it be?

Real different, as it turns out. I went into one of the worst slumps to start a career in major league history, going 0-for-20 and 1-for-32.

I was miserable. I was nervous. I wasn't sleeping. And it was in the papers every morning. I wasn't used to that, either. In the minors all they wrote about was the game, but in the majors a negative stat like that was going to be there every day.

"Rookie Ryne Sandberg is now 0-for-13 after going 0-for-3 Tuesday." And every day, they just added to it. It was my first real experience with the press and my first time seeing negative things about myself.

Every day I was reading about young players being sent out to the minors, and once or twice it was the Cubs doing it, so I was worried.

Then, about two weeks into the season, Lee Elia called me into his office. I thought, this is it. I'm going down.

"Ryne," Elia said, "you're my every-day third baseman and I don't want you to worry about it. We're sticking with you."

You know what? I don't think they had any choice. They didn't have anybody else. Still, it made me feel good to know I'd be around a while, and I kept playing good defense and rode out the storm.

I went on to hit .271, which wasn't bad considering how I started, and I set a club record for stolen bases by a third baseman with 32.

I also set a Cubs rookie record for runs scored with 103, which, when I think about it, is kind of amazing considering I wasn't on base the first month of the season. I don't know how I did that, but some positive things had happened for me despite the horrendous start.

I only made 11 errors in 140 games at third base and a lot of people thought I could've won the Gold Glove, but the Phillies' Mike Schmidt, another one of my heroes when I was in their system, had been at third forever and he got the award even though he made 23 errors.

I was feeling pretty good about things as we went into September. All in all, I thought, this isn't a bad way to finish and take some positive feelings into next season.

And then one day before the September call-ups arrived, I was summoned to Lee Elia's office again, where Dallas Green was waiting for me.

As soon as I saw Dallas I realized that every time I started feeling good and comfortable, something would happen.

I was right again.

"Ryne, the way that you hit the ball, and with your range, and with the type of player we think you might be," Dallas Green was saying, "we picture you as a Bobby Grich-type player. We think you can hit .275 or .280 with a little power, steal bases and score a lot of runs."

Wait a minute, I thought to myself, isn't Bobby Grich a second baseman?

In their minds, I'd shown too much range at third, and not enough power to be the ideal third baseman. In Dallas' eyes, I was playing the wrong position.

"We're going to move you to second base," Dallas said. "Tomorrow."

And that was that. The next day I played second base. My entire experience at second was a couple of weeks at winter ball, and now here I was in the major leagues and it was a new position to learn.

I'd been comfortable at third and figured that would be my position because Larry Bowa still had at least two or three more years left at shortstop. I played five months there and played well and got my offense going. I wasn't thrilled to be moving to second base but I wasn't going to tell Dallas that.

I played third one day and second the next.

Before that first game at second base, I got some of the best teaching of my career from that well-known second base coach, Billy Connors.

Yeah, that's right. I got my first real lesson about how to play my new position from the Cubs' pitching coach, who was about as agile as an elephant.

Billy is a funny guy and a good friend and he's also one of the best pitching coaches who ever lived. But on this day before my first game at second base, Billy was my second base coach, hitting me fungos at 9 a.m. and telling me what to expect.

He showed me, with that bad body of his, how to turn the double play and then jump afterward. He said the most important thing is releasing your feet after you throw.

But every time Billy tried to turn the pivot, I'd fall down because I was laughing so hard. I'll never forget watching Billy jump, but the truth is he showed me what I needed to know.

A couple of days after I started playing second, we had a game against the Phillies and one of my idols, Pete Rose, was standing on the bag.

During a pitching change, Larry Bowa went over to talk to his former teammate.

"This is gonna be our second baseman next year," Bowa said, pointing at me.

Rose sort of nodded, and said, "He'll be an All-Star second baseman."

They looked at me and I just looked at the dirt. It blew me away. I was thinking about getting his autograph and he was thinking about me going to the All-Star Game.

It's one of those things I thought about many times during my career and a moment that will stay with me forever. I still had some uneasy feelings about the move, but I figured Dallas Green must've had confidence in my ability to make the switch, and must've known what he was doing. And as I went home for the winter, I heard the words of Pete Rose over and over again in my head.

In December of 1982 we had our first child, our daughter Lindsey. Needless to say, Cindy and I were very excited because we had dreamed about having a baby and now we had Lindsey. It's the greatest understatement of all to say I never looked at my life in the same way once we had a child. It's simple, but true. From that day on, being a father was the most important thing in the world to me.

It was great being home with Cindy and the baby, but I started thinking about baseball again when I got a phone call from Larry Bowa in January of 1983. He had a new double-play partner and he had an idea.

"I'll be down the first week of February," Bowa said. "Be at the park and we'll get started."

He didn't ask me. He told me. Here was a guy 37 years old, offering to leave his home in Florida four weeks early to work with me because we were going to be partners.

I thought that was pretty cool and I was waiting for him when he got to Mesa. It was Larry, me and, of course, Billy Connors hitting us grounders for hours on end.

To the right; to the left; backhands; forehands; and double plays with Larry Bowa of every imaginable kind. I had four weeks of work in before the rest of the team was even in camp. This was good for me, because I was always a big believer in hard work, both during the season and in the off-season. I felt like the work I did ahead of time would carry me during the times when I might not be at my best.

Because of that spring, I developed a routine that I continued for the rest of my career. I would head over to Mesa from my home in Phoenix about a week before pitchers and catchers reported, and I'd take about 100 ground balls a day from that day until the end of spring training. During the season, I'd cut it down to 30 or 40, but I still took them every single day. To the left, to the right and right at me.

Routine was extremely important to me. I felt if I was consistent with that, I had a better chance to get into a rhythm and stay there, even during the times I struggled. I got into it in 1983 and never gave it up.

And going into that '83 season, I was feeling a little more comfortable about being in the big leagues. I knew my coaches and teammates and had a bit of an idea about what major league baseball was like. I was learning the cities and the ball parks, and I was breathing a little easier.

We'd finished in fifth place in 1982, so we were looking for much better things in 1983. Unfortunately, we got off to a bad start, and after one bad game at Wrigley Field early in the season, Lee Elia ripped the fans in a postgame tirade. It was pretty ugly.

Lee's a good guy but he was under a lot of pressure that season. It was his second year and the team was still not doing well. The new regime wasn't producing quick results and the media and fans were pretty hard on Dallas and Lee. Dallas had made some big promises and some remarks about a "New Tradition" when he came in, but so far the new one wasn't any better than the old one.

There were still only about 8,000 fans a game early and late in the season, and sometimes in the middle. It was that way when I got my one hit in Wrigley Field with the Phillies in 1981, and that way most of 1982 and 1983. That's the only way I knew Wrigley Field.

When Lee blasted the fans, it was out of frustration. A lot of guys were worried he'd get fired because of it, but actually, he didn't get fired until August — and it hit me pretty hard. It was my first experience seeing a manager get fired, although it was something I'd have to get used to. Lee was only my first of 11 managers in 13 years.

The thing is, it's never the manager's fault when a team doesn't win. It's the 25 guys who don't perform for him, and I always felt responsible when a manager got fired. Any player worth a darn felt the same way. I took it personally, as if I hadn't done enough.

Lee was very emotional when we said good-bye to him and I wished I had done more to help him.

Charlie Fox took over to finish the season. Because of the way we played, it wasn't a very pleasant ending to the '83 season. We finished fifth again with a 71-91 record, two games worse than the year before.

Offensively, I slipped from 1982. One thing you always hear in baseball is that once a pitcher has been around the league for a year, the hitters learn him and adjust.

Well, the same goes for hitters. I'd been around a year and in 1983 the pitchers were adjusting to me. Now it was time for me to think about adjusting because the pitchers were finding more ways to get me out.

I did, however, win a Gold Glove at second base, becoming the first National League player ever to win one in his first year at a new position. I was very proud of that. It was my first of nine straight, but I'll probably remember it more than any of the others.

Pete Rose's prediction hadn't come true yet about me being an All-Star, but now I was a Gold Glover and beginning to feel like an established major league player. It didn't feel right, though, because the team wasn't winning, and I had never been part of a losing team before in any sport.

I sure hope, I thought to myself as I flew home for the winter, that next year is a lot different for us.

5 **The "Sandberg Game"**

"Ryno was as tough as nails, but he never
caused trouble and he played every day
and kept his mouth shut. In some ways, I
think he didn't get the respect he
deserved because he didn't promote
himself and he didn't say much."
—*Former Cubs GM and manager Jim Frey*

There were a lot of questions going into the 1984 season. We were in store for a new manager and I was a little anxious to find out who it would be.

After the '83 season ended, Dallas Green went out and got Jim Frey. The only thing I knew about him was that he managed Kansas City to the World Series in 1980. That was the same World Series in which Dallas managed the Phillies to a championship.

I went on the Cubs Caravan in January, speaking in towns all over the Midwest. Three or four groups went to different cities, and I ended up on the same minibus with Frey, Thad Bosley and Scott Sanderson.

My first impression of Frey was that he was one of the funniest guys I'd ever heard speak. He was great at the luncheons and dinners, and I was thrilled with what I heard on the Caravan. A sense of humor is so important in baseball because the season is too long to be serious for every minute of every day, and Jimmy Frey could make me laugh like almost nobody else.

At the same time, I was really pleased by his positive attitude, so I liked him right away.

He had some good ideas he wanted to implement, and I found his optimism starting to rub off on me. Going into spring training I was feeling good.

In the spring of '84 came the turning point of my career—and it all began during a card game.

Frey, third base coach Don Zimmer, pitching coach Billy Connors and spring training coordinator Jimmy Snyder used to get together every night at the Mezona Hotel in Mesa to play pinochle.

One night Frey started talking about me, and he asked Jimmy Snyder, who knew me from the Phillies organization, why I never tried to pull the ball.

"Let me ask you something," Frey said to Snyder. "I'm watching this kid and every time he gets a 1–0 or 2–0 count he gets a base hit to right field. You've known him for a long time, why doesn't he hit it over the fence once in a while?"

"He's not a home run hitter," Snyder said. "That's not the kind of hitter he is."

They went back and forth with that discussion for a while until Frey got angry. He started yelling and stomping around and telling Snyder he was wrong. Everyone was already on edge because the team looked so bad and that night tempers flared.

"I'll tell you something right now," Frey screamed. "He's going to hit for power. You'll see what kind of a hitter he is. This guy's going to hit home runs."

In '83, I collected just 37 extra base hits and 48 RBI. Scoring runs and stealing bases seemed to be the focal point of my offense, but Jim Frey saw a guy who was 6-foot-2 and hitting ground balls every time he came up to the plate.

So it was after a couple of spring training games that Frey stopped me as I came in off the field after yet another ground-out.

"Ryne, it looks to me like you're trying to hit everything on the ground and run as hard as you can to first base," Frey said. "Is that any fun, doing that four times a game? I think you're either gonna get tired or pull a hamstring going down to first base."

Well, I had good speed and that's the way I'd been taught in the minors. I'd been told to keep the ball on the ground and use my speed to leg out some hits.

"But Ryne," Jimmy said in that great voice of his, "you're gonna be tired by June if you do that every time. Wouldn't it be fun to hit the ball out of the ball park once in a while and jog around the bases?"

I hit a total of 15 homers my first two years, so that sounded pretty good to me.

"That'd be great," I said. "How do we do that?"

"Come to the park early tomorrow," Frey said. "We'll go to the cage, just you and me."

So the next morning we had a private session. I didn't know at the time that he had made great strides with hitters like George Brett in Kansas City and Darryl Strawberry in New York. I just knew he wanted me to hit for power.

We had a one-on-one batting clinic in the cage beyond the right field fence at HoHoKam Park early the next morning, and for three more days after that. Jimmy would soft-toss me some balls, while trying to get me to open up and really pull the ball, as if to pull it foul.

After that, we'd go out to join batting practice and he'd stand behind the cage and say, "OK, for the next 10 pitches, try to hit that tarp in foul territory over there."

The rolled-up tarp was about 30 feet foul next to the left field stands, about 40 feet past the third base bag.

"I want you to hit that thing every time," Frey said. "Line drives right at it. Open up, and pull it right there."

I just listened to everything he told me and tried to do whatever he asked. I wasn't thinking anything one way or another.

I was taking a whole new approach and it was really more mental than physical. I had to learn to open up and be quick with the bat and hit that inside pitch, but the key was knowing when to do that.

On the very first day I tried it, I hit a home run, and when I came in off the field Jimmy gave me a big hug. For the rest of spring training, I'd look over at Jimmy before certain pitches and with certain counts, like 1–0 or 2–0. In the spring, the manager sits on a folding chair outside the dugout, so we could communicate with each other rather casually while I was at the plate.

Now even on 3–0, I'd look over at him and he'd nod at me as if to say, "This is your pitch." I used to take that pitch and try to coax a walk, or at the most hit it back up the middle for a base hit. But now Jimmy had me thinking, "Hit it out of the park."

I did hit some homers that spring, but in general I just hit the ball a lot harder and into the gaps quite a bit. The pitches that used to give me trouble the first couple of years—like the hard sinkers and fastballs inside—I was now hitting down the line, into the left-field gap or through the hole between short and third.

I was able to get to pitches on the inner half of the plate that I couldn't get to before, and I was still going with the ball to right field when it was pitched outside. So I was getting more plate coverage and was able to hit to all fields.

It was a big change for me, but I had no idea what was coming. I was still working extra hard and still felt like I had to prove myself, so I was taking nothing for granted.

While I had a pretty good spring, the team had a pretty lousy one. The Cubs hadn't made the playoffs since 1945. After we went 7–20 in spring training, it didn't look like 1984 was going to be the year the streak ended.

It was a mess. Mel Hall and Dick Ruthven got in a fight on the field, and Charlie Fox and Bill Buckner got in one off the field. We lost 11 straight at one point and finished with the worst spring training record in Arizona. It was hideous.

But on March 27, we made a trade that changed the entire season. Dallas Green sent pitcher Bill Campbell to the Phillies for Bobby Dernier and Gary Matthews.

It was huge because we needed a center fielder and leadoff man, and Dernier was both. And Matthews gave the team a new attitude, something else we needed. He was very positive and very aggressive.

The "Sarge" was always optimistic. Just his presence brought the team together. He'd sit around before a game talking to one guy about the pitcher we were facing, and before you knew it, there'd be 10 of us in a circle talking baseball. That started the first day he showed up. He was a true leader.

I have to give Dallas Green a lot of credit because Bobby Dernier was somewhat unproven and if the Phillies had known what he could do, they probably would've kept him. But Dallas, being the former Phillies farm director, had some insight because he watched him throughout the minors.

Me and Bobby D. were teammates in Reading (AA) and Oklahoma City (AAA), and we always batted 1–2 in the order with a lot of success.

So we began the '84 season with Matthews in left, Dernier in center and a platoon of Keith Moreland and Mel Hall in right.

When they moved me to second before the '83 season, they traded for Ron Cey, and he was our third baseman. Bowa was at short and Jody Davis was the catcher.

We did have a difficult situation after the trade because they moved Leon Durham from the outfield to first base, and that meant there was no place for Bill Buckner to play. Billy Buck was a great hitter and had a lot of guts. He played on some terrible ankles with a lot of pain for a long time. He was also very popular with the fans.

And for a veteran as good as he was to sit on the bench, well, it was rough on him. He could've made it difficult on us, too, but instead he handled it with a lot of class and dignity. When we opened up in San Francisco April 3, he was rooting for us as we won the first two games of the season against the Giants.

We scored 16 runs in two games, and all of a sudden that trade a few days before had given our offense and morale a big spark.

Personally, I was having success with my new batting style and hit a couple of homers on that first West Coast trip.

Meanwhile, Bobby D. and I picked up where we left off in the minors a couple years before. It seemed like every day he'd lead off the game with a walk or a hit, and then I'd get a hit and it'd be first and third and nobody out, with Matthews, Durham, Davis, Moreland and Cey coming up. We had the lead every day.

Dernier and I worked so well together that Jim Frey gave us the first seven innings of every game to do whatever we wanted. We had our own signs and if there was nothing on from Jimmy, we put on our own play.

If Bobby gave me the sign he was stealing, I might fake a bunt or crowd the plate or do something to give him a better chance. We had hit-and-run and bunt-and-run and run-and-hit plays we did on our own. We had a nice little game going within the game, which was a lot of fun.

Offense was definitely not a problem, but our pitching was not quite there yet. And on May 25, we got one of the pieces to the puzzle when Dallas traded Buckner to the Red Sox for Dennis Eckersley.

It was a heck of a deal by Dallas, because everyone knew we had to trade Buckner, and at the same time we got a great starter in Eckersley. I was happy for Buck because he was still a great hitter.

Buck's probably more famous for his error in the '86 World Series, which the Red Sox lost because of poor pitching in Game 6, not the error. But most people probably don't realize that he played more than 20 years in the big leagues and posted some big numbers, like 2,700 hits and 1,200 RBI.

In any case, he had some happy years in Boston ahead of him and we were happy to have Eck.

That wasn't the end of it, though. A couple of weeks later, on June 13, Dallas made the trade of the year. He sent Joe Carter and Mel Hall to Cleveland for Rick Sutcliffe, George Frazier and Ron Hassey. We already had some good starting pitchers in Steve Trout, Scott Sanderson, Rick Reuschel and Dick Ruthven, and a strong bullpen with Lee Smith and Tim Stoddard, but now we had Eckersley and an ace named Sutcliffe.

When that deal was made, it sent a message to everyone that we were trying to win it right now. We were in first place by a game-and-a-half and Dallas was telling us to go out and win it.

We knew Joe Carter was a can't-miss prospect. He was having a monster year in the minors at Iowa, but we got another true leader in Sutcliffe. Another gamer, like Gary Matthews. All the guys Dallas seemed to get were guys with good work habits who wanted to win and knew how to win, and Sut was another big piece of the puzzle.

It started to feel like something special was happening.

When I came to the park on June 23, I was already having a pretty good year. I had an 18-game hitting streak from April 24 through May 16, during which time our son Justin was born (May 6).

It seemed like every time something good happened to me, like my son being born or seeing the kids when they came to town, I'd go on a tear. And after Justin was born I was on cloud nine. I missed one game the day he was born, but then I went out and won my first Player of the Week award. I was unconscious.

So by the time June 23 rolled around, I was already among the league leaders in hits, doubles, triples, runs scored and slugging percentage, but there's no way I could've predicted what would take place on that Saturday against the Cardinals at Wrigley Field.

We'd lost six of eight and looked bad doing it, so the game wasn't supposed to be on national TV. But when the primary game was rained out, the Cubs and Cards were live on NBC across the country.

We were a game-and-a-half out, there were 38,000 people at Wrigley Field, and it was against the Cardinals—which was always a big deal.

The Cards jumped out to a 7–0 lead as Willie McGee hit for the cycle. But we battled back to within 9–8 after eight innings, and all of a sudden it was one of the most exciting games I'd ever been involved in.

We were still down a run, and I was already 3-for-4 with 3 RBI, when I came to bat in the bottom of the ninth. But the Cards had the best relief pitcher in baseball, Bruce Sutter, waiting for me to lead off the inning.

As I was getting ready to leave the dugout, a couple of the older guys gave me a hint. They said he had a great split-finger fastball, which acted like a forkball, and it would come down and in hard to a right-handed hitter.

At the same time, NBC's Bob Costas was announcing Willie McGee as the Player of the Game, because with Sutter on the mound, three outs were a mere formality.

As I walked to the plate, I thought, nobody expects me to hit this guy, so I have nothing to lose and everything to gain. I mean, if he gets me out, well, everyone expects that.

In 1982 and 1983, guys like Sutter had an easy time with me. I couldn't hit those hard, down-and-in pitches. But Jim Frey's program had me in a different frame of mind. I was hitting those pitches because I was looking for them, opening up quickly and swinging inside. That aggressive style was working for me the first couple months of 1984, and it was just what I was thinking when I went to the plate against Sutter.

"Open up and swing inside," I said quietly to myself as I stepped into the box. "Open up and swing inside."

Sutter always pitched out of the stretch, and I was still thinking those words as he set himself and delivered. And I'll be darned if the pitch wasn't exactly in the spot where Jim Frey had taught me to look.

I opened up and swung inside and...Boom!

It was gone off the bat and I knew it. I took off toward first as if it might go off the wall, but I knew it was gone and I was instantly numb.

It was a line drive into the left field bleachers and the game was tied up at 9–9. I reached second base but I couldn't even feel my feet. I was floating on air. Wrigley Field was up for grabs. I could hear the fans, sort of in the distance, but I was in a fog. I was there, but I wasn't really there.

I hit third base and our third base coach, Don Zimmer, was as excited as I'd ever seen him. Zim gave me a high-five and hit me real hard on the back. When he did that, I knew it was something special. And as I crossed home plate, I could feel the ground shaking.

I got back to the dugout and it was awesome. I don't remember ever feeling that great during a baseball game before. The guys were hugging me and jumping on me and I guess I didn't understand what a big deal it was, but I was starting to get the message.

It was one of those moments where you'd look at it on tape after the game and not really remember even being there. It was too incredible.

But the Cards stopped our celebration and grabbed the lead back in the 10th. It was an 11–9 lead and they still had Sutter for the bottom of the 10th. Once again, it looked like we were finished.

There were two outs in the bottom of the 10th when Bobby Dernier kept us alive by getting on base, and that left it up to me. I can't tell you how many fastballs I saw that year because of Bobby D., but this time I didn't know what to think.

They were rolling the credits on TV as if the game was about to end, and why not? St. Louis had Bruce Sutter on the hill, and at the time he was unhittable. For seven years, he had been the most dominating relief pitcher in the history of the game, and I had already touched him for one home run. Another was impossible. In his nine years in the majors, no player had ever hit two homers off Sutter in one game. Probably not even in one month.

And as I walked to home plate again, I could hear the crowd start to cheer in the background and I could see the people stand up. I knew what they were thinking, but I wasn't. I was trying to concentrate and figure out how Sutter would start me out this time.

Last time, he went with his bread-and-butter, that nasty split-finger on the first pitch. I didn't think he'd make the same pitch, but then again, it was his best pitch and 99 times out of 100, it was unhittable.

Again I was thinking, I have nothing to lose here. I stepped into the box and decided I'd try to open up quick again and pull the ball. Maybe he'd throw me the same pitch and I could pull it into the left-field corner for a double. That would score Dernier and I'd be in scoring position as the tying run.

Sutter went into his stretch, and paused. "Open up," I said quietly. "Open up fast."

Sutter delivered and it was the same pitch in the exact same spot. Identical.

Boom!

It was gone again. It was a line drive that cleared the left-center field wall by about 10 feet and landed in nearly the same spot as the first—and the fans were diving for it before I even reached first.

The game was tied again, now at 11–11, and I thought they would tear Wrigley Field down.

I peeked at Sutter this time, after I rounded first base, because I noticed his reaction. He was disgusted and he let everyone know it.

I floated around the bases again, kind of in shock. It was almost an out-of-body experience. I got another huge high-five from Zim, and by the time I got to the plate, half the team was on the field waiting for me and it was nuts. I thought we might get in trouble for celebrating on the field. I thought you weren't supposed to do that until the game was over.

The guys were jumping on me and high-fiving me to the point where my hands hurt. We were acting like we had won the pennant already, and the game wasn't even over. The fans were screaming at the top of their lungs and I was stunned by what was happening.

Finally, in the 11th inning, Dave Owen—who was a fine utility player for us—singled with the bases loaded to bring home a run and we won the game 12–11.

I was in the dugout when we won it, and I ran out on the field with the rest of the guys. I was in awe of what had taken place. "I can't believe what I did today," I muttered to myself, over and over again.

All Willie McGee did that day was hit for the cycle, but NBC awarded me the Player of the Game after my second homer off of Sutter.

I had gone 5-for-6 with 7 RBI, but had no idea what had really taken place. I didn't know we were on national TV and I didn't know how much the Cubs meant to Chicago yet.

For the rest of my career, fans would come up to me and ask me about "The Sandberg Game." I don't know how Bruce Sutter felt about it, but it changed my life forever and took my career to a whole different level.

When I came to the park on June 23, I was just 24-year-old Ryne Sandberg, Chicago Cub. When I left that day, I was Ryne Sandberg, national celebrity—whatever that meant. And much more importantly, the Cubs were not the lovable losers from Chicago anymore. For the first time in decades we were a real baseball team, and the country knew it. Better yet, the Cardinals, Phillies, Mets and the rest of the National League knew it. We were for real and the Eastern Division was ours for the taking.

Something about that game seemed to give us the confidence and the respect we'd been lacking. We had it now, and we were on a mission.

6 ◆ "Baby Ruth"

**"Ryne Sandberg is the best baseball player
I've ever seen in my life. He's Baby Ruth."**
*—St. Louis manager Whitey Herzog on
June 23, 1984*

Immediately after the "Sandberg Game," I ran back
onto the field and over to the visiting dugout for a
postgame show on a St. Louis radio station. I got the
feeling something had changed because there was a
big ovation and it seemed like no one had left the
park.

I was still stunned while I was doing the interview,
and I could hear the fans chanting, "MVP, MVP, MVP."
I have no idea what I said, but I was barely conscious so
I must've sounded completely out of it.

I ran back to our dugout and had to tip my cap
again, and when I got in the clubhouse, there was a big
group of media people waiting. I still wasn't used to the
idea of spending half my day with the press, but now I
had no choice.

Our clubhouse was loud, and the feeling was suddenly one of a winner. We felt like we couldn't lose and

the excitement after that game was like we'd won the pennant. We carried that feeling with us for the rest of the year.

After every victory, guys would be jumping around and high-fiving, and we never came down off that high.

For me personally, Jim Frey's tutelage and those two pitches from Bruce Sutter were the turning points in my career. The shock of it lasted through the night and I was in awe of what had occurred.

Most importantly, that one game took me up to a level of play that I'd never been to before. After I had accomplished that, I felt like I had to continue to play at that level and I believed that I could.

It also brought me national attention. The next Saturday I did a pre-game show with Joe Garagiola before the "Game of the Week." I won another Player of the Week and my first Player of the Month award.

Before that weekend I was a distant third in the All-Star voting behind the Dodgers' Steve Sax and the Padres' Alan Wiggins with only a couple weeks of voting left to go. But in the final week, I passed them both and got the starting nod at second base for the National League.

Not only was it my first start, but it was my first All-Star Game and the Cubs were only a half-game out of first at the break.

I still didn't understand what a big deal the Cubs were nationally, but I started to get the idea when I was mobbed by the media at the All-Star Game in San Francisco. It was around that time that I started to find out that the Cubs hadn't been in the playoffs in 39 years. It was all news to me. No one ever talked about it in '82 or '83 because we were never in the race.

There was early talk of MVP at the game and I was a little taken aback by the attention. While I was thinking about getting autographs from the other players, writers were asking me about being MVP.

I had my own press conference in front of a big group and I was answering a lot of questions about the Cubs. The only other Cub to make the team was Jody Davis, who was having a huge year, but Jody left me hanging there all alone. He was probably standing in the back of the room laughing at me while I suffered through the ordeal.

So I stood up there and did the best I could, not totally comfortable with it. But I'd come a long way in a couple years. I never had any college speech classes. I was just a baseball player and a pretty shy one at that. At least it was a nice change to talk about the team instead of me. But once I got to the locker room I felt really out of place. There was Mike Schmidt, Dale Murphy, Steve Garvey and Gary Carter. I was with the All-Stars. It took me back to the feeling I had when I was a September call-up with the Phillies, or on Opening Day of '82, and wanted to get everyone's autograph.

So you know what? I got everybody's autograph.

When I took the field on the first day, the American Leaguers were taking batting practice. As I walked down the first-base line toward the dugout, George Brett came over and introduced himself and said, "Hey, I like your style and I enjoy watching you play."

That blew me away. I still have a picture of that and it's one of my favorites. I was like a kid in a candy store. I knew I had brought up my level of play that year, but I still wondered if I belonged in that clubhouse with those guys.

I saw Bruce Sutter a couple of times but I was afraid to even look at him. I mean, he was the top closer in the game and I knew I'd have to face him again. And what was I, 24? He was 34 and I wasn't going to say anything that might offend him. If anything, I was going to get his autograph. It was a great time and a fun week, but I left San Francisco thinking about the second half of the season and how exciting it was to be in a pennant race.

I also wondered if Pete Rose remembered what he had said about me.

While the Cubs were becoming a national phenomenon, in Chicago it was pure hysteria.

For the first time in my career I was getting recognized away from the ball park. I'd be at a restaurant or a grocery store and people would come up to shake hands or get an autograph.

TV news teams were starting to come out to the house and meet the family and interview the kids. I was a pretty well-kept secret until June or July of that season.

Our assistant PR man, Ned Colletti, came to me in August and said he thought there was going to be a problem.

"I think you're going to have trouble from here on out because of all the media every day," Colletti said. "If you don't want it to affect your pre-game preparation, I recommend we set up a time every day when you can talk to the local media, visiting media and national media so you can get it all out of the way at once, and then go about your business."

So we held a daily briefing, for about five or 10 minutes, and I'd watch the clock. As soon as time was up, I'd say, "OK, it's time to go. I've got things to work on." And I'd hear comments like, "What do you have to work on?" I guess they thought it was easy, but I never felt it was and I never stopped working hard no matter what kind of season I was having.

There were also a lot of questions about the stats because I had a chance to become the first player ever to have at least 20 homers, 20 triples, 20 doubles, 20 stolen bases and 200 hits in a season, while batting over .300.

Guys would always ask about the triples, as if I knew how to get them. I was just a kid. I hit the ball and I ran as fast as I could. That's how I got triples.

Back then I was aware of stats, but I didn't wake up every morning and look at them. I looked at the wins and losses. So a lot of the records the media would talk about were stats I didn't know anything about or care about. I was just playing the game and trying to do whatever I could to help us win.

We were a half-game behind the Mets and 12 over .500 at the break (48–36), but there was a lot discussion about the 1969 Cubs and the heat of day games and 1945. Those were things this Cubs team knew nothing about, yet the press was saying the Cubs would fade like they always do.

We didn't know anything about the history. All we knew was we had the horses and 14 games left against the Mets.

We were three-and-a-half out when we arrived in New York for a crucial four-game series on July 27.

Dwight Gooden, who would go on to win Rookie of the Year, beat us Friday night to put the Mets up four-and-a-half, and we had to come up with a win on Saturday.

We had the lead late in that game, but Bobby Dernier dropped a ball in center field that allowed the Mets to go ahead. Bobby D. was spectacular that year and won a Gold Glove, but he made that one mistake and everyone at Shea Stadium was yelling something about a guy named Don Young.

Young apparently made a big mistake down the stretch in '69, but in 1969 I was nine years old, living in Spokane, and watching astronauts land on the moon.

Well, after Bobby D. dropped that ball, all we did was go out and score eight runs the next inning and win the game 11-4.

The next day Steve Trout began a double-header with a shutout and Scott Sanderson was almost as good in Game 2 as we swept the twinbill.

So after losing Friday, we had come back to win the last three and cut the Mets' lead to a game-and-a-half.

A couple of days later at Wrigley Field, on August 1, we came from behind to defeat the Phillies and then sat around and waited for the Mets game to end. They'd gone into extra innings, and we knew if they lost, we'd be all alone in first.

And those were the days when they didn't run the fans out of Wrigley Field right after the last out. The fans were allowed to stay and relax and let the traffic die down. But on this day, they stayed to see the results of the Mets' game.

I knew who won when I heard the roar from above the clubhouse. All the fans who stayed got their wish. The Mets had lost and now they got to see the scoreboard operator take the Mets' flag off the top spot on the pole and put the Cubs in first place in the National League East.

By the time the Mets came to Chicago a week later, we were a half-game up.

In an electrified Wrigley Field, where the fans were sick of hearing about past failure, we swept the four-game series to take a whopping four-and-a-half game lead. It was a madhouse.

The rivalry had become pretty intense and there were a couple of bench-clearing brawls, one of which involved Mets pitcher Ed Lynch and Keith Moreland.

Lee Smith got tossed out of one game after throwing a pitch over George Foster's head, and it got pretty wild.

It was my first experience in a pennant race and it was awesome. The fans were jacked up for every game and Chicago had the fever.

That's the most fun you can have in baseball and I enjoyed it, but I don't think I appreciated it as much as the veterans did. I was the youngest guy on the team and it was only my third year in the league. I didn't know how rare a pennant race could be, and I never really stopped to smell the roses.

The Mets, however, wouldn't let up and cut the lead to a game-and-a-half in mid-August. There was more talk of choking, until we got hot again and padded the lead. We were up seven when we faced the Mets in New York on September 7. We really only needed one in that series and we got it in the second game when Sut pitched another gem. The Mets came to town a week later and our lead was still seven. Once again, Rick Sutcliffe set the tone with a complete-game wipeout of the New Yorkers on September 14, and Jody Davis chipped in with a grand slam as the fans chanted his name. The fans were always chanting someone's name that summer, whether it was a "Jody, Jody" for Davis, or an "MVP, MVP" for me or something for almost everyone.

I think Harry Caray had a lot to do with it. A year or two before, Harry started calling me "Ryno" and it stuck. I'd never been called that before, but it's been with me ever since.

Harry was another guy brought in by Dallas Green when Tribune Co. bought the club. It was as if we were all on a mission to change the image of the Cubs and Harry's enthusiasm was a big part of that.

I'll never forget the day in early June when Pete Rose hit a line drive off Lee Smith's back. It caromed right to Davey Owen at shortstop, and he threw to first to double off a runner and end the game. Harry said, "I think God really wants the Cubs to win this year."

Another real character was veteran Richie Hebner, an outstanding pinch hitter and a guy who worked as a gravedigger in off-season.

Hebner played in the postseason eight times and Dallas Green liked the guys who'd been through the wars.

Richie would sit on the bench and not even warm up. When Jim Frey called for him, he'd stand up, walk over to the bat rack and grab a bat. He wouldn't even stop at the on-deck circle or take a practice swing.

On April 24, he walked right up to the plate in the bottom of the ninth of a tied game and hit the first pitch from Bruce Sutter into the bleachers to win it. That was Richie. The 1984 team had a lot of different personalities and the people related to them and took to them. It was special for the fans and for us.

On September 15, Scott Sanderson won and we were up eight-and-a-half games. But the Mets took the final game of the series and we'd lost five straight by the time we dropped Game 1 of a three-game series in St. Louis the next weekend. There were 10 days left and our lead was six-and-a-half, but the choke talk in St. Louis that Friday night was mind-boggling.

We were fighting the collapse talk, but we had some good veterans who handled it well and kept things positive in the clubhouse.

On Saturday, a monsoon hit and we never got out of the locker room. The rainout might've been a good thing for us. I know it was for me.

I was starting to feel some of the pressure, having finally figured out that the Cubs had consumed the city of Chicago and Cub fans everywhere.

I didn't even know what a magic number was, or what the "Games Back" column of the standings meant, so I didn't know if we were in good shape or if we should be worried. Every kid who goes to a game today knows how far his team is from first, but this second baseman didn't know in 1984. Honestly, the topic never came up in '82 or '83 because we were out of it on Opening Day.

So after they banged Saturday's game, Sutcliffe took me to dinner and tried to get me to relax. At one point I looked up at him, winced and said, "Sut, are we OK? Are we gonna win?"

There were only eight days left in the season, and I confessed that I didn't know what a magic number was. He just smiled that big Sutcliffe smile at me.

"Oh, we're gonna be fine, Ryno," he said. "We just need to win one of the two tomorrow, and I'm pitching Monday."

That's all. Just: "I'm pitching Monday."

He didn't have to elaborate. I knew, he knew and everybody knew he'd win Monday. He was 15–1 and hadn't lost a game since June. He was unbeatable, period.

That made me feel a lot better, and I slept fine Saturday night knowing we'd have a good day Sunday.

It was like a playoff atmosphere that afternoon at Busch Stadium, and a lot of Cub fans had come down from Chicago in hopes that we'd clinch it there.

The magic number was three going into the double-header so we still had a chance to wrap it up with a week left in the season.

In Game 1, we had Steve Trout on the mound, and I can't tell you how many big games he won for us the second half of the season. Billy Connors had taken him under his wing and given him confidence. Trout won six complete games, only one less than Sut, and by the time he beat the Cards in Game 1 that Sunday, he was as untouchable as Sut.

That knocked the magic number down to two, and some guys were breathing easier after Trout's great performance — including me.

We watched the scoreboard all day, and the Mets came back to win their game, but Dennis Eckersley pitched a beauty in Game 2 and we swept the double-header.

After the final out, Larry Bowa jumped up and down all the way into the dugout from shortstop while we high-fived and hugged each other. Jim Frey was congratulating everyone, and you could feel the excitement building. For all intents and purposes, the celebration had begun.

The magic number was one and we had Sut going Monday night in Pittsburgh. It was over.

There was no doubt about it.

7

Good morning, Chicago Cubs

> **"If ever there was a Hall of Famer, it's Ryne Sandberg. He single-handedly carried the Cubs to the playoffs for the first time in 39 years. Ryne Sandberg IS the Cubs."**
> *—1984 Cy Young Award winner Rick Sutcliffe*

The night of Monday, September 24, 1984, in Pittsburgh didn't feel much different in the locker room. The guys were relaxed and going through their normal routines. There was more pressure the day before in St. Louis, but now that we had those two victories, we knew it was over.

It was Sutcliffe Time.

Going into the game, though, there was big talk about me needing one homer and one triple and a couple of hits to reach the 20-20-20-20-200 package. So that was on my mind before the game, but once it started I forgot all about it. We were facing the Pirates' Larry McWilliams, and I had a pair of doubles that night over the third base bag. One of them took a weird hop in the left-field corner and I had an outside shot to get to third. But there was nobody out and the game situation didn't call for me to risk making the first out at third base. Don't think the reporters didn't ask me about it, though.

We cruised into the ninth with a 4–1 lead, and before we took the field for the ninth, Jody Davis walked up to Sutcliffe in the dugout.

"I want the ball, big fella," Davis said. "I want to catch the last out."

"You got it," Sutcliffe said.

Davis made it clear that once the Cubs got two outs, he wanted a strikeout to clinch the Eastern Division title. Sut got the first two outs easily and then got ahead of the Pirates' Joe Orsulak.

With the count 1–2, Sut wanted to waste one more fastball away, low and outside to the left-handed hitter, so he could set up his slider. That was probably his best pitch in 1984. I was watching all this from second and could see what pitches Jody was calling. Sut was going with the plan because he was trying to take care of Jody.

Well, Lee Wire was the umpire and he's well-known for having a wide strike zone. He always comes out before the game starts and sweeps about three inches on the inside and three inches on the outside of the plate. That dirt boundary then becomes home plate for Lee Wire.

I saw Jody set up well outside and Sut went into his windup. He threw the pitch just where he intended it to be, but before it had even crossed home plate and landed in Jody's glove, Lee Wire was ringing up Orsulak.

Sut was almost embarrassed. He was like, "No, no, no. That's not a strike."

But it was too late. We all charged the mound to get a piece of Sut and all the Cubs fans at Three Rivers Stadium were charging onto the field with us.

Rick had this expression on his face, like, "How could he call that a strike? What about my slider? I got a plan."

And Orsulak, who never took the bat off his shoulder, looked like he wanted to argue with Wire, but it was too late. Wire knew this was a big moment and he wanted to be a part of it. He could feel the excitement, too.

So before Orsulak could really even say anything, he realized he'd better get off the field before he got crushed in the stampede.

Thirty-nine years of misery had come to an end for Cub fans, and while the celebration in the locker room was great, I'm not sure we were as excited as the fans.

At one point we came out of the locker room and onto the field because they were showing Wrigley Field on the big scoreboard screen.

It was insane. There must've been 50,000 people at the corner of Clark and Addison, and I felt a little jealous that they were there and we weren't. That might've been the first time I realized what a big deal the Cubs were in Chicago.

But our party was pretty good, too. Ron Cey had been through all the celebrations with the Dodgers, and he said this one was the most emotional and the most fun he was ever a part of.

We'd been under a lot of pressure and this was the release. We'd grown close and stuck together through it all and proved all the naysayers wrong. We didn't just beat the East, but we beat all the critics, too. We did it and we were going to enjoy it.

We stayed at the park for an hour or two, and then went out on the town for a while.

But my wake-up call came quickly.

At 5:30 a.m., a crew from *Good Morning America* came knocking at the door and wanted me live, but I didn't answer. After a minute the knocking turned into pounding and the pounding turned into screaming.

"Come on," the guy was yelling. "We need you live in an hour."

I never answered, but they stayed for at least 30 minutes, pounding on the door. I never answered. I couldn't. I just couldn't move. I was too tired.

I did manage to get to the park that afternoon for the night game, and most of the starters got the day off. I played a couple of innings that day and the rest of the week, because I was a couple of hits shy of 200 and needed one homer and one triple for the 20-20-whatever thing.

I was long gone on the final day of the season when we trailed 1–0 going into the bottom of the ninth of a meaningless game against the Cardinals.

Our old friend Bruce Sutter was again on the mound at Wrigley Field and he was going for a major-league record 46th save.

Most of our regulars were out of the game, but none of the fans had left the park. It was much different than the years before, when we drew 8,000 fans a game. In '84 we set an attendance record with more than two million.

As was the case all year, different players chipped in on the last day. Henry Cotto, Tom Veryzer, Thad Bosley, Dan Rohn and Gary Woods led us back to defeat Sutter in the bottom of the ninth, and though the game meant nothing, we jumped all over each other and the fans went crazy again as we scampered in off the field and into the clubhouse.

We were in the locker room three or four minutes when PR man Ned Colletti came in and said, "They're not leaving. Nobody's left and they won't go."

So someone ran up to get Frey. When Frey heard what was going on, he came down in his T-shirt and shower shoes, threw on a jacket and said, "Let's go, men."

Half the guys were undressed already, but we put on some clothes and went out to see the fans. We had to. I was in my shower shoes as we walked back out onto the field and it was the loudest standing ovation we got all year.

We hadn't celebrated with the fans because we were in Pittsburgh for the clincher, but this was our chance. It might've been the most emotional moment for us all season, and it was a great boost going into the playoffs. It topped off the season with the best feeling possible.

Frey led us around the field from the left-field bleachers around to the right and then back to the dugout as we waved to the fans. It was unbelievable.

It was totally unexpected, just like everything that happened to us that year. What a way to end the season. When we came back in the clubhouse I saw Glenn Beckert and Don Kessinger and Ron Santo standing there smiling. They were all members of the 1969 Cubs and they looked like the weight of the world had been lifted off their shoulders. Over and over again they thanked the players for removing the curse.

There was definitely something more to this celebration than the story of one team and one season. Decades of agony had finally been buried for so many players and fans and we felt like we were carrying the torch for the entire city. I didn't get the 20-20-whatever thing, but I did finish with 19 homers, 19 triples, 36 doubles, 32 stolen bases and 200 hits.

I was more pleased with my defense, and the fact that I had improved my average to .314. I also made a big jump in RBI with 84 and piled up a league-leading 114 runs scored.

Mostly, I was thrilled because I was going to be in the National League Championship Series representing the Chicago Cubs, who were going to the playoffs for the first time since 1945.

I was nervous going into our first game against the Padres, but I was still riding the wave I'd been on since the "Sandberg Game" in June, and I knew we could beat the Padres. They were good, but we were better.

We showed it in Game 1 at Wrigley Field, crushing them 13–0, and knocking out starter Eric Show early. Bobby Dernier and Gary Matthews both homered in the first inning and it was easy after that.

Sut was awesome on the mound, and not bad at the plate, either. Before his second trip to the batter's box, he asked me if he could use my bat. I said, "Sure, take it. Hit it a long way."

My game bats that year were perfect. Nice grains and a good weight. Just a perfect game bat. And Sut's trademark was to take a bat from someone who was hot when he was pitching, so that day he took mine.

Well, he stepped up and hit an 0–1 pitch from Eric Show completely out of the park and across Sheffield Avenue, beyond the right-center field wall. It was the longest homer I ever saw hit to right at Wrigley Field. It was a bomb, and it might've even hit a house over there.

It took Sut about 20 minutes to circle the bases, and I got on him for it after the game.

"I thought they were going to call it on account of darkness," I told Sut. "When did you stop and pick up the piano?"

"But Ryno," Sut pleaded, "that's as fast as I can run."

It was a beautifully classic day at Wrigley Field and it was all going according to plan. Everybody in the starting lineup had at least one RBI, and we were red-hot. That carried into the next day and Steve Trout continued his streak of winning big games by defeating the Padres in Game 2. Lee Smith, who had 33 saves in the regular season, nailed it down.

We were extremely confident on the flight to San Diego. We needed just a win to reach the World Series, and there wasn't any doubt. The families were all with us and we were loose. We'd packed enough clothes and were ready to go to Detroit for the World Series, since the Tigers appeared on the verge of wiping out Kansas City.

We fully expected to sweep, but we lost Game 3 as Dennis Eckersley struggled, and we had an off-day before Game 4.

Then came the toughest decision of the series. Frey had pretty much decided during the Game 1 blowout, when he pulled Sutcliffe with a two-hit shutout after seven innings, that he'd move Sutcliffe up a day and pitch him in Game 4 or start him in the first game of the World Series.

It made sense because in the unlikely event that Sut lost Game 4, we'd have Steve Trout for Game 5.

Some of the guys even came to the park Saturday afternoon thinking Sut would start that might, but Frey decided that morning to pitch Scott Sanderson in Game 4, because he pitched well all season. I think Jimmy was still hoping we'd win without getting to Sutcliffe again, and then Sut could make three starts in the World Series if necessary.

With Sanderson on the hill, Game 4 turned out to be one of the most exciting playoff games in history.

The lead changed hands five times before we tied it in the top of the eighth against Goose Gossage on a double by Jody Davis, who had three hits and three RBI.

But in the bottom of the ninth, Steve Garvey homered to right-center off Lee Smith to win it.

The series was tied at 2-2 and we were a little stunned. I mean, Smitty was throwing about 95 mph at the time, and Garvey just stuck his bat out. Smitty supplied most of the power.

But you have to give the Padres credit for coming back from the dead to tie the series, and you have to give their fans credit, too. There had been some articles in the Chicago newspapers about how quiet the Padres fans were, and when those stories appeared in San Diego the fans became a different group.

They got too excited at times. After Game 3, my dad was pushed down a ramp. He wasn't seriously hurt, but it was scary. And the wives section was pelted with beer the entire series.

They were all whipped up and Jack Murphy Stadium was suddenly on fire as Garvey did his home run trot past me at second base, and their players jumped all over each other like we had done so many times before.

I still felt good because on Sunday we had Sut going and he hadn't lost in four months, but our locker room was a little tense Sunday morning for the first time all year.

We watched Walter Payton set the all-time NFL rushing record on TV, and then went out and ran right at the Padres.

Leon Durham blasted a two-run homer in the first inning and after Jody Davis homered in the second, we were up 3-0 and Eric Show was in the showers again.

We were cruising and Sut looked good as the 3-0 lead held up until the bottom of the sixth, when San Diego cut the lead to 3-2 on a couple of scratch hits, a walk and a couple of sacrifice flies.

But we were still in control. They weren't hitting Sutcliffe at all and we had the lead. Everything would be fine.

After I took infield practice just a few minutes before Game 5, I came in off the field and went straight to the Gatorade bucket. It was propped up awkwardly, and as I tried to get a drink, I knocked it right over — and it spilled onto Leon Durham's glove.

Leon tried everything possible to dry it off, including using towels and a hair dryer. It was still sticky when the game began, so he asked Don Zimmer if he thought Durham should still use the glove.

"Go ahead and use it," Zim said. "It might bring you good luck."

It was so hot that day in San Diego that the glove was dried out by the second inning, and Leon said it hadn't bothered him at all.

And by the bottom of the seventh, the Gatorade was a distant memory. We still led 3-2 and all we needed was to get nine outs to go to the World Series.

But Sut walked ex-Cub Carmello Martinez to begin the inning. With one out and Martinez on second, Tim Flannery hit a ball to Durham. It looked like a routine play and I was a little relieved. It would be two outs and a man on third.

Durham dropped down to one knee, but suddenly the ball hit the lip of the infield and never came up for him. He saw a bouncing ball and he lifted his glove a tad off the ground to meet it, but the ball stayed flat on the ground and it went right under his glove. Martinez scored and the game was tied at 3-3.

It's like this: When you see a ground ball coming at you, you get a certain feel for it. When you see it taking normal hops, that's what you plan for. What you can't predict is that one out of 500 hits a rock or a hole and either skips up or stays down. This ball hit the lip of the grass and stayed down and the Bull was looking for the ball to come up.

I didn't think too much about it because that happens every once in a while and it wasn't the Bull's fault. I figured we'd come back and get them the next inning.

But after another base hit put two runners on, Tony Gwynn hit a one-hop rocket just to my right. My first thought was, it's a one-hop, double-play ball. It's a do-or-die play, and I had one shot at it, but just as I was about to stab it, it took a big hop and almost ripped my face off as it went past me.

I turned around and the ball seemed to roll forever. That's what I remember most about that series. I turned around and that ball wouldn't stop rolling. It was torture. It rolled and rolled and rolled into right-center before Keith Moreland cut it off. Two runs scored on that play and another before the inning was over, and it was 6-3 after seven innings.

We had a couple chances to get them in the last two innings, but the Padres held us off and won the NL pennant.

It was sad to sit in the dugout and watch them celebrate what should've been our title. They were jumping around and the fans were going nuts. The fans at Jack Murphy finished us off with a chant of "Forty more years, forty more years."

In the clubhouse, a bunch of us went into a back room and just sat for about half an hour. I couldn't believe it. I could hardly speak. I looked around at the veterans for some direction and they all just hung their heads.

It was bizarre. We're not going to the World Series? The season is over? We're going home? I couldn't figure out what'd happened. It didn't seem right.

I knew we had the best team in baseball that year, so we had to be going to the World Series. I felt like there were about two weeks left to go. It couldn't be over yet.

It never entered my mind that we might not go to the World Series. Nobody had packed up their gear at Wrigley Field and no families had left. We had two more weeks to play, didn't we?

I was devastated. I had never suffered such a defeat and I could hardly muster the words.

The long flight back to Chicago seemed to take a month and it was very quiet. There wasn't much talking, but when we landed at O'Hare and got off the plane, we stood there. Guys hung around talking for about half an hour. No one wanted to go home for the winter.

That was pretty cool. We didn't want to break up the team and go our own ways. We were too close to let it go. We talked about getting together during the winter, and there was already talk about coming out early to spring training again.

I had obviously had a pretty good year. In the playoffs I hit .368 — but I felt empty.

While the media played it up, none of us ever thought much about Leon's error or the Gatorade. It was one play in a series that should've only lasted three games, not five. We had them down and didn't put them away. That's what I thought about.

When I flew home, it occurred to me that the next season they would be going to a seven-game format for the League

Championship Series. All I could think was I wished we still had those two extra games to play back at Wrigley Field.

Remember Bill Harper, the Phillies scout who watched me for two years in high school? Well, he got fired after that '84 season.

I guess he was pretty upset when the Phillies traded me and after '84 he got even more upset. You see, scouts don't make much money but they do get bonuses when the players they draft make it to the majors and perform well.

He let the Phillies know they had made a mistake and I think they fired him because of that.

And the fans who had chanted MVP for me turned out to be right. I was proud of the honor, but it wasn't much consolation after losing to the Padres.

I didn't think of it as a personal accomplishment anyway. To me it was a team honor.

If Jimmy Frey hadn't spent time with me in the batting cage and taught me to pull the ball with power, and our coaches hadn't spent extra time with me on the field, I never would've won the MVP.

If our great starters and relievers hadn't won games, it never would've happened.

If all the guys in front of me and behind me in the lineup hadn't had the great year they did, it never would've happened.

So my MVP was absolutely a team trophy. My stats were team stats, and that trophy was a team trophy.

The way we played was the way Dallas Green insisted we play: for the team and for each other. He collected only team-oriented players with solid character and baseball intelligence, and that team was a perfect Dallas Green team.

The 1984 team was special and the 1984 season was something I'll never forget. I'm sure Cub fans feel the same way.

But as great a season as it was, the ending was painful, and that pain would stay with me for an entire winter. All I could think about was what could've been. And I finally knew what it really felt like to be a Cub fan.

8 ♦ MVP—who, me?

"It's not often guys like Ryno come along. He was one of the cleanest-cut professionals I've ever known and one of the great leaders I've seen. Ryno provided leadership without ever having to say a word."
—*Former Cubs GM Dallas Green*

Before the 1984 season, I signed a six-year contract with the Cubs, but after my MVP season everyone was saying I'd made a mistake because it would cost me money in the long run.

I never saw it that way.

I didn't care about how much money I made. I was thrilled to know I was going to be in one place for six years, and to me that was true security.

In the minors I struggled to stay afloat. As a rookie in 1982, I made the major-league minimum, $45,000. That was more than my father ever made in one year, and I couldn't believe they would pay me that much to play baseball.

In '83, I jumped to $180,000 and it was a shock. So before '84, when they offered me a six-year deal that would carry me through the '89 season, at an average of $660,000, there wasn't any doubt in my mind it was the right thing for me. That was enough for my whole family for a lifetime. And more importantly, I knew where my family would be for six years, and that feeling of security helped me prepare for the 1984 baseball season.

Don't forget, this was before the '84 season and I didn't know how much I would improve or where my career would go.

Apparently Dallas Green had some foresight and knew something the rest of us didn't.

I had just turned 24 and I thought it was a long contract and a lot of money for someone as young as me. It was a big boost in confidence for me that they thought I would even be around six more years.

A lot of players were signing those deals back then, especially veterans, so I jumped all over it. At the time I signed the deal, Lindsey was about a year old and Cindy was pregnant with Justin, and I felt good about the long-term aspects of the contract.

What's ironic is that ball clubs hesitate to do that today, but if more teams did, they'd probably save themselves a lot of money. You wouldn't have heard years of talk about a salary cap and there might never have been a strike in 1994. Signing your core of young players to long-term deals is, in essence, a salary cap. Teams know what their costs are going to be and everybody's happy. Yeah, it may cost a young player some money down the road, but at least he's secure. That first contract did that for me and took my mind off the business side of baseball for six years. What I wanted was to be the best player I could be and not worry about finances. All my concentration and focus was on getting better, and I know that getting the deal before the season helped me in 1984.

It was during our division-winning 1984 season that I really became a public figure, and it was a difficult change for me. I was still a young, shy kid from a relatively small town. At least compared to Chicago, Spokane was small, and I didn't really understand why everyone wanted me at their banquets.

After the season, I traveled all around the country collecting awards at the major functions, and it really disrupted my off-season.

Don't get me wrong, I was appreciative, but I would rather have been home.

I had a baby boy and a two-year-old daughter at home in Phoenix and I had just been through an eight-month long baseball season. But instead of being home with them and getting my rest, my winter itinerary was packed. I was pretty uncomfortable with it and if I had my choice I probably wouldn't have done any of it.

It was also in 1984 that I first became identified as a role model, for reasons that just came naturally. I didn't do anything to get the label, but it happened and I felt an obligation to the fans to live up to it.

I never had a problem with that because I didn't have to change who I was in any way and it wasn't a burden. Part of being a professional athlete for me was knowing kids looked up to me and watched me very closely on and off the field, and that was OK because I was just being myself. I was never the type to go out every night and stay out until 4 a.m. I never had to drag myself to the park looking like I'd been out all night.

For some players it can be a problem or a burden, but it's their career and that goes along with it. For the most part players keep that in mind and are aware of it.

Let's face it, some athletes are role models and some aren't. Even Charles Barkley, who says he's not a role model, really is. Charles made light of it, but he's still a role model because he's a popular player, one of the biggest stars in the NBA, and kids watch him.

The way that he goes about the game—playing hard, playing to win, diving for balls, hustling all night long, putting everything he has into the game—is a very positive image and kids can get a lot out of that.

When you're in the public eye, no matter what you do, you're a role model. Whether you're on TV or playing a game in front of 30,000 people, you can influence people.

Away from the game, athletes are on their own time and some don't want to carry the responsibility 24 hours a day and I can understand that.

For me, it just so happens that it was easy because I just continued to be the same person.

There was always a common misconception that Tribune Co. was tight with the purse strings when it came to the Cubs, but that was rarely true.

I don't think the company was ever reluctant to spend money. It's just that some of the people spending it sometimes made horrendous mistakes, and occasionally they'd yank the purse closed and tell management to get its act together.

That was not the case in the winter after the 1984 season and we had a boatload of free agents to take care of. For starters, all of our starting pitchers needed to be signed. Rick Sutcliffe was coming off a Cy Young season. Steve Trout pitched the best year of his career. Dennis Eckersley gave us 24 starts with an ERA around 3.00. And Scott Sanderson was the best fourth starter in the game.

And they were all free agents.

But there was almost no way that Dallas Green could sit back and let these guys walk away. He couldn't break up a team that gave the franchise its first title of any kind in 39 years.

The players didn't even consider it a possibility. It was unspoken, but we all wanted to keep the club together and come back and get to a World Series.

So Tribune Co. and Dallas Green spent a lot of money to keep the team together. They signed all four of those pitchers to long-term contracts and the total just for the '85 season was about $5 million combined. That was a ton of money at the time.

Management went out on a limb for some guys and took care of a lot of families. But that went along with playing team baseball and winning baseball. That's what Dallas preached and so we did it.

Dallas is really interesting because he appeared to be this big, mean tough guy. And at times he could be, because he wanted to win so badly.

But Dallas is a good man and he treated his players well and he cared about them as people. All he expected was the best effort you could possibly give and he expected you to play baseball as a team, not as individuals. If you did that, he rewarded you.

But that was baseball in the early '80s, and unfortunately, that's a thing of the past, too.

Spring training in 1985 was a blast. It was like we'd never left that night at O'Hare Airport after the Game 5 loss to the Padres.

I was pumped because now I wasn't thinking about making the playoffs, I was thinking about winning the World Series. And personally, I felt I had a lot to prove after winning the MVP and getting so much publicity.

As I look back on it, I always had my best years when there was something to shoot for, like a pennant race, or if I felt I had something to prove.

Fear of failure is a great motivator for some, and that was always a big thing for me. A lot of great athletes are driven more by their fear of failure than by their desire to succeed, which is also essential. But I think the two go hand in hand and I believe a little fear keeps you sharp and makes you work hard.

That's "the edge," as athletes call it. When you lose that drive or that edge, you're done. That's what happened to me in 1994.

But in '85, I had it big. I wanted to prove that 1984 was not a fluke. I heard the "career year" phrase a lot and I didn't really know how to interpret it. I thought they meant, "Oh, this guy'll never do better than that."

I used that as an incentive for the entire 1985 season. I wanted to prove it wasn't a fluke.

As a team we had something to prove, too, because a lot of the guys had the best years of their careers and the critics were saying we couldn't do it again.

Well, we got off to a good start and were hanging right around first place when Sutcliffe pulled a hamstring in Atlanta on May 19. We lost the game, Sut for two weeks and a chunk of our confidence.

It was just the first of three times Sut went on the disabled list that year, because he kept trying to pitch through the injury.

The first time I saw it I almost got sick. I walked in the trainers room and there was Sut laying face down, getting treatment. His whole leg was purple and black and blue from his butt down to his ankle.

The tear in his leg was a bad one, but he was a team guy and he felt like he was letting us down if he wasn't out there pitching.

It wasn't until years later that he told me he thought he first hurt his shoulder that year, too, because his motion changed to favor his bad leg. Anybody who ever questioned whether this guy would pitch in pain simply didn't know him. Despite his pulled hamstring, Sut came off the DL and threw a complete-game, 1–0 gem against the Pirates on June 7 to move us back into a first-place tie. We won our next four after that and jumped out to a three-and-a-half game lead on June 11 with a 34–19 record.

Things were going great and we were cruising toward another division title. Everything was in place, so what could go wrong?

Everything. That's what could go wrong.

We proceeded to lose a franchise-record 13-straight games, and almost all of those defeats were by a run or two. Every team goes through stretches during a season when it can't get the big hit or the big out. That's what happened to us, but our stretch lasted about 10 games too long.

By the time it was over on June 26, we were in fourth place and four games out. We were done.

We never made another run at it after that because the most unbelievable things started happening to us. Injuries to half the starting lineup killed us, but that wasn't even the worst of it.

By the middle of August, we had all five starting pitchers on the disabled list at the same time. Sutcliffe, Trout, Eckersley, Sanderson and Ruthven were all on the DL, and we were calling up guys I'd never heard of from towns I'd never heard of before.

To lose five starters like that was insane. I don't think it had ever happened before in the majors, but it happened to us. We finished fourth, seven games under .500 and 23-and-a-half out.

It was a huge disappointment to me because I thought we would've been better in '85 than in '84 if we could've stayed healthy, but could'ves don't count for anything in baseball.

I won my third straight Gold Glove and made my second straight All-Star Game in 1985, but Tommy Herr of the Cards got the start. It's the only start I didn't make from 1984–1993.

All in all, I had a pretty good year and thought I had proved something to the critics who said I was just a flash in the pan.

I hit 26 homers, seven more than in '84, while batting .305. I also stole 54 bases, which as it turns out, was 20 more than I would have in any other year of my 13-year major league career.

I was very confident attempting steals that season because John Vukovich was our first base coach and whenever I was on, he'd help me pick my spots and tell me what pitches to go on. It worked because I was only caught 11 times.

I was at the top of my game in terms of speed and feeling comfortable on the bases and knowing the pitchers. But all those steals and all the attempts took a toll.

Playing second base every day, leading the league in total chances most years, batting 600 times like I usually did and stealing all those bases wore me down.

In the years after that I got away from running as much and concentrated more on the power aspects of my game and looked for more extra base hits.

I hit more than 25 homers five times in my career and stole at least 25 bases seven times, so people always asked me why I didn't go for the "magical" 30–30 in the years I hit more than 30 homers.

But I never even knew what 30–30 was until someone in the media told me about it. To me, that was just one of those personal stats that don't mean anything.

I'll bet you that guys like Willie Mays and Hank Aaron never thought about 30–30. They just did what was natural for them in the course of trying to help their teams win games.

I just wasn't into personal stats. If the game called for a stolen base and I got the steal sign then I'd steal the base. If I wanted to stay there and leave the hole open for a good left-handed hitter, like a Leon Durham or a Mark Grace, then I did that.

I always put the team first. It was the way I was brought up to play. I never had a problem with things like hitting to the right side and giving myself up. That's how you play baseball. At least, that's how I learned it in the Phillies' system.

There were times later in my career when I saw guys concentrating on personal goals, like a 30–30 season, and it offended me and a lot of my teammates.

Dallas Green had never allowed that to exist.

One question that was frequently asked of me was why I wanted to hit second instead of third. Well, the answer is, I never said that.

I came to the park every day and saw where my name was in the lineup and that's where I hit. I didn't care where the manager put my name. That was his job, not mine. I didn't think making out the lineup card was in my contract.

The fact is, I hit No. 3 a lot in some years, like in '85, '89 and '91, and in those seasons I had pretty big numbers so it obviously didn't affect me.

I think a lot of managers used me in the No. 2 spot because not only would I get RBI opportunities there, but I also averaged about 100 runs scored a year and they wanted to capitalize on my baserunning ability.

All I know for sure is that I hit wherever I was told to hit, and I didn't think much more about it than that. The idea that I didn't want to hit third is pure fiction.

I didn't always agree with Dallas, and I wasn't at all happy when he released Larry Bowa on Aug. 13, 1985. I guess he figured Larry was going to retire after the season because he was 40 years old.

It turned out OK for Bowa because he hooked up with the Mets and might've gotten to another World Series had the Cards not edged them out for the Eastern Division title.

But I just wasn't prepared to say good-bye yet. I owed Larry so much and didn't really get the opportunity to express that to him.

It's ironic that when I was in the Phillies' system, I always thought of Larry as the guy I hoped to replace at shortstop. But he turned out to be the guy who showed me the ropes in the big leagues.

He was a winner and a true team player, and he gave me the benefit of all of his baseball wisdom when we were together. I knew the day would eventually come that he'd leave, but it was tough to see him go.

Bowa taught me so much and looked out for me when I needed him. He's the one who, at age 37, wanted to come out weeks before spring training in 1983 to get to know his new double-play partner. At that point in his career, he could've easily played out the string.

Larry's going to be a great manager when he gets another shot. He's grown a lot since his first stint in San Diego, and he's got all the right characteristics for the job. Like all the old Phillies products, Bowa has the desire and the baseball knowledge, but he'll also be a good motivator and teacher. He's got a lot going for him and I hope it happens for him soon.

Bowa's departure in 1985 did, however, signal the arrival of a 22-year-old shortstop named Shawon Dunston. He was our first pick in the 1982 draft and he was pure talent. He was raw, but there wasn't any doubt he'd be an All-Star as soon as he learned how to take his incredible athletic ability and direct it into baseball skills.

Shawon and I went on to start eight times as the Cubs' Opening Day keystone combination, the first of which was Game 1 of the 1986 season. I played more years with him than any other player during my career.

We had hoped that the injuries that killed us in 1985 would be a thing of the past, and that 1986 would be a lot more like 1984.

It wasn't.

The Mets caught fire right off the bat and we were 10 games out by May 9, even though we were only five under .500 at 11–16. Still, the season seemed to be over for us before it even began, and that's a rough spot to be in by the middle of May.

That was not good news for Jim Frey, who got fired on June 12, only a year-and-a-half after we had won the division. I couldn't agree with that move, either, because it wasn't Jimmy Frey's fault we were losing.

It was very disappointing because the team that won in '84 would've been right there without the injuries in '85, and in '86 I thought we still had a chance.

In reality, the team was starting to get old and we were making changes. We were starting to pay a little bit of a price for trading some young players in '84 and '85.

Over the next year or two, most of the players from the '84 team would disappear, and I was starting to learn a major lesson in baseball about getting too close to your teammates.

I had always been told that you should never get too close to anyone in baseball because as soon as you do, they'll get traded. I was starting to see it happen.

I was starting to feel bad about seeing my friends, like Bowa and Gary Woods, leave. Woods and Bowa had been with me from the beginning, but I was learning that players come and go, and if you make the decision to become close friends, then you have to be willing to pay the price for it.

I remember in 1990 when our bullpen coach, Larry Cox, died suddenly in February. It was tough for the club because he was only 42 and in great shape and was such a great guy. Pitching coach Dick Pole had the roughest time of all because they were best friends.

Dick always told me that you should never get to close to anyone in baseball because they'll leave you at some point. I learned that lesson back in 1986 as guys were being traded or released or retiring or getting fired.

Dallas Green and Gordy Goldsberry were building a farm system and it would just be a matter of time before we got some kids to help out, so I thought the move was a little drastic.

The funny part about Jimmy getting fired, if there was such a thing, was that third base coach Don Zimmer was waiting outside the general manager's office when Jimmy came walking out and told Zim he'd been fired. So Zim kind of figured Dallas was going to make him the manager for the rest of 1986, since Zim had a lot of managing experience. And usually when a change is made during a season, they let one of the coaches take over. Well, Zim walked in and Dallas fired him, too.

Zim and Frey were buddies and I guess Dallas figured it was a package deal.

I wasn't happy because those guys meant a lot to me. If it wasn't for Jim Frey and his teaching, my 1984 season might've been a lot different. My whole career might've been a lot different.

But Frey and Zimmer were gone and Gene Michael was hired as the new manager. It was another big change for me and again I took it personally. I went through that period of wondering if it'd been my fault because I didn't do enough to help them keep their jobs.

Pitching coach Billy Connors was next to go after the '86 season, and he got the news while laying in a hospital bed after having hip replacement surgery.

Dallas didn't want to do it at all and certainly not then, but he was getting pressure from above to change the entire coaching staff and didn't have any choice. Strangely enough, Dallas hired Billy again in '89 when Dallas got the managing job with the Yanks.

I knew I'd miss Billy because he was another guy who really cared about me and tried to help me whenever he could. Not only did he teach me the pivot at second base, but he also pushed me to do things I didn't think I could do.

Even when we were on the golf course, he'd talk me into trying shots I didn't think I could make, and I'd usually make them.

On top of all that, and most importantly, Billy was a great pitching coach and I knew the guys would miss him.

The good news was we brought up some kids in September who looked pretty good. One was a young outfielder named Rafael Palmeiro and another was a 20-year-old pitcher named Greg Maddux, though he looked like he was about 12.

Greg, however, didn't pitch like he was 12. In his first major league start he threw a complete game and beat the Reds in

Cincinnati, and a few weeks later he out-dueled his brother Mike in Philadelphia.

The coaches told me that he was one of the few guys in the minors who wasn't afraid to pitch inside. In his first year of pro ball, he stood up at a meeting after the coaches had gone through the signs.

"You forgot one of the signs," Maddux demanded. "You didn't give us the sign for knocking a guy off the plate."

I was impressed with his poise and the way he handled himself after being called up. You can't teach heart and you can't teach desire, and it was pretty obvious that this kid had a lot of both.

As for me, unlike the scared kid of a few years before, I had finished my fifth year and was feeling very much like an established player in the major leagues.

But with us playing so badly, the All-Star Games were becoming the highlight of the season. I stole more than 30 bases for the fifth straight year, and made only five errors at second base.

But I wasn't feeling too good about the club. I didn't like losing, and it had been two long years of it now.

I wasn't blaming Dallas because he had the guts to go for it in '84, but we had gotten old and I didn't know what to think about 1987.

It was another winter full of questions, and I hated waiting for the answers.

9 ◆ Of might and men

"You could see the kid had a chance to make it. He had the body and he had the skills. I don't know if anyone knew he'd be this good. I think Ryne Sandberg just out-worked everyone."
—*All-time hits king Pete Rose*

During my career, I played against some of the greatest players who ever lived, and people always ask me who the best were.

It's very difficult to separate so many great ones, but I can tell you who I admired on the field and who I liked to watch play the game.

I have to start with Pete Rose, because he was a player I saw a lot growing up. He was on the Game of the Week frequently and that's where I got my major league baseball, since there wasn't a major league team near Spokane. I really liked the way Pete played the game, always aggressive and always working. Constant motion.

Mike Schmidt was another one of my heroes. He had that short, powerful swing, and his home runs looked effortless. He had style on the field and worked hard at his position. Just a tremendous all-around player.

Manny Trillo was a second baseman I watched a lot in the '70s and early '80s. He used his brains on the field and always seemed to know where the ball would be hit. He also had one of the strongest arms you'll ever see on a second baseman. When I came up he was the best second baseman around.

Tony Gwynn was probably the best hitter I ever played against. Year in and year out, he was consistently up around 200 hits. That's very difficult unless you're an exceptional hitter. He's another guy who makes hitting look effortless. He's the best I've ever seen at making the pitcher come to him. He makes the pitcher throw the pitch he wants and where he wants it. If you want to learn how to hit, you watch films of Tony Gwynn.

Ozzie Smith might've been the best defensive player I ever faced. Smooth is a word you have to use when you say Ozzie's name. Like Trillo, he's always aware of what's happening on the field, and that determines his positioning. Ozzie doesn't have the classic, shortstop's arm strength, either, but he makes up for it with a quick release and quick feet.

My all-time team of opponents might be Johnny Bench and Gary Carter at catcher; Keith Hernandez, Steve Garvey and Will Clark at first; Trillo at second; Smith at short; Schmidt, Terry Pendleton and Matt Williams at third; Gwynn, Dale Murphy, Barry Bonds and Andre Dawson in the outfield; and Pete Rose at every position, since he played almost all of them.

But I couldn't name them all and I'm sure I left out some terrific players.

I never liked hitting against Dwight Gooden, Nolan Ryan or Bruce Sutter, though Sutter tells me I owned him. He might just be thinking of one day, I don't know.

But the toughest on me was Steve Carlton. I think I was 0-for-1982 and '83 before I got a hit off him.

I was most uncomfortable against Nolan Ryan. He never hit me, but at least once every game he'd throw that 97-mph fastball so close that the wind would move the hair on my arm.

That was in the back of my mind the rest of the game, and that's what he wanted. I did have some success against him, though, unlike against Carlton.

The only guy I ever saw hit Carlton well was Gary Woods, who was a great bench player for us in 1984. From 1982–84, he hit .452 against Lefty and just plain wore him out. Nobody liked hitting against Ryan, though, and there was only one guy I know of who wasn't scared of him: Andre Dawson.

One time Nolan was trying to intimidate Hawk, but he wouldn't go for it. He stood up there and when Ryan threw it inside Hawk fouled it off. The next pitch was even more inside and higher up and the Hawk fouled it off again. This went on for about four pitches until Andre was standing in the on-deck circle tomahawking them into the left-field stands.

Nolan finally gave up. I think it's the only time I ever saw him give in to anyone.

Like the rest of us, Shawon Dunston was terrified of Nolan Ryan, but he was the only one who ever said it out loud. Shawon would look at the schedule and know three weeks in advance when we were facing Ryan, and then he'd talk about it until the day arrived.

There was one game against Houston in 1986 that I'll never forget because of Dunston and Ryan.

We'd all been up two or three times already and getting nowhere fast. But all day, manager Gene Michael was collecting baseballs.

He had about 10 or 12 of them that he said were scuffed up by Ryan, and he was screaming at the umpire all day that Ryan was cheating.

Finally, Michael had enough and when Shawon was about to go up for his at-bat, Michael called him back from the on-deck circle.

"Tell the umpire to check the ball," Michael said as Shawon poked his head into the dugout.

"Are you crazy?" Dunston said. "He'll hit me between the eyes."

"Tell him to check it," Michael repeated.

"I ain't checking no ball on Nolan Ryan," Dunston yelled back.

"Check the ball," Michael yelled.

"No!" Shawon said. "Forget it."

Dunston went up to the plate with Michael still yelling at him as he walked.

Shawon dug in with slim hopes he'd get a hit, but knowing in his heart he had no chance. Mostly, he just didn't want to get hit with that 97-mph fastball.

"Check the ball, Shawon," Michael was still yelling. "Check the ball."

Shawon just looked out at Nolan and said, "I'm not checking the ball, Nolan. Forget him. Just throw it. I'm not checking it."

Still, Michael was yelling and now the whole dugout was howling.

Shawon stepped out and yelled into the dugout.

"If you want to come up here and bat against him, then you check the damn ball," Shawon yelled at Michael, before looking back at Ryan.

Ryan fired the ball for strike one.

"Don't pay any attention to him, Nolan," Shawon said. "Throw it, scuff it, step on it. I don't care what you do to it. I'm not checking the ball. Just please don't hit me."

Michael turned his attention to home plate umpire Charlie Williams.

"Charlie, check the ball," Michael yelled. "Check the ball, Charlie."

This time Dunston didn't step out.

"Charlie," he said, head straight down. "Don't you dare check that ball."

Shawon stepped back in and took strike two.

"Check the ball, Charlie," Michael said again.

"Don't check it, Charlie. Please don't check it," Dunston said. He looked out at Ryan like he was about ready to cry.

"Nolan, pitch the ball."

Finally, Shawon struck out on three pitches and heard an earful from Michael when he got back to the dugout, but he didn't care.

He was just happy to be alive and looking forward to another day.

I was actually a teammate of Rose, Schmidt, Trillo and Carlton for about three weeks in September of 1981, before I was traded to the Cubs that winter.

That wasn't much of a chance to see them, but I always watched my teammates and tried to learn as much as I could from them, taking bits and pieces of their game and trying to include them in mine.

Bill Buckner was a guy I watched a lot. He was a great line-drive hitter and he always looked to shoot the gaps. Sometimes it looked like he was intentionally trying to hit those double-doors in the left-center field wall, because it would take a big bounce and was a sure double. He had a solid stroke and never gave away an at-bat. Tough out.

The years I spent with Andre Dawson, we took batting practice a lot together and I watched him during games. I learned a lot because pitchers pitched us similarly. He'd been around a long time, too, and I watched his mannerisms. He was quiet but very aggressive.

I took some things from Gary Matthews, too. His pre-game preparation was outstanding and he helped me with some mental parts of the game.

He was aggressive and he wanted to win. One approach he taught me was to go out on the field each day thinking, "I'm going to beat that pitcher today." He was into a lot of positive talk and positive thinking before a game and during a game.

I learned as much as I could from several different people, and developed my own hitting philosophy.

The first thing in my mind was always to use the whole field. That meant that wherever the ball was pitched, I would take it and hit it that way.

If the pitches were away, I'd go away or up the middle. If the pitches were inside, I'd try to pull it.

Next, I would try to consistently put the good part of the bat on the ball, the sweet spot. It's about a six-inch area halfway between the trademark and the top of the bat.

Third, in situational hitting, I was always very clear in my mind about what my job was when I went to the plate. I don't think enough hitters have a plan when they go to the plate, but I believe it's extremely important.

Sometimes the situation might call for a bunt or a hit-and-run. Sometimes it might be hitting to the opposite field or hitting behind the runner, or simply giving yourself up with a grounder to the right side to move a runner over. Or sometimes it might be a sacrifice fly.

But it all comes down to knowing the game situation, and not caring about your individual stats. Just because you're at the plate by yourself, it doesn't mean it's not a team game. I rarely tried to hit home runs because, for the most part, when I thought about hitting a home run I'd get overanxious and it wouldn't happen. You have to be in a rhythm at the plate, and you can't be overanxious.

Home runs are usually a result of just being relaxed and doing everything correctly.

Part of doing things correctly for me was a lot of thinking before the game about who the pitcher was and how he would pitch me, so when I went to the plate I had an idea of what to expect. You just can't walk up the plate and then start thinking. At least I couldn't.

I'd consider the pitcher and what pitches he has. Then I'd think about what pitches I'd see and what he likes to throw me in certain situations.

For the most part in the majors, we know what they throw. The only difference is that from year to year, their pitches might be better or worse than they were the year before, and you have to recognize that immediately and adjust.

A guy might have a mediocre slider this year and great movement on his fastball, and next year it could be the opposite. So you might be able to get his slider this year but next year have to lay off it.

A slider was the toughest pitch for me—and I guess for most guys—because it looks like a fastball coming right over the plate, and then it breaks down and away from you at the last split second.

A curveball, on the other hand, you can react to because it starts right at you and will break back over the plate.

Your job as a hitter is to try to pick up the spin on the ball in that split second when it's coming at you, and determine what the pitch is. Then, at the same instant you decide what pitch it is, you have to adjust your stride, hands and bat speed. That all happens in a split second and it's all in your mind, so that's why you've got to be prepared when you go to the plate.

That's the game within the game. It's a guessing game you play with the pitcher, based on your knowledge of each other.

The way I looked at it was the pitcher had to throw the ball across the plate eventually. A pitcher might stay away from me for a whole game on the outside corner and I'd try to recognize that as soon as possible.

When I did, I'd probably go the other way with it and take the base hits to right field or up the middle.

When I'd see that same pitcher a week or two later, he might try to bust me inside and I'd be looking for that because I got the hits the other way last time.

That's when the home runs would come because I'd be looking to pull the ball.

After that, we'd start a new game.

Like all hitters, sometimes I couldn't help myself. I would recognize that a pitcher's pitching me outside, but I'd still try to force it and pull that pitch.

That's when I'd get in trouble and go into a slump. All you can do then is go back to the basics of hitting. I'd take some extra batting practice and practice hitting balls up the middle and to right field.

I would take that into a game, too, and eventually the pitchers would come back inside again and I'd do some damage.

Some hitters don't have to guess as much as others because of their ability to pick up the spin of the ball out of the pitcher's hand.

I've heard a lot of great left-handed hitters, like Ted Williams, Tony Gwynn, Wade Boggs and Mark Grace, talk about how they can see the seams of the ball, pick up the rotation and react to it.

As a right-handed hitter, facing mostly right-handed pitchers, it was difficult during night games to see the spin, but during the day I could sometimes pick up the rotation on the ball and know what type of pitch was coming. That's tricky too, however, because a changeup is simply a fastball at a slower speed, and the rotation looks exactly the same. But that's why you keep your hands back. Even if you stride as if it was a fastball, your hands are back and you still have a chance to hit a changeup.

What I tried to do was watch the pitcher's release point. If the ball started right at me then most likely it would be a curve, because it breaks back over the plate. If a curve started over the plate, then it would break away out of the strike zone anyway, and I'd most likely lay off of it. If a pitch started out over the plate, then I'd figure fastball or slider, and we're back in the guessing game again.

Recognizing pitches comes with a lot of practice and facing a lot of pitchers. Then it's up to your hand-eye coordination. You hope you can hit the ball where you want it to go and the pitcher obviously has a different idea.

Another thing I'd take into consideration was the count. I considered myself to be a patient but aggressive hitter. I'd try to be patient early in the count and get into situations where the pitcher had to come in with a fastball. I'd try to get him to 1–0, 2–0 or 3–1 counts, and sit on those fastballs and try to pull them. That philosophy worked pretty well for me.

Many times a pitcher simply challenged me and said, "Here it is, hit it if you can."

That was the case on July 19, 1992, in Pittsburgh, which was a Sunday night Game of the Week on ESPN.

In the bottom of the eighth, Barry Bonds hit one of his classic bombs to tie the game at 2–2. After we waited half an hour for him to circle the bases, it was finally our turn to hit in the top of the ninth.

Doug Dascenzo led off the inning with a double, but after two were out, the Pirates brought in Stan Belinda, a fireballing right-hander.

We battled to a 3–2 count. Then I fouled off six straight fastballs that were about shoulder high. Belinda was coming at me with the gas and I was doing everything I could to stay alive. I was thinking only of a base hit that would give us back the lead.

With each pitch, I wondered when he would come down with the ball and throw a strike, but he never did. Finally, I adjusted my sights a little bit higher and he threw me another high fastball.

This time I was ready, and I crushed it deep into the left-field bleachers. It went up into the third or fourth level, where some people were eating dinner in a club, and one of the guys said it bounced right off their white tablecloth. It was probably the longest homer I ever hit. It was a combination of the catching the sweet spot with his 95-mph fastball. And it gave us a 4–2 victory.

I just put the bat down and ran around bases, and the announcers made a point of mentioning my lack of a home run trot, compared to Bonds' lengthy lap around the bases. I did the same thing every time I hit a home run. I wasn't going to show up the pitcher or the other team for two reasons. One is you have to face that pitcher and that team again someday. The other is that it just isn't right. You don't have to be disrespectful to have fun. When you get back to the dugout, you get the handshakes and the high-fives and you can have all the fun you want.

Not to belabor the point, but when I first came up, if you showed up the other team like that, you'd get a fastball at your head the next time up.

I always thought a lot of at-bats and games were still left and players, especially pitchers, have long memories. It also went along with staying on an even keel. I tried never to get too high or too low. If things were going great, I didn't let anyone know how I was feeling and tried to hold onto that feeling as long as possible. And if I was feeling down, I didn't let anyone see that either, because that's when the game will bury you if your opponents sense that.

It's important that you never change your style of hitting. I mean that in terms of swinging the bat. I changed my style from a mental standpoint when Jim Frey taught me to think differently, but not so much the physical part of my swing. Billy Williams, the Cubs' Hall of Famer and a great hitting instructor, hates it when he sees coaches trying to change a hitter's natural style.

When Michael Jordan first started with the White Sox in early '94, Billy was certain that Michael would've progressed more quickly had they allowed Jordan to swing naturally, like he did 15 years before, and then tinkered with him until he was comfortable and having success.

Billy said to start over completely at that point probably cost Michael an entire year of development. Besides, Billy said, why wouldn't you let a 6-foot-6, 200-pound man swing with two hands on the bat?

I admire Michael for what he's trying to accomplish and I wish him all the luck. But it'll be tough for him, starting baseball at age 31, trying to learn everything he can so he can perform at the major league level.

I know for me, baseball was very hard. It was harder for me than playing basketball or football. I had to work very hard for a long time and it took me four years in the minors and about five years in the big leagues before I even felt like I really knew what the game of baseball was about. Even though I'd already had success, it wasn't until about 1986 that I felt like a true major leaguer. That's nine years right there before I felt comfortable mentally and physically as a professional.

It's a huge mountain that he's climbing, but Michael seems to be enjoying it, and that's what it's all about. That's all that really matters. He's been good for the game, too, so I don't understand why some people are so upset about it.

In any case, I think he ought to swing with two hands on the bat. That's where the power lies. Once my hands were on the bat I felt like they acted as one, and I was taught to throw my hands at the ball. But you don't want a rolling-over effect with your hands when you make contact because you'll hit too much on top of the ball. So what I tried to do was throw my hands at the ball and try to hit the upper half of the ball while swinging down.

With my swing it looked as though I was swinging down on the ball, rather than lifting the ball in the air, which is what some guys do.

What would happen when I hit the ball just right is I'd get an overspin and that helped the ball carry because of swinging downward. I hit a lot of line drives that wound up as home runs because of that.

A lot of it becomes natural with years and years of batting practice and extra work. I never went up to the plate during a game thinking about how to get a certain spin on the ball. That'd be crazy.

I was taught in the minors to hit ground balls and hit the top part of ball. Then, when Jim Frey told me to drive the ball, I put the two together.

That allowed me to use all the facets of my game. I could hit the ball on the ground and leg out base hits or I could hit line drives and home runs.

Along with hitting it down, I also learned early to hit up the middle and to the opposite field, so when Jim Frey taught me to pull, I was able to use the entire field when I was up at the plate.

My first two years in the majors I used a 34-and-a-half inch, 32-ounce bat. I choked up with that bat, and more than anything else I was trying to put the ball in play.

In 1984, I started off with the same bat, but when Jim Frey taught me my new style of swinging for power, I wasn't comfortable. I needed to stop choking up and get my hands down on the knob of the bat for some resistance, so my hands wouldn't slip. But the old bat was a bit too long and too heavy.

So one day early in the '84 season, I picked up a Larry Bowa bat. He had a 34-inch, 31-and-a-half ounce bat. That black bat was just a half-inch shorter and a half-ounce lighter, but it made all the difference in the world.

I got hot with that bat and used it for about a month, which is a long time to use one bat without it breaking. But I didn't want to give it up, so I carried it with me on planes and took care of it and was very careful to make sure it didn't disappear.

That bat looked like a war club after a while. It was all beat up and splintered, and after a game at home I hammered a nail in it to get a couple more days out of it. I even won my first Player of the Week award with it.

I was still hot a few days after I put the nail in it, but the Phillies' Tug McGraw busted me inside and finally broke that bat. I watched in agony as the barrel flew into the stands over the third base dugout—while I held the handle in my hand.

But I never changed bat styles again after that. I used it for another 10 years and any time I even talked about my bat, Yosh Kawano would say, "Oh, no. You're not going to change, are you? Hey, it's not the bat's fault."

Some guys changed bats all the time and drove Yosh crazy, but I used that Larry Bowa model for the rest of my career. I'd order a dozen at a time and pick out the four or five I liked best, based on how the handle felt and which ones had the wider grains and hardest wood. Those would be my game bats, and I left the rest for batting practice.

The heavy bat I stopped using is the one Andre Dawson has always used, which tells you how strong he is. Power is bat speed, and a bat has to feel light enough to get through the strike zone quickly.

Pitchers today have so many different speeds and most guys need a lighter bat to be able to keep their hands back and still react to the pitch.

I found one and I stuck with it.

From a hitting and fielding standpoint, I had pre-game rituals that I rarely strayed from.

In batting practice, the starters for the day hit in three groups of three, but there's a limited number of swings each player gets so I tried to make mine worthwhile.

I'd always begin by bunting two or four balls down each line. Then, I'd think hit-and-run and I hit the ball wherever it was pitched and hit it on the ground. To get loose, I liked to hit the whole first round of eight or 10 swings to right field or up the middle. It was a good way to loosen up. Otherwise, you could pull a muscle with all that twisting around by immediately trying to pull the ball and rip it down the line.

The next round, I'd try to pull a few balls and then I'd have another round where I'd hit the ball hard no matter where it was pitched, like it was a game situation.

The last round of cuts was the most fun because then you'd get three or four swings and play games. It might be a game of total bases or most home runs or we'd do a power check on the last swing, and see who could hit one out.

I wouldn't do that for a whole batting practice because I didn't want to get into bad habits. But for the last round it was fun.

Sometimes we'd do it at Wrigley Field so we could get an idea of what the wind was doing that day and whether the ball would carry out of the park. On those days, everyone would watch our rounds, especially when Andre Dawson and I were hitting together.

The only glove I used at third base in my one season there was the Mike Schmidt model. I figured if I needed a glove, I might as well use the same one as the best third baseman in the game.

It was a big glove with some open gaps in the webbing and sometimes the ball would stick a little bit.

When I moved to second base, I asked Rawlings for a smaller glove with a more tightly woven web. When you're coming across the bag trying to turn a double play, you don't want to be fiddling around trying to find the ball in your glove.

I used that same model for the rest of my career. Every season I'd start with a new glove in spring training and break it in for the season. I also had a back-up glove that I used for pre-game play and had it ready in case my gamer fell apart, but I never once had to use it.

In all my years, I never lost or broke a glove.

Defensively, I learned a lot from Larry Bowa early in my career. His fundamentals and work habits and pre-game preparation were outstanding.

I watched the way he got jumps on balls even during practice. He took them all seriously. He always got in front of the ball if possible and his footwork and leg work in preparation for a throw was always the same.

What he taught me was that if you do it that way in practice, you'll do it that way in a game. But if you nonchalant it in practice, you might mess it up in a game. I developed a pre-game routine starting with 10 or 15 ground balls right at me to get my glove down on the ground and get loose. That would also give me an idea of what the grass and dirt were like that day. Each day and each field was different, depending on the weather and what time of year it was.

At the beginning of a series, the grass might be longer or shorter, depending on whose field it was and what the team's offensive strengths were.

At Wrigley Field, we might have the grass longer against a team that hit a lot of ground balls, or shorter against a team that liked to try to bunt for hits all the time. At Dodger Stadium, on the other hand, the infield was always like a putting green.

On artificial turf, the ball gets to you a lot faster than on grass so it's important to cut down the angle and I would practice that before the game. During a game, I would watch for the sign and know what pitch was coming and I'd know the hitters and try to think about where they'd hit it. That way you can cheat a step or two in that direction, and you might get to a ball you otherwise wouldn't have a shot at.

After taking grounders right at me, I would take 10 or 15 grounders to my left to get used to that reaching motion, and then the same thing to the right, where I'd have to plant and throw.

Then I'd ask for five farther to the right near the second-base bag, where I'd practice my one-hop throw to first base. I'd also make at least five throws to, and take five throws from, the shortstop at second base to get used to that motion. Mostly, I played with Larry Bowa and Shawon Dunston during my career, but one year I had seven different shortstops, and you have to make sure you both know what's going to happen on that double play. So a few extra throws never hurt.

All together, I'd get maybe 35 or 40 grounders and try to make the play just like I would in a game with a good, solid throw to first.

It's not hard to practice like that, but it does take some time and concentration. For me it paid off with nine Gold Gloves.

Some people think second base is a position that doesn't wear on you physically, but check out the total chances Shawon Dunston and I collected each year and you might think differently.

And as far as contact goes, the trainers can testify to all the bloody socks and all the scars on my shins from getting spiked over the years while turning double plays.

I was taught to use the base as protection, keeping the bag between myself and the runner whenever possible, but it didn't always work that way.

Some players always came in hard, like Bill Madlock and Lonnie Smith. They were fast and they were tough. They'd start their slide after the base, hitting you at full speed while sliding past the bag.

One guy who tried to get me was Kevin McReynolds in the '84 playoffs against San Diego. He threw a rolling, body block at me, but he missed and wound up breaking his arm. He missed the rest of the series and the World Series, too. Most of the catchers, like Darren Daulton and Gary Carter and Mike Scioscia, came in hard at second as well for a couple of reasons.

One is that they're big and physical guys, like football players, and they like that kind of stuff. Another is that they're always getting run over at home, so second base is the one chance they get to run over someone else.

Watch the next time you see a collision at home. I guarantee you the next time that catcher gets on base, he'll be looking to hammer one of the middle infielders.

That's when I'd look over at my double play partner, Shawon Dunston, and yell, "Make sure you get it to me quick, Shawon. Make sure you get it to me quick."

I was always aware of that situation. Another time I had to watch out was when one of our players went in hard on one of their middle infielders. It was an unspoken rule that if it happened to your guy, we were going to go after their guy, and vice versa.

As long as it was a clean, hard slide, I never had any problem with that. I just got up, brushed myself off and tried to do the same thing my next time on the bases. But for the most part nothing was said and it was just a little way to send a message.

That's the way it was supposed to be. Play hard and go on with the game. Not all the talking that goes on today. I didn't mind the rough play, because it wasn't going to take me out of the lineup. I played with a lot of stitches and bumps and bruises, not to mention colds and flus and fevers and all of that. If you're going to play 155 games a year, you just accept that as a part of the game and move along.

All the spring training work and all the pre-game work made it feel automatic once the games actually started, so it was more reaction than actual thinking on the field. If I felt uncomfortable during the season I'd go out early and get some extra work, and maybe think about getting my glove down quicker. Sometimes I'd go a few days without a double play, and then I'd want a few extra pivots before a game.

You have to realize, though, that I started from scratch every year. I began with the basics in spring training, getting hand-thrown grounders from side to side, 20 feet away. That's how basic it was.

I started spring training by hitting off of a tee, too, so to think that it was all easy and natural really isn't true.

If you saw the first day of spring training, you'd know there were balls bouncing all over the place, hitting me in every part of the body. But by April, after 40 days and hundreds of hours of work, it would all come back to me. I didn't just show up on the first day of spring training and hit home runs and catch every ball.

In terms of playing at the level I wanted to be at, and doing it against major league competition, I felt like no aspect of the game was easy for me.

In other words, I could've gone out to the batting cages any December with no practice and hit 90-mph fastballs. I could do that right now, just like I could field grounders right now, too.

But to hit all the other pitches they throw and turn double plays, and do it at the major league level, took a lot of work and in that respect nothing came easy.

That's why I went to spring training early every season. Each year I wanted that time to fine-tune my game.

I had a routine and I stuck to it and it worked for me. It was no different than when I was a kid, spending hours and hours, day after day, trying to catch a tennis ball or a golf ball taking funny hops off the stairs or off a wall. That's hard work, and that's how you become successful. You are only given so much natural ability, and I was given a lot, but then it's up to the individual to take it the rest of the way.

I played with a lot of great players during my career with the Cubs and if I had to pick an all-time Cubs team that I played with it'd be Jody Davis at catcher; Bill Buckner, Leon Durham and Mark Grace at first; Larry Bowa and Shawon Dunston at short; Ron Cey at third; Gary Matthews, Keith Moreland, Rafael Palmeiro, George Bell and Andre Dawson in the outfield; and pitchers Fergie Jenkins, Greg Maddux, Rick Sutcliffe, Dennis Eckersley, Goose Gossage, Lee Smith and Randy Myers—just to name a few.

But the best player I ever played with, and one of the greatest I ever played against, arrived in Chicago in the most bizarre way possible, and it happened in the spring of 1987.

10 The good, the sad and the ugly

"As an opposing player, you marveled at what the guy could do, because he could beat you in so many different ways. Then when you played with him, he's the type of individual who, every time you heard people talk about him, they wanted their kid to grow up like Ryne Sandberg. He was special. Everyone knew that."
—*Eight-time All-Star Andre Dawson*

After the 1986 season came the winter of collusion and no one was signing free agents. The owners had gotten together and decided they'd keep costs down by agreeing not to sign free agents. Of course, they did it behind closed doors, and they eventually paid dearly for it.

By the spring of 1987, some very big names out there hadn't found a team yet, and one of them refused to re-sign with his old club, the Montreal Expos. His name was Andre Dawson, and he'd been one of the best players in baseball over the previous 10 years, but he was caught right in the middle of collusion.

The incredible part was he wanted to play for the Cubs. He was begging the Cubs to sign him, but Dallas Green was caught in collusion, too, and he would've been strung up by his bosses, who had agreed to the pact with the other owners.

Still, there was so much talk about Andre wanting to play for the Cubs that I was excited. It seemed like every time he faced us while he was with the Expos, he just murdered the ball at Wrigley Field. But when he showed up at our camp in early March, the Cubs wouldn't talk to him.

It was sad watching him stand outside that fence, looking in at us. It was like we were a bunch of kids playing and we wouldn't let him in our game.

Some terrible things were happening to free agents at the time, but the worst was happening to Andre.

He earned $1.3 million from Montreal in 1986, but the Expos' best offer for 1987 was a pay-cut. Dawson was a 10-year veteran with six Gold Gloves and three All-Star Games under his belt, but all he could get from Montreal was a pay cut.

I know Dallas and I know he loved "Hawk" because he was a walking definition of the word "gamer."

But the Cubs wouldn't talk to him, so his agent, Dick Moss, walked into the Cubs' offices at HoHoKam Park one day and simply handed Dallas a signed contract.

It wasn't unusual except for one minor detail: There was no dollar figure.

Andre had signed a blank contract and then Moss went out and told the Chicago beat writers what he had done. There were big headlines in Chicago and now Dallas had no choice.

The players, coaches and fans were all excited, and there was nothing Dallas could do except fill in the amount. He did: $500,000.

Andre would make less than half of what he made the year before and be the lowest-paid veteran on the club, but he was where he wanted to be and we were thrilled to have him. What was great was he wanted to be a Cub and he wanted to play in Wrigley Field. He loved the fans and they loved him, and it made me feel good to know great players wanted to be there.

I thought having Andre would give us a chance to win, but I had no idea what a strange year it would end up being. It started four days before Opening Day when Dennis Eckersley was traded for three minor league players we never heard from again. I think you know what Eck went on to do for the Oakland Athletics.

Dallas had been ordered to dump salaries by his bosses, and when he dealt Eck he was just following orders.

Those four free-agent pitchers we re-signed after the '84 season had been hurt in '85 and went south in '86. Dallas must've been told his payroll was too high for a losing team.

We actually got off to a good start in 1987. Andre was hot, Sut was back in form and Lee Smith was Lee Smith. We were only a game out of first on June 3.

But that was about the extent of our pennant race.

On June 13, I suffered the first serious injury of my athletic career. I dislocated my right ankle during a collision with St. Louis first baseman Jack Clark, and I missed 26 games. I was averaging 155 games a year before that.

Two days later, Shawon Dunston broke a finger and we lost him for two months. We fell out of the race pretty quickly after that, but from a personal standpoint, my injury turned out to be a blessing.

My dad hadn't been feeling good during spring training, and he went into the hospital in May. I was keeping tabs on how he was doing over the phone and through my family. They'd tell me he was stable and doing fine and not to worry about him, but it was on my mind. They told me to keep playing, and I heard that right up until I dislocated my ankle.

About a week or 10 days after I got hurt, Dallas, who knew about my dad's health problems, came up to me and said, "Why don't you go home and be with your dad for a while, since you're going to be out a couple weeks anyway."

I said it sounded like a good idea to me, so I thanked him and took off for Spokane. I flew out that day and got there around noon.

I spent the rest of the afternoon with my father at the hospital — and that night he died.

I was devastated.

But thank God I was given a chance to say good-bye.

All I could think about for days was if I hadn't hurt my ankle, and if Dallas hadn't made the suggestion, I never would've seen my dad again.

I was close to my dad, but since I left Spokane for the minors in 1978, I never really got to see him much. During my career, he was working in Washington and I was working all over the country.

He'd come to see the Cubs play once or twice a year on the West Coast, and I might see him once in the off-season. But after I left Spokane, I never went back too much. That's life, I guess. There's no getting around it because everyone gets busy with their work and personal lives, but I missed going back to Spokane and I missed my family.

I really respected my dad. He taught us good values and respect and just plain common decency. I respect the way he raised his family and taught us a lot about life and took us to church every Sunday. He was a good human being and I don't think there's anything you can say about a person that means more than that.

My dad wasn't very involved in sports, because he never had the time. But he and my mom enjoyed watching sports and he always tried to make it to my games when I was a kid. Even if he couldn't be there for the start of a game, he'd get there as soon as he could after work. I knew it when he got there because I'd watch the stands. It was important for me to have my family there.

My dad worked hard as a mortician but he never made much money. He kept his business pretty private, too, so I never knew much about it. I don't think it was something he really liked talking about. He was depressed a lot of the time at work so he left it there and didn't bring it home.

I miss my dad, but I was fortunate that I got a chance to say good-bye, because I know not everyone gets that opportunity.

It was Dallas Green's idea for me to go home, but that was the kind of guy Dallas was, and the way a lot of baseball people were back in those days. Mean and tough and loud when it was time to be those things, and soft as a teddy bear when it was time to be that way.

Dallas cared about the players and their families and he always talked about taking care of your own. It was understood that he felt that way and he expected guys to bust their butts and give him that in return.

It was a great thing we had going with Dallas. He got the Cubs a winner in his third year and he brought two million people annually to Wrigley Field, which had drawn about half that before he arrived.

We were in a transition period in 1987 but the farm system was very close to giving us some terrific young players. He was paying the price for getting a winner so quickly, but I think everyone in Chicago, especially Tribune Co., felt it was worth it.

Another thing about Dallas was you never saw him hanging around the field or in the clubhouse, like you do with a lot of present-day GMs. My understanding of Dallas was he did his work during the winter to put together a club, and if there was nothing going on or no moves that needed to be made, then we never heard from him or saw him.

He picked a manager who he felt could do the job and he let him manage. He wasn't in the clubhouse or calling him on the phone every day. When you have a GM doing that, the players don't know who the manager is, and they don't know who's making out the lineup card or deciding who pinch hits. That's a bad way to run a club, and the manager gets no respect in that situation.

Dallas would come down from his office maybe two or three times a year and chew us out to try to get us going because he wasn't pleased with our performance, or sometimes when he thought we needed a little kick. He was a great motivator. But Dallas didn't play any games. He was honest and straightforward. Everyone knew where they stood with him and the organization, and you didn't have guys wondering what was going on.

There wasn't any confusion or speculation or lack of communication with Dallas in charge. You didn't have to see the rumors in the papers and reports on TV and we didn't have entire seasons of uneasiness.

There was no mystery. He didn't wait four weeks to make a trade, so it wasn't in the papers for a month. If you saw him on the field, then the trade was that day. If you heard a rumor, it was either bogus or it happened that day.

There's the difference. Nobody suffers. Families didn't have to wonder about when to start packing, because it either happened immediately or it didn't happen at all.

Players need to have some security and some information about their futures. You can spout a popular and easy theory and say pro athletes are spoiled brats, and I'll grant you that some are, but you'd be missing the point. It doesn't change the fact that players are still human beings and they have feelings. If they spend all day and all night for months at a time wondering what's going to happen to them, they will not perform at peak efficiency. It's important to communicate with them, even if it's to tell them bad news. At least it puts an end to the wondering.

I also think that if guys don't know if they'll be here next week or next year, you lose some loyalty. All players want to win, and if a player knows he'll be a Cub next year, he'll play harder for you.

If you make players feel wanted, make them feel appreciated and make them feel a part of the organization, while letting them know you care about their families, you will get a better performance from them.

You can respond to that in two ways. You can say, "They already make too much money, so why should we coddle them?"

Or you can say, "We've got this expensive commodity and a huge investment, so we might as well do everything we can to get the best return possible on our investment."

You figure out which approach makes more sense. It's no different than planting a crop or landscaping. If you spend the money to put it in, you don't just walk away for six months without watering it.

Dallas saw that and that's how he operated. The players worked their butts off for him and were extremely loyal. It was a very stable situation, not just for the players but for everyone who worked around Dallas. He let everyone know what was expected of them and there was no mystery. There was no whispering or guessing games. If there was something on his mind, Dallas told you. If he didn't tell you, then you were OK with him.

In my mind, it's the way baseball is supposed to be.

It was tough for me to return after my dad's funeral, but I came back when my ankle healed. My family wanted me to play because they felt it was good for all of us, and I'm sure my dad would've wanted that, too.

He was a realistic guy and I think he probably would've said, "There's no sense in sitting home. You can't do anything here, so go take care of business."

I was always able to play through tough family times because once I got out on the field, I was usually able to concentrate and do my job.

In fact, in my first at-bat on the day I came back, July 11, 1987, I homered off the Dodgers' Tim Leary. I thought about my dad when I crossed home plate and got a little emotional in the dugout, but I won't sit here and tell you I predicted it.

There was another strange twist to my being activated that day, because as I came off the DL, I took the roster spot of Gary Matthews, who was sent to Seattle for a player to be named later.

That was a sad day, too. The Sarge meant a lot to me and taught me so much about the game on and off the field. When I started out, I was the youngest guy on a team full of veterans who knew how to win and were determined to win. Now another of them was gone.

So was our season, for the most part. We were in second place but had slipped to nine games out of first and seven games over .500 (47-40) on July 11. Today if you're seven over you're probably in first place, but that's another way the game has changed.

Two days after I came back Dallas continued dumping salary by trading Steve Trout to the Yankees. I think Dallas figured he better get what he could after Trout had pitched two straight complete-game shutouts.

One of the guys we got in return was Bob Tewksbury. He had arm trouble and hardly ever pitched for us, but he eventually got healthy and went on to do some outstanding work for the St. Louis Cardinals.

One thing I missed while I was gone was the "Eric Show Incident" on July 7, when Show hit Andre Dawson in the face while he was in the midst of home run streak.

Andre told me that he always thought Show threw right at him, though Show denied it. The thing is, Show always had great control and knew exactly where the ball was going, and that one was going right at Andre's face.

My old pal Larry Bowa was the manager of the Padres at the time, and I know he never would've told someone to throw at a guy's head. Show might've known he had to do something, and probably meant to hit him in the butt, but it got away from him.

Most major league pitchers have incredible control and can brush you off the plate or hit you in the butt without coming anywhere near your head. So you can see why Andre was upset.

Show was lucky Hawk didn't get to him that day, because Andre didn't get mad often, but when he did you didn't want to be the one he was mad at. It took a lot to get him that angry, but I've seen him pick up guys bigger than him and throw them into lockers.

Normally, he was very friendly and soft-spoken, but about once a year someone would really make him mad and he'd take care of it quickly.

The maddest I ever saw him was on July 23, 1991, when home plate umpire Joe West called him out on a pitch a foot outside and in the dirt. Hawk went nuts and Joe threw him out. After he got back to the dugout, Hawk grabbed every bat he could find and threw them on the field. I think it's the only time I ever saw him get tossed out of a game, and if you saw the pitch you know why he was upset.

Well, all Andre did that year for his $500,000 in 1987 was win the MVP award. He hit 49 homers, drove in 137 runs and was simply awesome.

That was the best performance by a player that I ever witnessed during my career and no one else came close.

Andre led our offense and we put up some amazing numbers. That team set club marks for homers at Wrigley Field (114) and total homers (209).

Offense definitely wasn't the problem, but we didn't have much pitching after Sutcliffe. We were still in that transition time when we were starting to get some young pitchers, like Greg Maddux, up from the minors but they weren't quite ready yet.

Toward the end of the year we saw more position players getting their feet wet, like Rafael Palmeiro, Damon Berryhill and Darrin Jackson.

We finished last, but Andre walked away with the MVP award and Sut, who won 18 games, lost out by a couple points to Steve Bedrosian for the Cy Young in the closest voting ever. Greg Maddux was 6–14, but I can say with a straight face that he really pitched a lot better than that. His stuff was very good and all he had to do was learn how to pitch. We did not, however, make it through the year without a managerial switch. Gene Michael believed he was going to be fired at the end of the year, so he re-signed on September 8, and Frank Lucchesi finished out the year.

I knew we'd have another new skipper to start the '88 season.

That's something I learned to expect.

The missiles of October

> "Ryne Sandberg is probably the best thing that ever happened to the Chicago Cubs. On the field he was almost perfect. Off the field, he was perfect."
> —*All-time saves leader Lee Smith*

When we finished 1987 without a manager, there was a lot of talk about John Vukovich, the third base coach, taking over.

It would've been a good thing for us because Vuk was probably ready for the job. He has all the great characteristics of a Phillies product — tough, compassionate and baseball smart.

Vuk is a hard worker and he wants to win, which is what Dallas Green looked for in all of his people, whether they were players or managers or front office workers.

Dallas interviewed several candidates, including Joe Torre, but he wasn't satisfied with what he'd heard and he ultimately decided he'd go back down to the dugout himself. Dallas won a World Series with the Phillies in 1980 as a manager, so he knew how to do that, but he wanted to keep his role as president and general manager while training Vukovich to be the manager.

He wanted Vuk next to him in the dugout, and as soon as Dallas felt Vuk was ready, even if it was midseason, he was going to turn the club over to him.

In the meantime, he wanted his right-hand man, scouting and minor league director Gordy Goldsberry, to keep an eye on things as the general manager until Dallas got back up to the front office. The two of them were building a foundation with a strong minor league program and didn't want to give that up.

But the Cubs' Board of Directors—which is made up of Tribune Co. executives—wouldn't agree to Green's plan. They said he could become manager, but they wanted Don Grenesko to take over as president and decision-maker. Green, however, was not at all excited about the prospect of Grenesko—a Tribune Co. executive and vice president of the Cubs—taking over control of the organization Green was building.

So Dallas said, "Forget it. I'll hire Vukovich as the manager and I'll keep running the team."

Vukovich flew in on Oct. 29, 1987, to meet with Dallas and then had to go in front of Tribune Co. executive John Madigan. That meeting went well and it looked like it was a done deal.

Dallas had already put out the word to call a press conference to annoint Vuk as the new manager when Madigan suddenly showed up at Wrigley Field and called a halt to the proceedings.

He told Dallas again that he could manage the team, but that his other powers would be taken away. It wasn't just an option anymore. It had become an order. Dallas finally couldn't take it anymore. Enough was enough. The interference from above was driving him crazy and he decided it wasn't worth it.

Tribune Co. was taking control of the team and wanted its corporate man, Don Grenesko, in charge of the operation.

Dallas said, "No," and Madigan told Dallas he was fired, while giving him the opportunity to resign. Any way you look at it, the disagreement cost us the best GM in the business, and Vukovich as well.

The radio stations were all reporting that Vukovich had been named as manager, and when reporters showed up for a late afternoon press conference expecting to see the new manager, they instead saw Green get fired.

In my 13 years with the Cubs, that was unquestionably the biggest mistake ownership ever made. There were some big ones later on, but they never would've occurred had Dallas been in charge.

Dallas Green had been hired to do a job and he did it better and faster than anyone could've expected. He brought the Cub fans a winner, he was developing a farm system and the Cubs had drawn over two million people for three of the last four years. Before Tribune Co. bought the team and hired Dallas, the Cubs were drawing about a million less than when Dallas left the ball club.

But after five years, Dallas felt there was too much interference from above, and he didn't much care for advice if it wasn't coming from "baseball people."

There's no way to know how different my life would've been had Dallas not insisted on my being a Cub in the Larry Bowa deal. And Dallas did so many other things for me, like sending me home to see my dad before he died.

I knew I'd lost a close friend who often looked out for me. I'd never really been apart from Dallas Green. I didn't know him well when I was a Phillies farmhand, but he knew me when his people drafted me and when he came to the Cubs, one of the first things he did was trade for me.

He found me a position to play, gave me a major-league job and then gave me a six-year contract and security for life when I had only been in the majors for two years.

Dallas had taken care of me and my family since I signed my first pro contract in 1978, and now he was gone. I owed him a lot, and I felt a little empty knowing he wouldn't be around any longer.

I really believe, now that I look back on it, that we had an incredibly good thing going in 1984.

We had the late Jim Finks as president, and he was a terrific person who took a lot of pressure off Dallas by handling the business decisions. We had Dallas as the GM, Jimmy Frey as the manager and Don Zimmer as a third base coach. Everyone was very good at those jobs, and if it had stayed that way, I'm certain we could've won five or six division titles during my career, maybe more.

But Finks left after the '84 season because he was tired of the interference and didn't want anything to do with the push for lights in Wrigley Field. The company was trying to make him the front man on that and Finks, who understood tradition, didn't want to be known as the man who brought lights to Wrigley Field. Dallas begged him to stay, but Finks couldn't do it anymore.

And I'm sure Dallas would've gotten us back in the playoffs because his farm system with Gordy Goldsberry was producing. But that was not to be. All of them were gone by the end of the '87 season, and I was sitting home in Phoenix wondering where we were going from there.

There were times during my career when the non-baseball execs made baseball decisions, and the results weren't good.

This was one of those times.

The bad news was Dallas Green was gone.

The good news was I was about to be reunited with some old friends.

Jim Frey, who was fired in 1986, spent 1987 in the Cubs' radio booth, and he was darn good at doing color commentary. But Jimmy wanted to get back into baseball and that's what he did when the Cubs hired him as the general manager a few weeks after Dallas resigned.

The first thing Frey did was bring back Don Zimmer as the manager and I was pretty happy about it.

I liked and respected them both. I spent my early years with them and it was a good feeling to have them back. Jimmy had never really left so he knew the club well, and he was very well liked from his managerial days.

The best part was Frey and Zimmer could work together and you didn't have to worry about them not being on the same page, as is sometimes the case with a GM and manager.

Jimmy was a lot like Dallas in the sense that he was very personable and easy to talk to when you saw him. He always wanted to know how you were as a person.

Like Dallas, he did most of his work in the off-season as he put the team together.

Like Dallas, Jimmy had faith in his manager, so Zimmer got full control of running the team during the season. Jimmy hired him because he thought he could do the job, and he let him do his job. No meddling. No calls on the phone about the lineup.

That doesn't mean they didn't talk, because they talked all the time. They communicated and Jimmy always asked Don if he needed anything or what he wanted to get to improve the club.

But he didn't go down to the manager's office every single day to tell him how to run the club. It was a great combination.

Jimmy was also similar to Dallas in the way that he cared about people, and Jimmy did things for people that you probably never heard about.

Like in the spring of '89, Jimmy had Eric Yelding penciled in as a utility guy for us. Eric was sitting in Frey's office about to sign a contract when the Houston Astros called.

Jimmy wanted to keep Eric as insurance in the middle infield, but the Astros had put in a waiver claim and seemed interested in having him play a lot more than that.

"What do you want him for?" Jimmy asked Houston, with Eric sitting right there. "What's he gonna do?"

Jimmy listened and put the Astros on hold.

"Eric, they said they want you to play every day," Frey told Yelding. "That's a pretty good opportunity, isn't it?"

"That's a great opportunity," Yelding answered. "I'd like that."

So Jimmy let him go on a waiver claim. He didn't have to, but it was good for Eric's career and that's the way Jimmy looked at things.

In the spring of 1991, he did a similar favor for Gary Varsho.

The Cubs couldn't find a roster spot for Varsho, a solid bench guy who played a few different positions for us and did well as a pinch hitter.

Frey could've sent him to the minors again as insurance, but he and Zimmer thought so highly of Varsho as a person that Jimmy called around until he found him a major league job. He traded Varsho to Pittsburgh, where he got to sit next to Jimmy Leyland every day and play in a couple of playoff series with the Pirates.

Varsho's one of those guys who could be a great manager because he's very dedicated to the game and studies it. No matter what team he's on, he sits near the manager and tries to learn as much as he can.

He's one of those guys who had to struggle to make it to the majors and stay in the big leagues, and those players usually are the best managers.

But Jimmy did him a favor because he was unselfish and cared enough to do something for Varsho and his family.

Jimmy wasn't perfect, either, and he made mistakes like we all do. He'll tell you right off the bat that trading Lee Smith to Boston in the winter of '87–'88 for Calvin Schiraldi and Al Nipper was a huge mistake.

The thing about a man like Jimmy is he admits his mistakes and moves on. He didn't spend the next two years trying to show the world he was right and compound the mistakes by making the team live with it. He tried to do something about it. General managers compound mistakes all the time because they're more concerned with their image than the team. Dallas Green and Jim Frey weren't like that.

During the 1986, '87 and '88 seasons, I didn't have great years at the plate, at least not like '84 and '85 when we were in the race. Those were the dogs days of my career and something was missing.

Personal stats didn't mean anything to me, so the lack of a pennant race hurt me. I was playing good defense and racking up Gold Gloves and All-Star appearances, but I was unhappy. By the time the '88 season started, Lee Smith and Keith Moreland had been traded, and Bob Dernier left as a free agent. Leon Durham was next to go in May, and our cast from '84 was nearly gone.

In our first year under Jim Frey and Don Zimmer, we went through a rash of pitching injuries early again and were 10 games out by May 20. We finished fourth, 24 out at 77–85 and it was our fourth straight losing season.

The good news was a lot of those young players that Dallas Green and Gordy Goldsberry had developed were showing up in full force.

Rafael Palmeiro proved he was for real and Mark Grace arrived on the scene in May to hit .296 and finish second in the Rookie of the Year voting. Greg Maddux took a big step up and went 18–8.

For the first time since 1977 we had nine players on our Opening Day roster that had played only in our organization, and by mid-season that number was up to 14.

We also placed six players on the All-Star team: Andre Dawson, Shawon Dunston, Vance Law, Palmeiro, Maddux and myself.

But the shock of the year took place when the Cubs announced in July that they'd be adding lights to Wrigley Field, which is something I honestly never thought would happen. I didn't love the idea because I thought Wrigley Field was perfect the way it was, and it sure was nice having all those day games when Lindsey and Justin were in town. But I didn't have a major problem with it because I thought it would help to play a few night games on certain days, and there were only going to be 18 of them.

Before the lights, we were at a disadvantage when we'd fly in late on a Thursday or Sunday night and have to play a day game the next day. Sometimes the opposing team would be in half a day before us and be nice and rested up. So a few well-placed night games throughout the season could actually help us get a few more hours of sleep, and I, for one, always needed my sleep.

There was another problem with having no lights. Any year that we were in contention or near the top of the division, the TV networks would threaten to make us play our games somewhere else, like St. Louis or Atlanta.

I wouldn't have been too happy playing our home playoff games on the road, so that was a benefit.

And I was getting tired of the 3:05 p.m. games. You'd play five or six innings in light and then you'd have shadows. That made the balls into short right field very tough, and I had my share of collisions or near-misses with right fielders out there because neither of us could see.

I loved tradition and I hated to see that one come to an end at Wrigley Field, but as a player I didn't have any say in it and we still had 65 games a year during the day at home, so that was pretty good.

I figured it was just a matter of time before we had lights anyway and it was exciting to be part of it when it happened. The date was 8-8-88, and it was a pretty neat deal. The atmosphere was great, like a playoff game, and seeing the stadium so different at night made it feel like we were characters in a movie.

Fittingly, Rick Sutcliffe started the game and gave up a home run to the Phillies' Phil Bradley on the fourth pitch, but the biggest play of the night came in the bottom of the first, when I came to the plate after a Mitch Webster single.

As I was stepping in, Morganna the Kissing Bandit came galloping out of the right field stands and toward me at home plate.

I was stunned, frozen solid. I had never been chased by anyone of her, uh, magnitude before, and I just stood there. But right before she got to me, the Wrigley Field security force ran her down from behind and wouldn't let her near me. The crowd booed, and actually I didn't see the harm in it, but that was Wrigley Field security for you. They never had much of a sense of humor.

Still, the excitement must have inspired me and I hit the next pitch from Kevin Gross out of the park.

It was the best atmosphere at Wrigley Field since the '84 playoffs, and a great deal of fun, but the game was rained out after three-and-a-half innings and the first "official" night game didn't take place until the next day.

I figured the way the heavens opened up — and we're talking Brazilian rain forest here — was a message to the Cubs about messing with tradition like that.

It was great that Sut started the game, but it was strange that Damon Berryhill got the start behind the plate and not Jody

Davis. No knock on Damon because he was a brilliant young catcher at the time, but Jody had been a fixture for so long.

He wasn't playing much and when he didn't start that big night game, I knew his days were numbered. The first four or five years of my career, I never would've picked up on things like that, but there comes a point when you begin to sense that something's going to happen.

You can tell when a manager's going to be fired or a player's going to be traded. When Jody didn't start that night, I knew they were going to deal him.

Sure enough, on September 29, Jody was traded to Atlanta and the only guys left from '84 were Scott Sanderson, Sut and me. It was tough saying good-bye to good friends like Jody, but we were a young team again.

We still needed a lot of help if we were going to compete in 1989, but at least there were reasons to be hopeful.

I realized I had become a Cub fan, because I was starting to believe in the saying Cub fans made famous: "Wait till next year."

12 A glove full of dollars

"He made so few errors that when he made one you thought the world was coming to an end. Then he hits 30 or 40 homers and scores 100 runs. I saw them all...I saw all the best second basemen who ever played, and in my opinion Ryne Sandberg is the best second baseman who ever played baseball."
—*Former Cubs manager Don Zimmer*

When I signed my six-year contract before the '84 season, I couldn't have known the kind of year I would have and I never would've predicted the year the team would have.

The same holds true for the 1989 season.

I arrived in spring training knowing I'd be a free agent at the end of the season, and that's when I first put a March 1 deadline on wrapping up negotiations — contract or no contract.

I didn't want to deal with it during the season because my focus was on baseball. I think sometimes the Cubs thought my March 1 deadlines were artificial, but they weren't. Unless you've ever been through a protracted, personal negotiation while attempting to do your job at the same time, then you've got no idea how truly distracting it can be. For me, that was no cliche.

I saw some guys completely go to pieces during a season because they were on the phone with their agents 10 minutes before a game. Walking onto the field with that on your mind is no way to play the game.

I wasn't ever going to lose a year of baseball because that was in my head. It was either do it now, or wait until after the season.

And, believe me, my agents knew what they were doing. Each time it got down to less than a year, they encouraged me to take it all the way to free agency, where the opportunities would be much greater. But I always felt like it was best to get it done sooner than later.

If it hadn't gotten done before March 1 in 1989, I would've gone through the season and become a free agent. It doesn't mean I couldn't have re-signed with the Cubs, but in a lot of cases bad things happen and you don't wind up with your old club.

I wanted to stay with the Cubs. I didn't want to leave Wrigley Field and the Cub fans. I didn't want to leave Chicago. I didn't want to learn a new city and new stadium. And most of all, I didn't want to give up my dream of winning a World Series with the Cubs.

So it wasn't an artificial deadline to me, and I stuck by that deadline. In 1989, I was prepared to play out the season and by early evening of March 1 it looked like it would happen that way.

But it got done just before midnight, and I was relieved. I'd been very well taken care of again by the Cubs and Tribune Co., and it was a huge burden lifted off me before the '89 season.

The three-year contract extension would take me through the '92 season, and again people said I had made a mistake because I would be underpaid when the contract was over.

It's true that I would've made more money as a free agent seven months later.

But again I said, who cares? The point was, I didn't want to go through the whole '89 season wondering where I would play the next year and where my family would have to live.

In the deal I got a $900,000 signing bonus; $1.1 million for '90; $2.2 million for '91; and $2.1 million for '92.

And I was supposed to be upset about that? Uh-uh.

That was more money then we'd ever need for the rest of all of our lives, so why did I have to go through a year of agony and the unpleasantness of free agency for a few dollars more?

More importantly, I again had the security of knowing where we would spend the next four years of my career.

Just as before the 1984 season, I was excited as could be to be done with negotiations, and I was primed for a big year. Had I thought about it, maybe I would've seen the obvious comparisons to 1984, but there was no way I could've seen what was going to happen to me or the ball club in 1989.

In 1988 we suffered without a closer. Getting one was Jim Frey's priority when he arrived at the winter meetings in December. He knew it was going to cost him plenty, but he gambled and made the blockbuster trade of the year when he sent Rafael Palmeiro — who everyone knew was going to be a star — Jamie Moyer and Drew Hall to Texas for closer Mitch Williams, infielder Curtis Wilkerson and pitchers Steve Wilson and Paul Kilgus.

Williams was the key to the deal, and Jimmy Frey got hammered for making it. He was raked over the coals for weeks.

But we lacked depth and pitching and Jimmy made a deal that would bolster those areas. We were still short some power, but we were a young team and very enthusiastic.

We were making a nice transition with young players from the farm system. On Opening Day, we started two players — center fielder Jerome Walton and catcher Joe Girardi — who'd spent 1988 in Double-A.

As usual, we didn't have a good spring training and we finished up in Minneapolis to play the Twins for a couple of exhibition games.

Privately, Jim Frey told Don Zimmer that he'd throw a party if this young club could finish .500, but I didn't think that was unreasonable.

During the last game in Minneapolis, Zim got kicked out in the third inning. I got my two at-bats in and after I did my running, I walked into the manager's office to kid Zim about being kicked out of an exhibition game.

Zim was totally relaxed, sitting back in his chair in his underwear like he always did. He was watching the game on TV and every once in a while he'd take both hands and rub his face as if to say, "I'm worn out from this team already and the season hasn't even started."

Zim looked at me, smiled and said, "Ryno, I don't know how we're gonna do this year, but it might not be too long before I'm down in Treasure Island, Florida, doing some fishing and playing some golf."

We laughed. But it wasn't too funny because things were really going badly. And on that note, spring training came to a close— with Zim thinking he'd be fired and fishing before the All-Star break.

Opening Day was always a fresh start for everyone. If you couldn't be optimistic that day, then you never had a chance to be.

And Opening Day 1989 against the Phillies at Wrigley Field erased all the bad memories of spring training.

Rick Sutcliffe started his fifth straight opener and pitched a terrific game. Walton and Girardi each got a couple of hits and everything clicked. It was like night and day from the way we played in spring training.

And, of course, it had its drama.

Mitch Williams came in to pitch the ninth with a 5–4 lead, and already Jimmy's trade was on the line.

As we came to learn quickly, nothing Mitch ever did was simple. All our new closer did was load the bases on three scratch singles with nobody out and the meat of their order coming up.

But before the crowd could get surly, Mitch struck out the great Mike Schmidt and Chris James, too.

Now the crowd was going bananas and Mitch was so pumped up he was throwing about 95 mph. He finished it off by striking out Mark Ryal and that was the ball game.

We won the game and Mitch jumped up as high as he could and we danced all over the field. It was really the first time I could remember celebrating a win like that since Game 2 of the 1984 playoffs against San Diego.

But it was really quite different from 1984. We didn't have nearly as many veterans — only me, Hawk, Sut, Scott Sanderson and Vance Law.

The rest of the guys were young and we didn't know how we'd win games, but we played good ball. Zim had us squeezing and had the hit-and-run going constantly. We'd hit behind the runner and sacrificed properly and just played good baseball.

It was a good mix of veterans and young guys and it made me feel like a kid again.

One thing Jim Frey and Don Zimmer were always careful about was having good people on the club, and that made for good chemistry.

There are some people in baseball who don't believe in chemistry. They say, "Go out and play baseball, who cares about chemistry."

Well, those guys are executives and they don't have to play, so they don't care what it's like. But people who don't think chemistry matters, don't know what they're talking about.

Jim Frey — and Dallas Green before him — made sure the chemistry was good. Sometimes they traded good players and got criticized for the moves, but what the fans might not have known was what a bad influence certain people were. I watched Mike Ditka build the Bears into a Super Bowl winner using the same philosophy. He shocked a lot of people in the early '80s and cleaned out a lot of lockers before some veterans got the message.

Like Ditka, Dallas and Jimmy would occasionally sacrifice talent for the good of the team, to try to put together a group of guys who would fight for each other and play as a team.

Chemistry can be as simple as getting together a group of players who follow the rules, have the same goals and have the same attitude. Guys who respect each other.

That's what baseball is all about. That's the way it's supposed to be.

And that's the way it was in 1989. We had guys going to lunch together every day on the road, six or 10 in a group. Not 25 guys going in 25 different directions.

It seemed like all the guys wanted to win. It was a team-oriented clubhouse with great atmosphere and a lot of that came from the leadership of Don Zimmer.

You had to love playing for Zim. His rules were so simple: Be on time and play hard. Zim was an old-school guy who felt that "90 percent of life is showing up." If you couldn't enjoy playing for him then you had a problem.

Boy, did we have fun in '89.

I think Zim felt like he didn't know how long he'd be around, so he threw all caution to the wind. That's when you play the best baseball, and everything Zim tried that year worked.

We pulled some plays on teams that they couldn't believe — and neither could we. It'd be bases loaded and one out and maybe a 3–1 count and Zim would run everyone. Or we'd have guys on first and second and nobody out on a 3–0 count and Zim would send them.

It was the most fun I'd had in a long time.

We were a team. When you came in off the field, guys were cheering you on, even if they weren't playing. We had great bench guys like Doug Dascenzo and Curtis Wilkerson and Lloyd McClendon and Rick Wrona.

They weren't mad that you were playing and they weren't. They just wanted to win and didn't care about their playing time.

If you're a guy who plays 155 or 160 games a year, the last thing you want when you come into the dugout between innings is to hear guys complaining about their personal situation or their playing time or how much money they can make at arbitration if they play more.

You want a little support. We had bench guys in '89 who supported the regulars, and then when they were called on to do the job, they did it. That's a definition of chemistry right there. If everyone's goal is to win, the rest of it takes care of itself.

Mitch saved six of the first 10 games and right off the bat it gave us the confidence we didn't have the year before. Mitch was a great character, too. They started playing the song "Wild Thing" over the P.A. system whenever he came in because that was his nickname. It was an obvious steal from the movie *Major League*.

Mitch loved it, but the pitching coach, Dick Pole, didn't like it and made them stop.

"He's wild enough as it is," Pole said. "I don't want him thinking about that when he walks in from bullpen."

Mitch kept everyone loose, except Zim. He drove Zim crazy on the field because he loaded the bases every time he pitched, and off the field because he was a little tough to handle at times.

Mitch needed to know he was the man, and he needed that reassurance. That's OK, because there are a lot of players like that. You just have to know how to handle players and understand that everyone is different and know their needs are different.

Some players are high-maintenance and some are low-maintenance, like Andre Dawson. Leave him alone and let him play and you'll never have to say a word to him. At the same time though, you can't let the stars get away with anything. You have to make sure everyone plays by the same rules and does what's asked of them.

A manager's dream is a star who works harder than everyone on the team, leads by example and never has to be told when to show up and or when to do his work.

I took pride in the fact that I was always early and always prepared. I'm amazed by what goes on in today's game, with the laziness and lack of work ethic and preparation, and just the way some players don't follow the rules.

It's such basic stuff. How hard is it to set your alarm and get to the park on time? How difficult is it to run the bases during batting practice? How tough is it to learn the signs and pay attention to them?

I never thought it was too difficult.

Our 1989 season was wild from start to finish. We began by winning eight of the first 10, and then put together these streaks for the rest of the year:

We lost eight of nine; won eight of 11; lost five straight; won 16 of 22; lost six of eight; won five; lost seven; won eight of 10; lost four of five; won 22 of 29; lost six straight; won four of five; lost five of seven; and finished the season by winning 16 of 23.

We had already lost 16 of 25 from April 17 to May 14 when things really got ugly.

Our entire starting outfield — Andre Dawson, Jerome Walton and Mitch Webster — went on the disabled list in five days from May 9–14.

So up from Des Moines came Doug Dascenzo, Lloyd McClendon and Dwight Smith, who nearly made the club out of spring training.

And all we did was win 10 of 13.

By May 28, before we started getting any of the outfielders back, we went from three-and-a-half games down to two-and-a-half games up in first place.

That was probably the key time of the season. Instead of falling apart, we rallied and took over first.

It took about 35 guys to play that 1989 season and they all contributed in some way.

In his first at-bat as a Cub on May 15, Lloyd McClendon hit a three-run homer and helped us break a five-game losing streak.

Dwight Smith hit about .400 for a month and never went back to Iowa. Doug Dascenzo caught every ball that was hit near him.

But the injuries didn't stop there.

We were in first place and up a couple of games on June 4 when we creamed the Cards 11–3 at Busch Stadium. I hit two homers, Shawon hit two and our total of six that day was a Busch Stadium record for homers by one team in a game.

Late in the game, Frank DiPino threw inside on Mark Grace and nearly hit him. Those two didn't much like each other from the previous year they'd played together in Chicago. So after the brushback, Grace charged the mound and got DiPino pretty good. But the benches emptied and Grace wound up on the bottom of the pile.

Bad things can happen to you down there and sure enough Gracie got stepped on and suffered a separated right shoulder.

Again, we overcame the injury.

Gracie was having a great year, but McClendon stepped in and did the job at first.

The next night at Wrigley Field, Greg Maddux pitched a beauty and we hammered Mets ace David Cone 15–3. That sent them a little message, because here we were all banged up and they were supposed to walk away with the division in '89.

We took three of four in that series and took a three-game lead. But a couple of weeks later we lost six straight on the worst June homestand in club history (0–6), and fell out of first for the first time since May 21.

It was late June and all the old talk of choke was beginning to creep back into the newspapers.

In any championship season, there are big comeback wins that propel you to a title and in '89 we had 33 comeback victories.

Twenty of them came after July 20, but July 20 in itself was a memorable night at Wrigley Field when the young Cubs played the Giants on national TV.

We were two-and-a-half out of first and this night we trailed the Giants 3–0 in the bottom of the ninth facing Steve Bedrosian, one of the best closers in the game at that time.

With two outs and two on, Dwight Smith singled to score Mark Grace from second, and when right fielder Candy Maldonado tried to get Grace at home, the ball skipped away from catcher Kirt Manwaring, allowing Damon Berryhill to move up to third and Dwight Smith to second.

That was a big play because moments later, Curtis Wilkerson took an 0–2 pitch from Bedrosian and slapped it through the left side for a 100-foot single that scored both runners and tied the game at 3–3.

Lester Lancaster took over on the mound after that. Les was another guy we couldn't have won without in '89. He came up June 24 and was absolutely on fire for about seven weeks. He pitched 30 consecutive scoreless innings and was virtually unhittable.

On this July 20 night against the Giants, he set down the heart of the order and it was still 3–3 going into the bottom of the 11th.

Les wasn't much of a hitter, though I'm sure he'd tell you differently, but Zim had no choice but to let him hit with two outs and Curtis Wilkerson on first.

Somehow, Les punched a double down the left-field line and into the bullpen. Wilky was running on the pitch and barely beat the throw home, sliding head-first across home plate with the game-winner.

We went nuts. We jumped all over Wilky and all over Les, but what we didn't know was that Wilky had swallowed a whole mouthful of tobacco when he hit the dirt at home plate.

And while we were climbing all over him, Wilky's eyes were watering and looked like they'd pop out of his head. All he wanted to do was go in the tunnel and throw up. We finally let him go take care of himself, and he never did join the celebration that night.

But from that point on, we won 21 of the next 28 and were tied for first with Montreal when the Expos came to town August 7.

For the first time since August of '84 against the Mets, we were playing in a series with first place on the line. I was pumped. I lived for the crowd excitement that went along with a big series.

We lost a tough 18-inning game in Pittsburgh the day before, so I was glad this was a night game, 364 days after the first one ever at Wrigley Field.

With 39,000 people on their feet all night, Greg Maddux tossed a complete game for the victory and we were all alone in first place.

The bizarre move of the night went to Montreal starter Pascual Perez. The guys had been on him all night because they knew they could rattle him with enough chatter.

After a while he couldn't take it any longer, and during a conference on the mound, he turned and tossed a ball into our dugout — and it hit Sutcliffe right in the arm.

"It didn't hurt," Sut said. "It was going so slow I thought Scott Sanderson threw it."

Yes, we were loose and we were hot.

The next night Mike Bielecki, who was having the year of his career, pitched another beauty and Les Lancaster picked him up with the save.

Jerome Walton, meanwhile, had the crowd on edge the entire series because he was in the midst of a Cubs' record 30-game hitting streak.

Sut pitched the final game and got the win with help from Mitch. We had swept the Expos and never looked back.

I homered in all three games and I was making life difficult for Zim. The afternoon before the first Montreal game, Zim came to me and told me he wanted to give me a day off. All of the managers I played for tried to find days off for me, but they never could really find them because I'd get hot or the team needed a win and he wanted his best lineup out there.

I mean, I played 157 or 158 games a year, except for in '87 (dislocated ankle) and '93 (broken hand and finger). So I got one day off a month or less during most seasons.

Well, Zim called me into the office before the Montreal series and was looking at the schedule. I think I had played about three months without a day off.

"I need to get you a day off," Zim said. "And there's a stretch coming up where I'd like to get you one. You can relax and be strong to finish the last six or seven weeks."

He always gave me about a week's notice. I loved when a manager did that because I knew then that I could take the family out that night for dinner or the night before or make plans for after the game.

But from the time Zim told me that until the day he wanted me to take a day off, I hit a home run in every game. I hit six homers in five games, including at least one in five straight, tying Hack Wilson's club mark and I came within three of the major league record held at the time by Dale Long and Don Mattingly.

Zim was on the spot because my day off was the next day. He told the reporters that he had promised me a day off and so I'd be off.

The response from the reporters was that everyone would be going to Wrigley Field the next day to see me hit a home run, and Zim said, "What do you want me to do? The guy needs a day off. He can't play 162 games, and I promised him. I'm thinking in terms of September here."

He was put in an uncomfortable situation but he gave me the day off against a pitcher who threw a lot of nasty sliders and I don't know how I would've done anyway.

The following day I did play and didn't hit a home run. I felt bad for Zim because he was being criticized, but I didn't care about the record anyway. Those days off were precious. I never asked for them and over the course of the season, I probably needed a day off every six weeks to stay strong and the manager could usually sense that.

It never failed, though, that if I was going to get a day off, I'd have three straight three-hit games and everyone would be yelling at the manager about giving me a day off while I was hot.

I was certainly hot in August of '89, hitting 11 homers for one of the biggest months of my career.

But it was near the end of the month that we played what might've been the biggest game of the year.

# 13 Hot town, summer in Chicago

"I once saw Ryno make an error two straight days. It was unbelievable. I said, 'Are you OK? Is something wrong?' He didn't say anything. He doesn't show emotion. His emotion is he gets the fingernail clipper and does his nails. That's how you know he's mad. But he won't say a word."
—*Double-play partner Shawon Dunston*

We'd lost seven of 10 and nothing much was going right when the Astros hit town in late August of '89. They swept us the week before in Houston and we looked terrible in the process.

Maddux opened the series at Wrigley with a complete-game victory and our lead was two-and-a-half games, but the next day, August 29, we spotted the Astros a 9–0 lead after five innings.

At that point, Zimmer took out Andre Dawson and came down the dugout toward me.

"Ryno, I'm sorry," Zim said. "But there's a full house here today. I already took out the right fielder, and if I take out the second baseman, too, there's 30,000 people here who are going to run me out of town."

So I stayed in, and we began to chip away at the deficit.

It was 9–4 in the top of the eighth when Dwight Smith took over the game. Playing right field for Andre, he threw out a runner trying to score to keep us within five.

I had an RBI single in the eighth to start the scoring, and we didn't stop until a few minutes later when Smitty flew out to deep center to score Lloyd McClendon with the tying run.

If that weren't enough, Smitty won it in the 10th with an RBI single, and there we were on the field again celebrating like we'd won the World Series.

The 10–9 victory marked the biggest comeback by the Cubs in the 20th century, and it sent us on a 19–12 run.

Zim was celebrating just as hard as the rest of us. He came running into the clubhouse whooping and hollering and jumped up onto a long card table. The leap itself would've been enough for me, but then it collapsed and Zim went flying.

He was OK, but the table was a goner, and we were all hysterical — except for Yosh Kawano. Yosh was so upset he went a little nuts. But Zim couldn't control himself any more than the rest of us. It was just too much fun. The young guys had made us all feel like rookies again.

All the kids — Dwight Smith, Jerome Walton, Joe Girardi, Rick Wrona, Doug Dascenzo, Gary Varsho, Shawon Dunston, Mark Grace, Les Lancaster, Greg Maddux, Mitch Williams, Steve Wilson and Jeff Pico — had filled our clubhouse with excitement and enthusiasm.

That Houston win also marked the first Cub victory for Paul Assenmacher, who came to us four days before that from the Braves. He turned out to be a great guy and he fit right in with our group. He also did a great job in relief down the stretch.

On August 31, Jimmy Frey picked up a couple more veterans. He got Luis Salazar and Marvell Wynne from San Diego for Calvin Schiraldi and Darrin Jackson. The new guys fit right in, too, and the moves Jimmy was making told us we were going for it all.

I appreciated the title chase much more in '89 than I had in '84, knowing that so many factors can stop you from making another run. I knew I had to enjoy it while I could, and I was more into it during the second half of 1989 than at any part of any season during my career.

In '84, I was so young. It's not that I took it for granted, but I didn't know those pennant races would be so few and far between. At the time I figured we had a lot of chances to get in the playoffs — or at least enjoy the heat of a pennant race.

And even though this '89 club was young, I'd learned that a lot of things can sidetrack you on the way to another division title.

This team was special, too, because it was the closest team I ever played on — even closer than the '84 team, which was a very tight group. The guys genuinely cared about each other and liked being together.

There were so many surprises and that made it exciting. Both young and old players were coming out of nowhere to have big years.

Mike Bielecki, for instance, had made only 47 big-league starts and won 33 games prior to the '89 season, but at age 30 in '89 he went 18–7 with a 3.14 ERA and finished 11–3 against the Eastern Division.

A lot of the credit has to go to pitching coach Dick Pole, who worked with Bielecki in winter ball and helped him re-create the forkball that had been Bielecki's bread and butter years before.

Pole, who actually pitched for Zim in Boston in 1976, had worked wonders with Greg Maddux in the minor leagues. And after Maddux went 6–14 in 1987, he went to winter ball with Pole and came back to win 37 games the next two years.

For me, 1989 represented my first power surge since '85, when I hit 26 homers. In '86, '87 and '88, I hit a combined 49 homers, but in '89 I came back with 30 homers and 104 runs scored.

I know it had a lot to do with the excitement of the team being in the race. That pumped me up. There's no getting around the fact that when I was having fun I performed better.

The jump to 30 homers also had something to do with the fact that I was getting bigger and stronger. I had just turned 30 and I was in my prime both physically and athletically. In '86 and '87, I worked hard with the strength coach, Phil Claussen, who was the first to show me a weight program that worked nicely for a base-ball player's body. It's something I still use today.

I also became more aggressive at the plate in '89 and I knew the league and had a lot of confidence. I was peaking, plain and simple, and it was a good time for it.

Our lead was back down to a half-game after we lost the first of a three-game set with St. Louis at Wrigley Field on September 8.

I homered twice in that game and we were cruising with a 7–1 lead, but Pedro Guerrero's eighth-inning homer to right off Mitch Williams capped a big comeback for the Cards and we lost 11–8.

Every time we lost a big game in '84 and '89, the same talk of choke would return, and this day was no different. But our attitude was nothing like that. The kids in '89 didn't know any more about '69 than I did in '84, and we were very positive going into the next game.

So on Saturday, Game 2 of the series, we played the Cards tough. Luis Salazar made his impact felt when he tied the game at 2–2 in the eighth with an RBI single.

The crowd was thinking the same thing in the 10th when he came to the plate with Andre Dawson on first. Hawk was really suffering with a bad knee at the time, but there was no way he was coming out.

Salazar reached out and poked a Ken Dayley pitch into the right-field corner for a double, and Hawk was digging as hard as he could. He rounded third and it looked like it might be close, but Hawk beat the throw and as he crossed home plate he jumped right into the arms of Shawon Dunston.

That's the picture I remember most from 1989, Andre and Shawon jumping up and down and hugging each other. Andre, like me, didn't show much emotion out there, but that's what Shawon brought out of him. Shawon kept Hawk young and Hawk helped Shawon grow up. They were great for each other, almost like father and son.

Well, Assie got the win in that big game, too, and we ended up winning five more for a six-game streak. We were now two-and-a-half games up on St. Louis.

All year, every time we faced adversity, we turned it up a notch and fought off the criticism. We were a very loose team and we weren't bothered by those tough losses.

And when we finished a sweep of the Pirates on September 24 at Wrigley Field, to go up four games on the Cards, the magic number was down to two with only six games to play.

We drew almost 2.5 million fans in 1989 to set a franchise record, and just like in '84, the fans wouldn't go home after our final home game in 1989.

The difference was we hadn't won anything yet. But there was no way the fans would leave, so we came back out of the club-house for a victory lap and celebrated with the fans, because we were going on the road for the final week of the season.

The papers had a nice time with that, because it would've been the worst victory lap in history if we failed to win the division in the final week of the season.

In 1984 it was only fitting that Rick Sutcliffe pitched the division-clincher, and if we were going to win in 1989, that job had to belong to our new ace, Greg Maddux.

The 23-year-old started the year 1–5 but went 18–7 to finish 19–12 and third in the voting for Cy Young.

And on Tuesday, September 26, in Montreal, with our magic number still at two, it was up to Maddux to end the suspense with only five games left in the season.

We needed some help from the Pirates and we watched the scoreboard all night. Finally, it was posted: The Pirates had beaten the Cards and we just had to finish off the Expos to clinch the division.

When the St. Louis final went up, we were tied at 2–2 in the eighth with Dennis Martinez and the Expos, and I was standing on first base. Dwight Smith was the hitter and he promptly singled to right. I got a good jump on the play and was well on my way to third when Hubie Brooks bobbled the ball in right field. Chuck Cottier, the third base coach, never stopped waving and I slid home ahead of the throw to put us up 3–2.

Maddux started the ninth but got into trouble, and he left with Otis Nixon on second and one out.

I guess since Mitch Williams started our season with his dramatics, it was probably appropriate for him to close it out, too.

Mitch got the second out and then Nixon stole third while Mitch got Mike Fitzgerald in the hole at 1–2. Just like in Pittsburgh five years before, most of the fans in attendance that night in Montreal were Cub fans, and they were all on their feet.

Mitch was pumped, and when I saw the sign for a fastball, I knew the pitch wouldn't be anywhere near the strike zone. Mitch went into his stretch, and Nixon was bluffing at third. A wild pitch or a passed ball or anything in the dirt would've meant a tie game.

Mitch fired it about a foot high and two feet outside, and Fitzgerald tried to check his swing almost the same way Joe Orsulak did in Pittsburgh in '84.

But the result was the same. Before Joe Girardi could even ask for an appeal, home plate umpire Dutch Rennert rung him up and our party began.

Mitch jumped about 10 feet into the air and we all followed suit. It was like a group of Little League kids crawling all over each other and tackling each other.

The celebration was tremendous, and the outpouring of affection was something I'd never seen before in baseball. Everyone felt great for Zim, who said it was the proudest moment of his baseball career. He'd been in baseball 45 years at that point and he had come so close in Boston in 1978, but lost a one-game playoff to the Yankees. But this time there was no Bucky Dent and Zim walked around the locker room and kissed every one of us and thanked every player for playing so hard for him. When he hugged me I wanted to cry.

People thought Jimmy Frey hired him only because they were friends, but Jimmy would say, "I got a lot of friends, and I didn't hire them all to be manager of the Cubs. I happen to think Zim's a great manager and the guy for this team. That's why I hired him."

Zim won Manager of the Year in '89 and he should have. Everything he did worked.

In June, he went to a four-man rotation and sometimes even a three-man with days off. He got criticized for that, too, but Maddux, Bielecki and Sutcliffe were having huge years, and Zim always believed in playing the hot hand.

He called those three into his office and said, "Raise your hand when you can't pitch, and I won't be mad about it. I need you guys to bring us through this, so when you can go, I'm sending you out there."

That's when we made our big move in June and those starters kept us in every game. I doubt we would've won the division if Zim hadn't gambled on that decision.

But Zim would always say, "I never got a hit, I never made a pitch and I never caught a ball. The players did this, not me." Zim just wanted to win. He didn't go looking for any credit.

We stayed in the clubhouse for about three hours celebrating and the guys didn't want to leave. Once again, we watched on TV as the fans celebrated at Wrigley Field and I wished we were there with them.

After most of the guys had left the clubhouse, I walked in and sat down with Zim. He was still so emotional.

"Ryno, when I looked up and saw St. Louis lost, I knew we clinched a tie," Zim said. "I said to myself, 'OK. That's the best I've ever done in baseball. That's what we got in Boston.' And when we got that last out, a feeling came over me. It was the most satisfying feeling of my baseball life." And then Zim started to cry again.

Zim had finally satisfied the critics, who really didn't know anything about him. Baseball was life to Zim and he put his heart and soul into it.

And baseball had finally given him a team he could be proud of.

That was a late night, like the one in Pittsburgh in '84, but this time *Good Morning America* wasn't knocking on my door at 7:30 a.m.

That's good, because I don't think I could've answered that morning either.

And it's a good thing we won the night we did, because after the next night in Montreal, we ran into trouble at a Montreal airport.

When we got there, hydraulic fluid was leaking all over the place, and there was no way the plane was going to be ready that night.

But the bus that brought us there had left and the truck that brought all our equipment was also gone. So there we were at midnight in Montreal, stranded at the airport with no bus, no truck, a broken plane and no way to get to St. Louis.

We wound up at the other Montreal airport and didn't take off until 6:30 a.m. for St. Louis. We finally got to the hotel at 10 a.m.

The Cards had been right on our heels all season, so if we hadn't clinched in Montreal, and had to face the Cards in those final three games under those conditions, I shudder to think what might've happened.

It's a good thing the games in St. Louis on the final weekend didn't matter.

It was such an exciting run from beginning to end, and I know personally I was more emotional than at any other time in my career.

I've always been intense on the inside, but some guys told me they saw a fire in my eyes in the second half of '89 that hadn't been noticable before. In some ways, I felt like that was my team in '89 and I felt a responsibility at times to carry the club. We had a lot of injuries to key players that year and I felt like I had to elevate my game. Especially when Hawk was out, I felt like it was my responsibility to make things happen.

With Hawk out, they weren't really pitching to me, and for one of the rare times in my career, I had to expand my strike zone and swing at some pitches I normally wouldn't have gone for.

At the All-Star break I was hitting .262 with 11 homers, 34 RBI and 44 runs, but in the second half I hit .321 with 19 homers, 42 RBI and 60 runs.

From July 28 on, when we trailed the Expos by three-and-a-half games, I hit .346 with 18 homers and 38 RBI. I was totally zoned in and I was leaving it all out there emotionally and physically.

It was so satisfying for us on so many different levels.

I was happy for Jimmy Frey. Although he had been heavily criticized for the Palmeiro deal, he had proven the critics wrong. There's no way we would've won it that year without Mitch Williams, so while it cost us a great player like Palmeiro, as did Sutcliffe-for-Carter in '84, it had been worth it. Mitch was a big part of the excitement that year, too. He was always running around jumping up and down after games. Constant energy and motion. People may say a lot of things about Mitch, but he wanted to win and he gave you everything he had, no matter what the outcome was.

Everyone on that team was in it together, and no one talked about our injuries that year because we overcame them.

We lost a whole outfield in three days, but we overcame that. We lost our starting catcher, Damon Berryhill, but we overcame that.

Every time you turned around, someone was coming up big. Shawon Dunston was superb at the plate, and in the field he was running all over the field catching balls and throwing runners out.

Dwight Smith was amazing, on and off the field. He kept us all laughing in the locker room, and on the field he made opposing pitchers cry.

He hit .324, the highest average by a Cubs rookie since Bill Madlock in 1974, but he finished second in the Rookie of the Year voting to Jerome Walton, who was simply spectacular.

The real job still lay ahead of us, and we were going to need everyone to defeat the NL West champion San Francisco Giants.

We had a better team than the Giants in '89, but right from the time the series started, they seemed to get all the big hits when it counted.

In Game 1, we were down 3–0 early, but cut it to 3–2 after an inning. We still trailed 4–3 in the fourth, but we were scrapping to stay in the game.

Greg Maddux was struggling, and Zim had the lefty, Paul Assenmacher, ready in the bullpen when he went out to see Maddux with the bases loaded, two outs and Will Clark due up.

I know what Zim was thinking. Mark Grace homered in the first, I homered in the third and we were hitting Scott Garrelts hard. We're a run down with our ace on the mound, and if he gets out of the jam, the game turns in our favor. So Zim came out to see Greg, who said he was fine. Not that Mad Dog would ever tell you he wasn't fine.

As they were speaking, Will Clark walked back to the visitor's on-deck circle and stood next to Kevin Mitchell. And while Zim and Greg spoke, Clark read Greg's lips. Clark already had a double and a homer off Greg, but he saw Greg repeat what Zim said: Fastball in.

Clark knew what the pitch was going to be and sure enough it was a fastball in — but not far enough in for a guy who knew what pitch was coming. Clark was looking for it, got it, fully extended and hit that fastball in, out onto Sheffield Avenue for a grand slam.

It was 8–3 and Game 1 was basically over.

That was Clark's second grand slam of his career, and the other one had come earlier that year against the Phillies' Mike Maddux. At least Greg wouldn't have to hear about that on the golf course from his brother.

After we heard about what Clark had done, we were amazed. We've all tried it before, but I don't know anyone who has known for sure what the pitch was going to be by reading someone's lips. It reminded me of high school football when we tried to listen in on the other team's huddle to hear the play and cadence.

I know one thing: Since that day, Greg Maddux has never had a conversation on the mound without putting his glove over his mouth.

We lost Game 1 11–3 as Kevin Mitchell added a homer and that tough Giants lineup just didn't let up.

These were the first playoff night games in the history of Wrigley Field and it was cold.

That's one thing about October in Chicago. It might be 70 and beautiful during the day, but it's cold at night.

I remembered wanting lights for playoff games but now I was seeing what the wind off Lake Michigan does on an October evening.

Game 2 was delayed by rain and affected by the cold, but we knew we had to have it. We couldn't go to San Francisco down 2–0 in a best of seven series. We got out of the blocks quickly, hitting my former teammate, Rick Reuschel, for six runs in the first inning while sending 12 men to the plate.

Mike Bielecki started but Les Lancaster was credited with the win after pitching four innings in relief. We won 9–5 and felt pretty good about our chances. All we had to do was win one of three games at Candlestick Park to get back to Wrigley Field for Games 6 and 7.

Of course, I thought to myself, we only needed one of three in San Diego in '84 to go to the World Series. So while I was certain we had a better club than the Giants, overconfidence was not a problem.

Rick Sutcliffe had another terrific year in '89, but when he took the mound for Game 3, he really looked like he was pitching with a bad shoulder.

He battled hard despite the pain and we led 4–3 in the seventh, but for the first time all year we didn't get the relief we needed from Les Lancaster.

In the seventh he relieved Paul Assenmacher with a runner on and a 2–0 count to Robby Thompson. But Les didn't know the count. He thought it was 3–0 and with Will Clark on deck, he figured he needed to throw a strike.

He threw a fastball right down the middle and Thompson crushed it for a two-run homer to put the Giants up 5–4. That's the way it ended, we were down two games to one, but we had Greg Maddux going in Game 4.

Once again, however, we were down early. Zim took out Maddux in the fourth, and in the top of the fifth we came back to tie it at 4–4.

But in the bottom of the fifth, Matt Williams took Steve Wilson deep for a two-run homer and that was the all the scoring for the night. The 6–4 loss put us on the brink of elimination, but all we had to do was win Game 5 and we could head back to Chicago.

Mike Bielecki pitched his heart out in Game 5. I don't know how else to describe it.

We were leading 1–0 going into the bottom of the seventh when they tied it at 1–1, and that was still the score in the bottom of the eighth.

It seemed like a harmless inning when Bielecki got the first two outs. But Candy Maldonado worked the count to 3–2 before he fouled off a couple of pitches. On the 10th pitch to Maldonado, Bielecki looked tired. He missed low and away for ball four.

Mike fell behind on Brett Butler, but came back to even the count at 2–2. Then he threw a fastball on the outside corner and we were running in off the field. It was a strike, but it was called ball three. Butler then fouled off two pitches before Bielecki missed high and away for ball four.

He had pitched the game of his life, but he was up around 130 pitches and he was done.

The problem was, the bullpen hadn't done the job in this series, and Zim was concerned about that.

Even so, when he came out to the mound, we were patting Bielecki on the back because we thought Zim would call for a reliever.

When Zim got to the mound, Bielecki walked up from the back of the mound, reached out with the ball and prepared to give it to Zim in full stride on his way to the dugout.

But Zim folded his arms and Bielecki stopped dead in his tracks. "You're my man," Zim said.

Bielecki had already shut it down mentally, and physically he was done. He walked Robby Thompson on four pitches and Zim went to the bullpen.

Then came the match-up everyone had been waiting for all week. It was Mitch Williams against Will Clark with the bases loaded, the scored tied at 1–1 and the series on the line.

Mitch was ready. The first pitch was a fastball right down the middle. Strike one. Clark fouled off the next pitch and Mitch was up big, 0–2.

He wasted the next pitch high and away, but Will didn't bite and it was 1–2. Mitch went back at Clark again, and he fouled off another pitch.

Again Mitch challenged him with a fastball down the middle and Clark fouled it straight back. They were battling, but no one was giving in.

There were so many times in that series when we just needed one hit or one pitch to win a game, and here we were in Game 5 needing one strike to stay tied and have a chance to win. But Clark didn't miss the next pitch. He lined a base hit right up the middle past Mitch for two runs and the Giants took the lead 3–1.

We came back in the ninth to score once and close the gap to 3–2 on three hits with two outs, and that gave me another shot at Steve Bedrosian.

We had good luck with Bedrosian all year, but in the series he was sharp and had saved two games already, and throughout my career I'd never done much against him.

I knew with the tying run on second and the lead-run on first, he wasn't going to give me something inside I could pull down the line, so I was looking for something on the outer half of the plate.

I also expected him to start me with a slider because that was his bread and butter. I was just hoping for something I could take up the middle or drive into right or right-center.

The pitch was in the location I expected, but I didn't get a good swing and his sharp slider nearly broke my bat. I grounded out to second baseman Robby Thompson for the final out of the series.

That was the way it ended and I had to walk back to the dugout through their celebration.

We had lost the last three games by a total of four runs and it meant I had to watch another celebration from the dugout. That was the worst part about losing. Those first four or five minutes when the Padres or Giants jumped all over each other.

It made me sick.

This was a bitter defeat because we didn't play badly. We did a lot of things well, but there was just too much Will Clark, who hit .650 against us.

Every game was close but the Giants were unconscious offensively when they needed to be.

And you can't fault Zim for any of it. He gambled all year and we won every time. He went against the book for an entire season and we won a division. You can't change your style just because it's the playoffs.

It just stopped working for us at a bad time.

A really bad time.

It hurt a lot, but I hurt more for the others, most of all Andre Dawson. Hawk had a rough series because his knees were killing him. But he never used that as an excuse and stood up after those games and answered every question from every reporter. Andre is one of classiest and most professional guys you'll ever meet.

But it was tough watching him after the series was over. You could see the disappointment in his face.

I also felt terrible for Frey and Zimmer, who lived and died with the young club.

Before he opened the doors to the press, Zim pulled us all together. He was bawling like a baby, but he said, "Before this year I never would've believed in what chemistry could do for a team, but I've never seen 25 guys pull together like you guys did for each other this year. I'll never forget you guys as long as I live."

Zim might've been a grizzled, 40-year veteran of the baseball wars, but he was as caught up in that team as the rest of us, and I was sorry for him that we fell short. I felt bad, too, for Mark Grace, who had such a phenominal series, and Mitch Williams, who took every loss so personally.

Those guys were young, at least, and would get other chances. For some of us, I knew it might've been our last chance ever to get to a World Series.

I was happy about my season because we won the division. I set a major league record for consecutive errorless games at second base, and offensively I led the league in runs (104) and was fifth in at-bats (606), hits (176) and total bases (301).

Those are the kinds of things I looked at in terms of overall production, because those are the stats that help the team.

My goal each year was to play every day, play solid defense and score 100 runs. I generally thought the other things would take care of themselves if I did that.

In the series with the Giants, I hit .400 with a homer and 4 RBI in 5 games with 6 runs.

In total bases, I trailed only Mark Grace and Will Clark, who were the big stars of the NLCS.

It had been the most emotional year of my career and I probably had more fun that season than any other.

So much was unexpected, so much of it was exciting.

We had a good mix of veterans and youth, and there was no reason we couldn't repeat as division champs. But one thing I learned from 1984 was that you never know what the future will hold.

You just never know if you'll ever get back.

14 **Home and homers**

"Ryne Sandberg's a good person. He's an honest person. You had to earn his trust before he let you get close to him, but how many people ever really tried?"
—*Former teammate and close friend Doug Dascenzo*

By the spring of 1990, Lindsey was seven and Justin was five. As the kids were growing up, it was getting tougher and tougher for me to be away from home.

Leaving spring training every year was different for me than it was for most of the players, because I was leaving home and leaving the kids. That was always a really tough time of the season for me.

Every year I'd get on the team bus at HoHoKam Park as we prepared to leave for the airport. We'd be on our way to Chicago or wherever we were starting the season, and I'd have to say good-bye to the kids as they cried their eyes out.

"Daddy, don't go away," they'd say, because they knew they wouldn't see me for a while.

I'd be crying, too. I'd get my last hugs for maybe a month or two before I saw them again.

I'd get on the bus and as we were pulling away, I

could see them waving and crying.

My whole life became a contradiction.

I worked so hard in the off-season to prepare myself physically for the upcoming year. I'd work extra hard in spring training, and now the season was ready to start but I'd have mixed emotions about it.

On the one hand, I was trying to look forward to the upcoming season. It was a new season and there was always hope that something good would happen for the team. But on the other hand, it also meant I was leaving the family behind in Arizona. That happened for quite a few years and it tore me apart.

It occurs to me now for the first time that maybe the reason I started off so slow almost every year was because I wasn't 100 percent there mentally.

It makes sense, because on one side I was being tugged back home, but on the other side I was trying to convince myself that I had worked so hard for a reason and it was time to kick it in.

I'd leave and we'd start the season; I'd be sad about the kids and anxious to play games at the same time. I usually started to heat up around the middle of May, and that's when I knew I'd be seeing the kids soon.

During my career I averaged .235 in April and .297 the other five months of the season, so there might be a connection.

A lot of times during the season I would count down the days to their arrival, and when it was close I'd take that good feeling on the field with me. There were also times I'd drop them at the airport and that night feel sluggish.

Since the two days that my kids were born, Lindsey and Justin have been the most important part of my life — more important than baseball or anything else.

Cindy and I did the best we could to move the kids back and forth from Phoenix to Chicago, so they could be with me as much as possible. When they were young it was easier because they weren't in school yet and they didn't have as many commitments with friends and activities.

But as they got older it became much more difficult to bring them to Chicago for the whole season. Once they were old enough for school, I wouldn't see them for two months to start the season and a month and a half at the end of the season.

Let's face it, it was more fun for them to be in Arizona at basketball camp or gymnastics or camping, than in Chicago when I didn't have a lot of time for them anyway.

What hurt was they were camping with their friends and their friends' parents. I told them to do it because I didn't want them to miss out, but I missed out. It was killing me. Out of Justin's baseball season, I'd see maybe five games while I was still home for spring training, but then I'd miss the next 30.

During my season, he'd tell me on the phone how it was going, and I'd be thinking, I wish I was there to see it and help him. I'd go through the same thing with Lindsey and her gymnastics meets. It got to the point where I felt like I'd rather be there supporting them, than doing what I was doing.

Baseball was becoming a burden in that sense, and I missed my family terribly.

With six games to play in the 1990 season, I hit my 39th dinger in New York, and I went into the final three days of the season still needing one to reach 40 for the first time in my career.

We were finishing the season in Philadelphia, and in the first of three games at Veterans Stadium, we were facing a hard-throwing righty in Jose DeJesus.

In my first at-bat, DeJesus struck me out on a high fastball, but in the third inning Doug Dascenzo led off and walked on four pitches. I looked over at Dougie at first base and he knew what I was thinking.

DeJesus had gotten me out on high fastballs the first time up and he had just walked Dougie on four pitches, so Dougie knew what was on my mind.

I was up there looking for a high fastball because I knew he needed to throw a strike. Sure enough, he gave it to me and I crushed it deep into the left-field bleachers.

Dougie scored in front of me to give me 100 RBI on my 40th homer.

I got back in the dugout and Zim shook hands with me and said, "That's enough, you're done."

I said, "For tonight?"

"No," he said. "You're done, period."

I said, "OK."

That was good because it gave the kids a couple of days to play and gave me a couple of days off to relax and have some fun and watch a couple of games.

The next night, Dougie led off the game with a base hit and two outs later, Andre Dawson drove him home with a base hit, giving him 100 RBI.

Zim immediately pulled Andre off the field and he was done for the year, too.

Some people tried to say he wouldn't even be able to play in 1990 because he was coming off another knee surgery, but they didn't know Andre. His knees wouldn't stop him from playing until he decided he was done.

So all he did was hit .310 with 27 homers, 100 RBI — and 16 stolen bases just for good measure. Not bad for someone they said would have to retire, huh?

And to top it off, Zim let Andre manage the final game. Mad Dog won his 15th and Assie got his 10th save and Hawk really knew what he was doing, too.

It was a fun way to end a disappointing season.

We got cheated in 1990, because we'd all looked forward to spring training. It was a chance for us to enjoy what we had accomplished the year before, like in the '85 spring when we had a blast.

But '90 was the year of the lockout, and we didn't get our six weeks of fun and that dampened the enthusiasm. It was finally settled March 18, but a lot of players didn't get to camp until three or four days later, so it left us only 15 or 16 days of spring training.

From a workout standpoint, it was great because six or seven weeks of camp is way too long anyway. The position players only need about three weeks, and the pitchers feel like three to four weeks is enough for them.

But from an excitement standpoint, we definitely got cheated out of enjoying our title as division champs and we lost something there.

When we finally started playing baseball, 1990 seemed eerily like 1985. We starting losing players to injury immediately.

From a team standpoint, it was a rough year, but personally, it might've been my best.

I surprised myself a few times during my career, but my biggest surprise was when I hit 40 home runs in 1990.

I never imagined hitting doing that in the big leagues, but I got into one of those grooves when everything was working.

There were times during a game or a season when I'd get in that groove and stay there for a week or a month or a summer. It was a timing thing with my body, combined with the right swing and right strength. If I got the pitch I was looking for, it was gone.

You have to have the right mental approach, too. Coming off '89 and hitting 30 homers and winning the division, I was definitely pumped for the '90 season. I wanted to do everything I could to help us repeat and I got on a roll.

I only hit one homer in April, which wasn't unusual for me, but then I got hot in May, hitting nine, and caught fire in June, hitting 14 — one shy of the June record held by Babe Ruth and three others.

July was rough and I only hit one after the All-Star Game before I came back with six in August and nine in September-October.

I hit 26 homers three times during my career and 30 once, but 40 was a big jump.

I also led the NL in total bases (344) — something else I never thought I'd do — and hit .306.

I stole 25 bases, but once again I hadn't thought about the 30-30. Zim gave me the green light almost 100 percent of the time, but I didn't steal just for the sake of it.

It might've been the best individual season of my career, but '84 and '89 were awfully good, too, and those years we won divisions, so it meant more to me.

In '90 I became the first player to ever have a 40-homer and 50-steal season during a career, and I extended my errorless streak from '89 to a record 123 games before I lost it in Houston on May 17.

Personally, it was perhaps my most complete year, but we finished fourth and without a pennant race it didn't mean too much to me.

It never was much of a pennant race, and I knew we were in trouble when we lost Rick Sutcliffe before we even made it out of Arizona. He was on the disabled list most of the year after having surgery in May.

It turns out he'd been pitching hurt for about five years, but he still averaged 16 wins and 230 innings the three years before he had surgery. Sut was always able to pitch with pain, and people kidded him about being a "human rain delay" out on the mound. But he told me it was the only way he could pitch. He needed those few extra seconds between pitches to get rid of the pain. That's why he was always walking around out there or faking throws to second or third.

It didn't stop him from winning 16 games and pitching 229 innings in '89. He was one of the toughest guys I've ever seen in baseball.

Not having Sut around all of 1990 really hurt us. He was not only a great teacher for the young pitchers and a leader on the team, but he kept us laughing. He was constantly pulling practical jokes and harassing everyone in sight.

In fact, whenever I pulled one I could just blame it on Sut because he did 99 percent of them anyway.

In 1991, Sut really got Doug Dascenzo.

Dougie's a great guy and one of the best friends I ever had in baseball, but he was a favorite target for Sut. One time Sut talked him into giving away his game glove for a good cause, and Dougie figured Sut knew what he was talking about, so he did it.

Well, Dougie had the longest errorless streak from the start of a career by an outfielder (242 games), and he was about 20 games shy of the overall, all-time errorless streak by an outfielder.

Sure enough, the night he gave his glove away, Aug. 25, 1991, Dougie got in and made the first error of his major league career.

The guys were all over him for that, even though it had nothing to do with the glove.

Sut was also the master of the pie in the face while you were doing a TV interview, especially a live one.

Another favorite of his was the Gatorade trick, made especially for rookies. There was a bucket of red Gatorade in the dugout and any time rookies were around, Sut would poke a hole in the side of the cup, put his finger over the hole and fill it with the red stuff.

When the rookie came in off the field, Sut would say, "Can I get you some Gatorade? It's hot and you should keep your fluids up."

And the kid would say, "Yeah, sure," and think it was so cool that the great Cy Young Award winner, Rick Sutcliffe, was doing him a big favor.

Sut would keep his thumb on the hole and then hand it to the kid so when he drank it the red stuff would come out all over his uniform.

Here's this nice white uniform and the rookie's all messed up with the red stains on television and Yosh Kawano would be all over the kid for staining his uniform.

Sut was merciless.

He'd also nail the rookie bat boys with the "keys to the batter's box" trick.

He'd tell the bat boy to go ask the opposing manager or the second base umpire for the keys to the batter's box before the game. They would send him somewhere else and everyone he talked to would send him to a different place.

He'd be running to the bullpen or to the parking lot attendant or the concession stand. The kid would be running all over the stadium.

Finally, he'd come back and Sut would say, "Where's the batter's box?"

The kid would point right to the batter's box.

And Sut would say, "Is there a key that fits that?"

"No," the kid would say.

"So why," Sut would reply, "are you looking for a key?"

And everybody would burst out laughing.

Andre Dawson would surprise you once in a while, too. He liked to get George Bell by sticking an exploding cigarette in George's smokes.

The Hawk was surprisingly mischievous, like me, but Sut was the culprit most of the time.

Not having Sut with us hurt in a lot of different ways in '90. He was also one of the most caring individuals around. If you ever really needed something, Sut was there before you could ask for help. Great guy.

One reason I trained so hard in the off-season was so that I had the physical and mental strength to make it through the tough times — and in 1990 I needed all the strength I could muster.

We were 12-and-a-half out by June 7 and it was like all those other years when we were out of it before the All-Star Game because we couldn't overcome injuries.

But with the All-Star Game coming up at Wrigley Field, I wanted to get off to a good start.

I was having a great year, but we were on our second West Coast trip of the season right before the All-Star break when I got another one of those phone calls that can change your life in a heartbeat.

Cindy's brother, Dan White, had fallen into a diabetic coma, and he died July 1. This wasn't Don White, the guy who followed me around in spring training in '82. It was Cindy's other brother, and it was a terrible shock.

I got the call in San Diego and I was ready to go to Florida, where the Whites lived, but the advice I got from Cindy and our relatives was to stay and play ball.

They said they would take care of everything and that I could show my respect by playing ball and continuing to play well. They said it's what Danny would've wanted, so I continued to play.

The trip ended with a double-header disaster in San Francisco and was followed by an all-night flight back to Chicago to get ready for the All-Star Game at Wrigley Field. I was the National League's leading vote-getter, and had in many ways been designated the host because it was at Wrigley Field. That became a tiring experience because of all the promotion and interviews during the weeks before the game. After flying half the night, we got in at about 4 a.m. Monday and had to be downtown for a press conference at nine. Straight from there it was back to Wrigley Field for the workout and home run hitting contest.

I was at the top or near the top in almost every offensive category, so the home run contest was all set up for me. They had me hitting last so I was going to be hitting for the personal title and a chance to win it for the National League if I came through.

It was tied at 1–1 after four American League hitters and three National League hitters.

The wind was blowing in pretty good and guys like Jose Canseco, Mark McGwire, Cecil Fielder, Darryl Strawberry and Matt Williams were all trying to hit high, towering home runs, which were being caught 50 feet behind shortstop. I was sitting on the side laughing and thinking, man, they didn't hit any out, I have no chance here.

But we had a full house and the Cub fans were cheering me on, so I had to deliver.

On that day, if you were thinking about hitting it out, you'd have to keep the ball lower than the upper deck or there's no way the ball would go out. That's pretty typical of Wrigley when the wind's blowing in. It isn't really the home run hitter's park that a lot of people think it is, because the wind blows in or across more than half the time. For this contest, I knew I couldn't get the ball in the air, so on my second swing I hit a line drive that stayed low and went right over the left field wall.

I hit two more just like that to win the personal title and give the NL the win. It was pretty neat to win that at Wrigley Field in front of the home fans.

For the most part during my career, when I went up to the plate thinking about a home run, it didn't happen. My approach to Wrigley was always to hit the ball hard and hit line drives.

Even in 1990 when I hit 40 home runs, or the years I hit 26 or 30, I had that same approach: Hit hard line drives. If I hit it just right with the right trajectory, then it's a home run. If not, they're base hits or gappers off the wall.

I didn't have to adjust my swing every day based on the wind because my approach was always the same. There were ways, however, like the day of the home run hitting contest, that I did consciously remind myself to keep the ball low. It was nice to win it at home, and the game itself was great, but I was exhausted afterward.

With a death in the family, two West Coast trips before the break, and flying all night to get back for 48 hours of being in the spotlight with promotions, contests and games, I was done.

It was probably more mental than physical, but it was the worst I had experienced up to that point in my career. On top of all that, Cindy and I worked hard to set up a press conference for later in the month and, in memory of her brother Danny White, a donation program based on my performance to raise money for the Juvenile Diabetes Foundation.

All of it combined took a toll on me.

Despite our fourth-place finish in '90, the Cubs still drew 2.24 million. That's when the National League counted actual attendance, not tickets sold.

And it was typical of the Wrigley Field faithful.

The fans had always been supportive of the Cubs, but once we won in '84, the annual attendance went from about 1.2 million a year to over two million, and it's never varied much from that.

That one season, 1984, took care of a lot of years for the Cubs as far as attendance went. It carried all the way to '89, and '89 has carried the Cubs ever since.

It was such a great feeling to come home to Wrigley Field. It was always full and the fans were incredibly supportive. I always played well at Wrigley Field and the fans were a big part of that.

What the fans want is for the Cubs to win that day. That's all they ask. No miracles. They want you to win today, and if you don't, they come back tomorrow and hope you win that day. Honestly, Cub fans are the most amazing group of people you could find anywhere. Such a thing does not exist anyplace else in sports.

Cub fans are very educated about the game and the way it's supposed to be played, and they recognize it when someone isn't trying hard. All they ask is your best effort and good fundamental baseball. If you do that, win or lose, home run or no home run, they'll support you.

That's as fair as you can be, and as a player it's all you can ask from the fans.

They love hustle and great plays and they respect achievement. There were many times an opposing player made a great catch and got a standing ovation from the crowd at Wrigley.

It always made me feel good that the fans appreciated good effort no matter what team the player was on, because I knew opposing players appreciated it.

That was neat for me to see. You never heard one of our guys say, "I can't wait to get to this city," or, "I can't wait to get to that city." But you always heard visiting players say how much they loved it at Wrigley Field.

I remember the game in 1985 when Andre Dawson hit three homers against us when he was with the Expos. He actually hit two three-run homers in one inning that day. When he came to bat for the fourth time he got a standing ovation at Wrigley Field. He got a base hit to right and the fans were disappointed for him — not for themselves — that he didn't hit another home run. That's pretty cool.

Where else could you find fans like that?

I saw Pete Rose tie the all-time hits record of Ty Cobb at Wrigley Field in 1985. It was a base hit off Reggie Patterson right over my head. Standing ovation.

I appreciated the fans and I was proud of them when they did something like that for an opposing player. I thought it showed so much class and it was good for Wrigley and good for Chicago.

Driving to the park every day I had a good feeling because I knew it would be a full house and I wanted to play well for the fans. The players also knew it would be on the superstation across

North America and our peers would see the game. But mostly, it was those fans that made me want to play well.

And if anyone thinks Cub fans just show up and don't care about quality of play, they're wrong. They can see it when guys don't hit cut-off men; or don't run out a ball; or don't get down a bunt; or score a runner from third with less than two outs. They may be loyal and forgiving fans, but any Cubs executive who thinks they're stupid is dead wrong.

There were other parks I liked playing in, but not as much as Wrigley Field.

Busch Stadium in St. Louis was enjoyable because it had a nice atmosphere for baseball. It was all very professional there and the fans are very knowledgeable.

It helped that the Cubs-Cards rivalry is so strong because the games are meaningful in St. Louis even when both teams are out of the race. It also helped that I seemed to see the ball very well in that park.

I loved playing in Atlanta because Fulton County Stadium is a great hitter's park and the ball carries very well. I always enjoyed playing in the hot weather because I could get loose in a hurry, and it was always steamy in Atlanta.

Believe it or not, I hit the heck out of the ball in Candlestick Park and my highest career average against any team was .345 against the Giants. I was one of the few players who hit well there even though I didn't enjoy playing in Candlestick. Nobody does because it's miserable, but I was able to focus on the game and not worry about the cold and wind and fog and rain. During a game in 1987, Ed Lynch was pitching when one of those hurricane wind gusts took the hat right off his head. It was going about 30 mph when I tried to make a play on it up the middle, but it got through the infield. After that, it kept on going and center fielder Davey Martinez failed to make a grab, too.

It wound up stuck against the outfield wall like an invisible man was holding it there. We all just stood there staring at it, but that was classic Candlestick Park. I didn't care much for

I loved being a part of baseball, whether I was on the field or in the dugout. Here I am with Ozzie Smith (left) and Jack Morris during the Japan All-Star tour after the '86 season.

Photos courtesy of author and *Daily Herald*.

Catching fish at Thomas Lake was a part of my favorite summer trip. This was taken in 1966.

Here I am sliding headfirst into the bed at five months.

My first time in a baseball uniform was as bat boy for my brother Del's Legion team when I was 12. At the time, Del was about half a tree taller.

A hairstyle fit for Little League in the sixth grade.

As a senior in high school, I was an All-American quarterback, an all-city basketball player, and an all-state baseball player. During my years at North Central High, I ran up against the likes of Mark Rypien and John Stockton.

On June 16, 1978, I chose baseball.
Moose Johnson (left) and Bill Harper
signed me to my first pro contract.

Mom and Dad came to see me in
Helena in 1978...

Lifelong Chicagoan and Cub fan Ray
Borucki was my best man and roommate at Spartanburg.

... but they never saw
this broken-down stadium in Asheville,
North Carolina, when I was playing
with Spartanburg in '79.

When I made it to the big leagues, I met people I'd always heard about, like Steve Garvey (below) and Ryne Duren (above), for whom I was named.

I looked up to a lot of players during my career. One of them was Ozzie Smith, who was a real professional and the best shortstop I ever played against.

Making the All-Star team was a dream
come true. In '84 I got to meet two of
my idols, Mike Schmidt (left) and
George Brett, who said he liked my style.

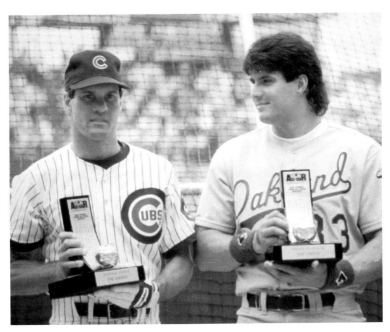

At the 1990 All-Star Game at Wrigley Field, I won the Home Run
Derby, despite competition from fierce sluggers like Jose Canseco.
Here we are holding our awards for leading the leagues in All-Star
balloting.

One that got away as Bo Jackson slides under me at the '89 All-Star Game in Anaheim.

The Japan tour in '86 was fun ...

... but not as much fun as facing
the Giants in the 1989 playoffs.

I never liked showing up my
opponents, but the fans forced
me to take a curtain call after
my second home run off Bruce
Sutter on June 23, 1984.

I always enjoyed working with the coaches, like Chuck Cottier (above).

I often worked with Billy
Connors (left, shaking my hand),
who could make me laugh even
while hitting me ground balls.

Spring training was a time for remembering how to hit, field and sign autographs.

In 1993, it also meant a broken hand.

On July 22, 1994, I made my first trip back to Wrigley Field since I retired. I sat in the bleachers for the first time ever with my good friend Peter Bensinger.

That was the day I was inducted into the Cubs' Walk of Fame which includes (l to r) Ernie Banks, Billy Williams, Ron Santo and Don Kessinger.

I was happy as could be the day I signed the contract that kept me with the Cubs for the remainder of my career.

But that was cut short when I retired, sooner than anyone expected, on June 13, 1994.

At home in my trophy room, there is a lot to reflect on and be thankful for.

But I'm even more thankful that, for the first time in my life, I can spend 12 months of the year with my children, Justin and Lindsey.

I left baseball a lot sooner than I ever thought I would, but I'm
filled with great memories. Many of them include Cub fans
everywhere, who were with me every step of the way.

Astroturf or indoor stadiums, because it was tough to see the ball inside. I was an outdoor, warm-weather kind of guy.

While the fans of Wrigley Field treated me like a king, the fans in every city treated me very well and I have no complaints. Even in New York, Mets fans weren't as nasty to me as they've been to a lot of visiting players over the years. They're also some of the most knowledgeable fans in the game. They could be mean, but they knew good baseball from bad baseball and they also knew who could play and who couldn't.

It's terrible that Shea Stadium is so broken down and falling apart. Dodger Stadium is two years younger and looks and feels like it's brand new. But New York is a rough town and I guess the stadiums, like the people, have to be tough to survive there.

There's one guy who lets us know how he feels about visiting teams when the bus passes by his store every afternoon before the games. Just as the bus goes by, he runs outside, drops his pants and moons us. I guess it's his way of wishing us luck. Most of the guys I knew were pretty careful and didn't go out much in New York. Everyone, that is, except for Harry Caray.

Harry would go off on his own and not be seen again until the next morning. There was one morning in 1990 when I was heading down into Grand Central Station about 8 a.m. to get my coffee and Harry was just rolling in.

He's an amazing guy and the only one I know who managed to take a normal 24-hour day and stretch it into 30.

While 1990 was a good year for me, it wasn't for the team. But we still had a good young team and we just needed to plug up a couple of holes and stay away from injuries, and we had a real good chance to win in '91.

I was confident of that.

 **15** **Nightmare in New York**

"I've played with a lot of great players, but Ryno was different than most. He didn't care about all the things that went along with baseball. He just wanted to play baseball and have fun. How can you fault him for that?"
—*Former teammate Paul Assenmacher*

In the spring of 1991, I had two years left on the contract extension I signed before the '89 season, but the Cubs wanted to talk about another extension.

They extended Andre Dawson during the All-Star break in 1990, and over the winter they spent about $25 million on free agents Danny Jackson, George Bell and Dave Smith.

We agreed to talk, but again I put a March 1 deadline on it because I didn't want it to go on during the season.

With two years left on the deal, my agent was telling me that at the end of '91, I'd be only a year away from free agency, and I ought to think about playing it out to see what the conditions were like out there.

That actually made a lot of sense. You wait a long time for the opportunity to become a free agent, and I was always passing it up by signing long-term deals.

Still, I wanted to remain a Cub, and if it could be done right away, then I'd be happy to get it over with. As usual, it would probably cost me a lot of money and save the Cubs a bunch to do it early, but that was fine with me. This time, though, the Cubs weren't as interested. The process started late and we didn't get it done by the deadline. In fact, we weren't even close.

I think because I had two years left, Cubs president Don Grenesko didn't really take us seriously. They had their toughest negotiators in the room and the talks never got very far.

So we shut it down just like I said we would. I was surprised that it didn't happen, but it wasn't going to affect me one way or another. I knew I'd play the 1991 season and I'd have a year left on my contract, but the difference now was I'd have to seriously consider taking it all the way to free agency.

Spending money certainly hadn't been a problem for the Cubs when it came to free agents, and we got three big ones during the winter of 1990–91. We signed George Bell, Danny Jackson and Dave Smith and everyone was pretty pumped up going into the season.

I was reunited with George Bell for the first time since our days at Helena and Reading, and it was great having him around.

George was a joker and always picking on guys, and he's one guy who could really get Shawon Dunston going. Shawon could trash-talk like nobody I'd ever heard, but he met his match in George. George would get on Shawon and the two of them were so loud you could hear it for miles. George was fun but he also knew when it was time to play, and he knew as much about hitting as anyone around. If he was near the cage, he'd watch everyone hit and help them out, because he knew what he was talking about. George had a reputation for being a bad guy, but that wasn't true at all. If you put George in the right situation and left him alone and let him play, he would perform for you, and that's exactly what Don Zimmer did with George.

The first day of camp, Zim brought George in and explained things to him. He let him know that Doug Dascenzo would be his late-inning replacement, and George said, "That's great. All I've ever asked was to know my situation. That's been my only problem, not being told the truth."

George gave us a clutch hitter and he gave Andre Dawson some protection for the first time in a long time. Hawk hardly ever had an RBI guy behind him, which make his numbers seem even more incredible. The only time I can think of that Andre had a good No. 5 hitter before George was in '87, Andre's MVP year, when he had Keith Moreland behind him. Moreland was a terrific RBI man.

But now George was hitting behind him and you had to pitch to Hawk because if there was a runner in scoring position, George was a threat. It was a nice situation to have in the meat of the order.

We also picked up Dave Smith, who had been one of the best closers in the game the previous six years. We all knew that meant Mitch Williams was on his way out and, sure enough, right before the season began, Mitch was traded to the Phillies for young pitchers Chuck McElroy and Bob Scanlan.

Mitch was hurt in 1990 and his performance suffered, but his time off meant too much time for he and Zim to be together, and that didn't turn out to be such a good combination.

It doesn't mean they didn't like each other, because I know Mitch still called Zim frequently even after he was traded, but it was probably better for everyone at that point. We got a couple of good young pitchers in return, and the 1991 season held a lot of promise for the Cubs.

Now it was just a matter of delivering on it.

The Dave Smith signing looked perfect as he got off to great start, going 4-for-4 in saves and we won six straight. The last victory in that streak on April 18 in Pittsburgh was Rick Sutcliffe's first major league win since the last day of the '89 season.

And that was about the last good thing that happened for the Chicago Cubs in 1991.

In Game 2 of that series on Friday night, Danny Jackson made only his third Cubs start and severely pulled a groin muscle.

His Cubs career was messed up before it had even begun, and it was a big blow to us. We were counting on him to provide our staff with some toughness and leadership, and that's something a proven winner like Jackson was supposed to deliver.

But the injury was so bad that it wasn't until 1994 with the Phillies that Jackson returned to form and pitched like he did before he was with the Cubs.

The same night Jackson got hurt, we trailed 3–0 with two outs in the ninth and the bases loaded. Down to our last out, Zim sent up Hawk as a pinch hitter and he blasted a grand slam to put us up 4–3.

But Dave Smith started the ninth and gave up two runs for his first blown save, and we suffered a tough 5–4 defeat. That was a difficult loss after Andre's heroics. Saturday we got creamed but we went into Sunday's game at 7–5 and tied with the Pirates for first place in the NL East on April 21. The Pirates had also won the division the year before.

Once again, we had a lead in the ninth and Dave Smith on the mound. With two outs and a runner on, it came down to Smith against our old pal Gary Varsho, whom we had so generously given to the Pirates a month before.

As you've probably guessed by now, Varsho tagged Smith for a pinch-hit double that scored the run and tied the game at 7–7. Jimmy Frey must've been thinking, "That's what you get for being nice to someone."

It was still 7–7 in the top of the 11th when we grabbed an 8–7 lead, and Andre Dawson came to the plate again with two outs and the bases loaded.

Any kind of a base hit here, and we grab a big lead, leave town with a split and sole possession of first place, right? Andre did better than that. He crushed a ball to deep right-center for his second grand slam in three days, and we had a whopping 12–7 lead!

We had overcome a tough weekend of baseball, and we were back on track.

Almost.

We forgot to get three outs in the bottom of the 11th and the Pirates mounted one of the greatest comebacks in their history. They scored six runs in the bottom of the 11th to win it 13–12.

We had wasted two Andre Dawson grand slams in three days and lost three out of four in the series. We left Pittsburgh in second place after a tough weekend in which we suffered two of the most brutal, heart-breaking losses you could imagine. Smith had been amazingly consistent throughout his career, but now he might've been pitching too much. He'd averaged only about 50 games a year, but now he was pitching almost every day.

The next night in St. Louis, we led 2–1 going into the bottom of the ninth, but it was the same story. This time Felix Jose got Smitty for a two-run homer and a 3–2 Cards victory.

After saving his first four, Smitty had blown three straight and he had a swelling on his tricep the size of an egg. You don't have to be a surgeon to know that's not good news. That St. Louis defeat left us at .500, and we hovered around there for the next month.

But we didn't quit.

Smitty got healthy again and saved his next six opportunities, and we were playing pretty good baseball. After we won a tough, 10-inning game in Philadelphia on May 19, we were 18–19 and only five-and-a-half games out of first.

The guys were confident because we'd gone through our bad spell early and we knew we had a strong club. There wasn't a team in the division we couldn't compete with, including the Pirates.

At the box office, meanwhile, the Cubs were again on their way to their second highest attendance total at 2.3 million. It was still early and things were going just fine. We weren't where we wanted to be, but there was no reason to panic.

The day after the Philly game was an off-day on Monday in New York. Some guys went sight-seeing to the museums or the Statue of Liberty. A few guys traveled down to Atlantic City. And those who were too afraid to leave their rooms just rested, ordered room service and watched TV.

But in Chicago, Cubs president Don Grenesko was preparing to board a plane and fly to New York Monday night.

There was only one purpose for his trip: On Tuesday morning, May 21, 1991, he planned to fire Don Zimmer.

Back in mid-May, Grenesko was quoted as saying Zimmer would be "evaluated after the season," and that he had no plans to discuss Zimmer's contract, which was up at the end of 1991.

Well, Zim went nuts when he saw the story.

He had usually worked on one-year deals with the Cubs and while he didn't like it, he was used to it. But he didn't at all care for Grenesko, because he wasn't a "baseball guy" and Zimmer figured he knew nothing about the game.

Those two never got along at all. One was a 40-year baseball man and one was a corporate officer. It wasn't a match made in baseball heaven.

Well, when Zim saw the quote about being evaluated, he went to Grenesko and told him he wanted to know by July 1 if he would be back for '92. Zim said he'd manage out the year regardless of the answer, but if he wasn't told by July 1, then he wouldn't be back for '92 under any circumstances — not even if the Cubs won the World Series.

Jimmy Frey tried to talk Zim out of it, but Zim wouldn't hear it. Ten days later, on May 21, Grenesko fired him. Just like that.

I can't really blame Zim because he was frustrated. From what I hear, Grenesko was going to fire him anyway and was just looking for an excuse. If it hadn't been that, he would've found another reason.

But the firing of Don Zimmer started a chain of events that the Cubs were still trying to recover from as late as December of 1994.

That one decision eventually set into motion a series of decisions that brought down an entire regime from top to bottom, and cost a lot of people their jobs along the way. The hirings and firings were still taking place three-and-a-half years later, and it all began with Don Zimmer's dismissal on May 21, 1991.

The biggest mistake I had witnessed by the Cubs up to that point was the firing of Dallas Green in 1987, and now I had seen another colossal blunder.

It didn't actually take place at the hotel, because Zim was always at the park extremely early. So Grenesko had to travel out to Shea Stadium from mid-town Manhattan to make his move.

Zim was at the park and in uniform at 3 p.m. when Grenesko caught him in the visiting manager's office at Shea Stadium. He closed the door, and Zim knew what was going to happen. It wasn't his first time being fired.

After Grenesko gave him the news, Zim told Jim Frey what he thought they should do to improve the club and that was it.

It was done, just like that.

Zim shook hands with Jim Frey, caught a cab back to the hotel in Manhattan, packed his bags and flew back to Chicago before most of us even knew what had happened.

It was awful. It was almost exactly like the time Jim Frey got fired in '86. As was the case in '86, it had only been a year and a couple of months since we won a division title and Zim had been named Manager of the Year, just like Frey in '84.

We were only a game under .500 (18-19) and only five-and-a-half out. It made no sense to us.

Another manager had been fired that I really liked and respected. Once again, I took it very personally. I felt responsible for it.

Coaches and managers work so hard and they don't get paid a whole lot compared to the players. They live and die with each game, but not just because their livelihood is on the line. They care and they want to win.

And whenever I saw a coach or a manager lose his job, it made me unhappy. I was certainly unhappy that night at Shea Stadium.

It was a circus atmosphere, because it happened in the media capital of the world and Don Zimmer was a very popular guy around the country.

Joe Altobelli managed the game that night and got thrown out for arguing with home-plate umpire Steve Rippley. Altobelli went bananas because Doc Gooden was hitting guys and brushing them back and Joe wanted something done about it. But more than anything else, I'm sure he was upset that his buddy Zim had been bounced.

Frey's reaction after the game was the same. He was blasting everyone; Rippley, Gooden and anyone else he could think of. Seeing Zim get fired right in front of him was especially tough on Frey. Grenesko had fired his good friend and Jimmy was left out of the decision-making process.

I'm not sure Jimmy was ever the same after that. I'm not sure any of us were.

The following day, Grenesko hired Jim Essian, who had been the Triple-A manager at Iowa and had done a nice job of developing players and winning all throughout the Cubs' minor-league system.

A lot of our players in '91 had played for Essian in the minors and even though they were sad about Zim, they were happy when they heard Essian was the new manager.

There was a positive feeling about the situation and right off the bat we won the first five under the new skipper and pulled to within four games of first.

We were 30–29 and seven-and-a-half out when we headed out for our first West Coast trip in mid-June. It started off well enough when Danny Jackson won his first game of the year in the first game in San Diego.

But then the roof caved in.

We proceeded to lose the next nine straight, and five in our opponents' final at-bat with three more blown saves. We concluded the trip in Pittsburgh by splitting the first two games and Frank Castillo made his major-league debut in the final game.

He was winning 3–0 after eight innings, but Dave Smith was down with a torn knee ligament and the bullpen gave away another game.

We lost 4–3 and the nightmare was finally over on June 27. We lost 11 of 13 and went from seven-and-a-half out to 11-and-a-half out, while falling to 32–40.

End of road trip, end of season.

They were some of the most crushing defeats you could ever imagine. We just couldn't get three outs when we needed it that year.

The rest of the season was ugly.

Injuries mounted and Dave Smith was hampered by a bad knee and elbow. He went 17-for-23 in saves, so there's no telling how different things might've been had he been healthy all year.

But we had some of the toughest losses that year that I can ever remember. We were right there all year as far as offense and defense and starting pitching, but we couldn't get three outs in the ninth.

We blew 27 saves and lost 26 games in our opponents' final at-bat. Every day it was the same thing. It got to be where I'd be out there standing in the field, looking at Mark Grace or Shawon Dunston or Andre Dawson, wondering how we were going to blow it this time.

That's why a closer is so important. It's a big confidence factor when you know you've got that man down there. We simply could not get three outs. Period. Other than that the team was right there.

By the last weekend of the '91 season, all kinds of rumors were going around.

The word was out that Essian would be fired after a total of four months on the job, and Jimmy Frey would come back down onto the field and manage, which sounded a lot like 1987 when they tried to force Dallas back onto the field and take away his GM position.

Essian tried to keep his head up despite the rumors and some nice things happened on the final day of the season.

Mad Dog pitched a complete game for his 15th win, and Andre hit two homers to get over the 30 mark.

I needed one RBI for 100 and it went down to my final at-bat of the season in the seventh inning.

With two outs, Mark Grace singled to give me a chance.

Facing Omar Olivares, I took the ball the other way and drove it into the right-center field gap.

Mark will tell you that he's not very fast, but he's an excellent base runner because he studies the game. He knows off the bat if a ball is a hit and he makes all the right moves on the bases. He scores a lot of runs that faster guys don't score because they don't know what they're doing. On this play, Gracie was off with the crack of the bat and running hard. He scored easily and that gave me my second straight year with 100 RBI.

But now I was only a year away from free agency, and so was Andre Dawson, and we were becoming quite an offensive combination.

With George Bell hitting 25 homers and driving in 86 runs behind Andre, the Hawk smacked 31 homers and had 104 RBI. I hit .291 with 26 homers, 100 RBI and 104 runs scored, and I led the majors in All-Star voting.

But it had been a very tough year. We were sixth in hitting and last in pitching and we needed to know who our closer would be in '92.

Of course, at that point, we didn't even know who our manager would be.

Jimmy Frey came to me the last weekend and said he'd like to get together and talk about a new contract for me, but only a few days remained and there wasn't really time.

And once the season ended, Tribune Co. tied Jimmy's hands and everything was put on hold.

Essian was supposed to get fired, but then the day after the season ended they told him to go home to Detroit. He didn't know what to think.

We were all waiting to hear about that situation when suddenly the news came on October 17 that Don Grenesko had been removed as president of the Cubs and was being shifted back to Tribune Co. as Chief Financial Officer.

That's not exactly a demotion if you consider that when most people get fired in baseball, they're out of work. Don Grenesko not only had a job, but one of the most important and lucrative jobs at a Fortune 500 company.

Don did some really good things for the Cubs during his time with the club and he really cared about the organization, and he cared about people. But the players felt like the corporate execs got too involved in baseball decisions at times. The firing of Don Zimmer was just one example of that and it really backfired.

Now with Grenesko gone, it wasn't clear who was in charge, but it wasn't Jim Frey. He'd been told by the company to sit on his hands and wait — though he didn't know for what. Finally, the day after the Grenesko announcement, Frey was told by ownership to fire Essian. They made the poor guy wait for 12 days after the season was over, and in the process they probably led him to believe he had a chance to keep his job. But then they fired him anyway.

It was bad enough that they had taken Essian's blossoming career as a manager and ruined it in one quick move, but then he was hung out to dry, sitting home in Detroit wondering if he might still keep his job.

Essian had been put in a tough spot with a GM who loved the former manager and a coaching staff that was equally loyal to Don Zimmer.

Essian simply never had a chance.

After Grenesko and Essian were axed, it got a little weird. Jimmy Frey wasn't allowed to conduct any business, so he sat in his office for the next month and waited for the other shoe to drop.

And we waited.

I knew bizarre things were happening when I read in the paper that Stanton Cook, a longtime Tribune Co. executive, had offered Grenesko's job to Toronto's Pat Gillick, but Gillick turned him down.

Cook had apparently taken over the operation and after a couple more weeks went by, the other shoe dropped on Jim Frey.

He was fired on Nov. 14, 1991, and Larry Himes was hired as the new general manager.

Frey and Essian each had a year left on their contracts, so they were given scouting jobs, but Frey was given some ridiculous title like "special player consultant."

At the press conference, a reporter asked Frey how he felt about being kicked upstairs, to which Jimmy replied, "Upstairs? Upstairs? I'd say it's more like out-stairs, wouldn't you?"

And this was all the result of Gresnesko firing Zimmer.

It began a chain reaction of events that didn't stop until Zimmer, Essian, Frey and Gresnesko had all lost their jobs. Pitching coach Dick Pole had also been fired not long after Zimmer, and he was replaced by my old pal Billy Connors. It had become such a circus that they cleaned the whole thing out. It wasn't Jim Frey's fault. He didn't fire Zimmer with the team a game under .500. And it wasn't the fault of Jim Essian, who was set up for a failure under the circumstances.

But everyone paid the price, and three years later they were still adding up the receipts.

◆ 16 ◆ A Cub for life

"Having Ryne Sandberg play second base behind you was like having a security blanket. You name it and he could do it — offensively, defensively, on the bases. In his prime, he was probably the best all-around baseball player I've ever seen."
—*Perennial Cy Young Award winner Greg Maddux*

On Nov. 14, 1991, I heard the news that Larry Himes had been hired as the new general manager. I didn't really know much about him.

I knew he was given a lot of credit for building a terrific young White Sox team on the strength of draft picks by Al Goldis, but what I couldn't figure out was why he had been fired by the White Sox if he had done such a good job.

In any case, we had new leadership again and I was willing to give Himes a chance. He had impressive credentials and my hope was that he'd find us the missing pieces to the puzzle for the 1992 season.

Once again we had a strange ending to a season with all the upheaval. We went into the winter not knowing the direction of the club and not knowing what the game plan would be for the next year.

We ended the season needing a closer and not much

more than that. Heck, if Don Zimmer could've been a closer and gotten three outs himself, he'd still be managing the Cubs today. I felt bad for Jim Essian, who'd had a nice career going in the minors before that was interrupted, and now he was out of a job, too.

I was going to miss Zimmer and Frey. It was really disappointing, once again, because Jimmy Frey had been a big part of my life and a good friend. He helped me a lot with my career and had been a big part of our two division-winning clubs.

Those were the only titles of any kind the Cubs had won since 1945. Jimmy won in his first year as manager and second year as general manager.

He always communicated with the players, and made them feel like they were a part of the organization, not just employees. The players felt comfortable with him around and that helps when it comes time to perform.

Jimmy had some ideas, too. He was looking for a closer, a third baseman and a leadoff man, but he never got the chance to make the deals.

We were right there, maybe a player or two away from being back in the thick of it. It was a young club and we didn't need to be torn up. We just needed to fill a couple of holes, and we had a chance to compete.

But we had turned it over again, and I had no idea what to expect.

After Himes was hired, we put my contract situation on hold because we wanted to do some research. We were thinking that maybe the West Coast would be a good place to play because it's closer to Phoenix, and I could see the kids on the weekends.

We told the Cubs we'd get back to them because we wanted to think about it — and we thought about it very seriously. I had been through so much change and I wanted to get a feel for what the new regime would do and what direction the organization would go.

I was 32. This was probably going to be the last contract I signed, and I wanted the opportunity to play for a winner. I wanted to feel things out and see what would happen before I committed to the Cubs again. I wanted to see what they would do during the winter meetings and how they would handle negotiations with Maddux, Dawson and Sutcliffe. They were all important players and I didn't want to see them gone and me left behind.

Andre, Greg and I were all going to be free agents at the end of the 1992 season, but Rick Sutcliffe's contract was already up.

Jim Frey had been informally trying to discuss things with Rick when control of the team was taken away from him. Frey knew the Cubs had been paying Rick a big salary while he got healthy again, and he didn't want him to leave and pitch well for someone else.

He knew Rick would stay for a small guaranteed contract loaded with incentives, and it made a lot of sense after they had worked so hard to get him ready to pitch again after shoulder surgery.

It wasn't like they didn't have any proof, either. Sut went 4-1 with a 2.25 ERA in his last nine starts of 1991, dating back to mid-August. He was getting healthy again.

But I got a clue that something had really changed at Wrigley Field when Sutcliffe called me in Phoenix around December 1. He told me he and his agent, Barry Axelrod, had been calling Himes for about three weeks and Himes had yet to return a phone call.

Nothing.

Even if you don't want a guy, doesn't an 18-year pro deserve the courtesy of a phone call?

The Cubs had spent literally millions of dollars to rehab him while he was coming back from surgery, and now they were letting him go for nothing.

Why not give him a contract and load it with incentives?

What's the worst thing that can happen?

Here was a great leader and a wonderful teacher, and we didn't even try to keep him.

Sut called me and he was very depressed. He considered himself a Cub and wanted to retire as a Cub.

Well, a few days after he called me, he got hold of Larry Himes in his office by accident. He called the office to try to leave yet another message, and Larry just happened to pick up the phone.

"Larry, this is Rick Sutcliffe," Sut said. "I've been trying to reach you."

"Yes, Rick," Himes responded. "What can I do for you?"

Sutcliffe paused, stunned by Himes' response.

"Well, the reason we've been calling all these weeks is we were wondering if you were interested in keeping me," Sut said. "I'm a free agent and I want to stay with the Cubs. That's why we've been calling for all this time."

"Oh," Himes said. "Uh, no. No, I'm not interested."

"OK," Sut said. "Thanks."

And that was it. If he had told him that three weeks before, Sut would've been saved a lot of aggravation and could've been out looking for a team.

But this was a new Cubs organization, and it was something I was going to see a lot of. I'd heard from White Sox people about how Himes couldn't communicate, but I didn't know it was so bad that he wouldn't even return a phone call.

The Orioles then signed Sutcliffe for less than $1 million and put about another $2 million in incentives in the deal, so if Sut proved he was healthy, he'd get paid nicely.

All Sut did in 1992 was go out and lead the American League in starts (36), pitch 237 innings and win 16 games for the Orioles, while imparting every ounce of his baseball wisdom on Mike Mussina, who jumped from four wins in '91 to 18 in '92, and Ben McDonald, who went from six wins to 13.

The Orioles thought so much of him that he was given the first start in the history of Camden Yards, and responded with a five-hit shutout.

The Cubs, however, couldn't return a phone call to him.

Sut and I had been close for a long time and it wasn't the same without him. I missed him personally and the team missed him professionally.

I'd be shocked if he doesn't wind up as a major league pitching coach someday, because he knows so much about baseball it's unbelievable.

Unlike so many of us from that '84 team that had the Dallas Green/Phillies training, Sut had that great Dodger teaching and he's a brilliant baseball guy.

I'm sure he'll wind up in a prominent position in baseball someday if he wants it.

At the winter meetings in Miami in December 1991, there was a lot of talk about the Cubs trying to trade Mark Grace. Himes had only been on the job a month but he was apparently ready to make major changes already. He was talking trade with Kansas City, but when he failed to trade Grace for a starting pitcher, he told the media he was "disappointed" that he couldn't complete the deal.

Well, there were only two problems with that. The first was that the night he said he was talking with the Royals, they were busy signing free agent first baseman Wally Joyner, so there was something wrong with that story.

The second problem was he still had Grace on the team!

He just told the world he was sorry he couldn't deal a lifetime .300 hitter, and in the process forgot he was on the club. I'm sure that made Mark Grace feel pretty good. Himes had already shown Rick Sutcliffe the door and when I read what he said about Grace, I knew something weird was going on.

I was going to be a free agent after the '92 season, but I wasn't going to sit down and talk to the Cubs until I got to spring training in 1992 and saw what the deal was.

Normally, I'd start showing up a couple of days before pitchers and catchers, but in mid-February I got some bad news: My oldest brother Lane had passed away.

I flew up to Washington to be with my family and spent about a week there with all of our relatives. It was tough to come back and think about getting started, but as usual my family insisted I take care of business on the field. When Cindy and I got home the phone was ringing off the hook from reporters wanting to know about the contract situation, and I wanted no part of it.

It wasn't very pleasant, but at least baseball would take my mind off of things.

The last thing I wanted was to talk about contracts, but the March 1 deadline I always imposed was coming quickly again and we only had a week to get something done.

I wasn't ready to commit yet because I wanted to see what it'd be like in another new camp with another new manager. After my first day of working out with the pitchers and catchers, I went in and sat with the new manager, Jim Lefebvre, and I took a real liking to him right away. We talked for quite a while and I was impressed. He was a good motivator and he took a very positive approach. Everything was upbeat and I got a good feeling from our talk.

I felt so good when I got home I called my agent, Jimmy Turner, and said, "OK. Call the Cubs and see where they are with this."

As had been the case in two prior negotiations, it went down to the last minute again. We spent a week talking about it and got nowhere fast. I don't think Larry Himes was in on many of the sessions, but maybe it didn't matter to him. I don't know.

"This isn't going to happen, is it?" I asked my agent, Jimmy Turner, on March 1.

"Ryne, I don't know," he said. "Their negotiators are holding firm to their position."

The day went by and very little happened, and we were sitting in the hotel when the clock struck midnight. It was March 2 and it was all over. I was shocked.

That's the first time it struck me that maybe I wasn't coming back, that maybe I wouldn't be a lifetime Cub. It was a strange feeling. I always thought the Cubs wanted me as much as I wanted them. I couldn't believe it had come to this, and I didn't know what to do.

The unfortunate part was we could've done it the spring before. That would've saved the Cubs about $10 million and it would've saved me the aggravation of another negotiation. For a split second, I actually wondered what it would be like to play in Dodger Stadium every day.

But I stopped myself and I said, "Jimmy, what do you think about me going over to see Stan Cook personally?"

Cook was the Cubs' Chairman of the Board and had taken Don Grenesko's place. He didn't take the title of president, but he was in charge.

I had spoken with Cook a few times and I thought maybe something could be done.

"Take a shot," Jimmy said. "You have nothing to lose."

So I called Stan Cook at his hotel and asked if we could see him. "Sure," he said. "Come on up."

Cindy and I drove from the hotel in Phoenix, where the negotiations had taken place, to Cook's hotel in Mesa.

It was about 1 a.m. when we got up to his room.

"I want to be a Cub," I said. "I want to stay a Cub and I want to retire as a Cub. Is there anything we can do? There is no deal working."

The three of us sat there for 90 minutes just talking about the situation, but not really about contracts or money or any of that. It was about the Cubs and who we were and where we wanted to go with the Cubs.

"Ryne, I want you to be with the Cubs forever," Cook said. "Now, and for many years."

But it was late, maybe 2:30 a.m., and we were all pretty tired.

"Let's get everybody together in the morning," he said. "And we'll start all over again."

Cook was great and very supportive. We hadn't heard anything like that from Himes or any of the other negotiators.

So we started again at 8 a.m., and this time everyone was in the room. All the negotiators from each side were there, and Stan Cook, myself and Larry, too. It wasn't easy, but somehow we got it done in about three hours. I finally signed the contract that would keep me with the Cubs for the rest of my career.

It had been a rough couple weeks for me personally, and I felt like I hadn't even had time to think about my brother. I took a deep breath after it was over and was thankful it was done.

As was always the case, I was pleased with the amount of years that I got, because that was what gave me a feeling of security.

That's all I worried about, and then it was Jimmy Turner's job to put that together with whatever the market value was at the time.

In some ways, though, I was still as naive in 1992 as I was in 1982, because I was shocked by the way the press handled the settlement.

Right away, it was called the first $7 million-a-year contract in the papers and on TV. In fact, at a league meeting a few weeks later, another owner yelled at Stan Cook about it. "The market was $5 million," the owner screamed. "Don't you know there's a number between five and seven? It's six!"

I was amazed by all of this.

Not that it really matters, because I know for 99 percent of the people in the world there's no difference between $5 million and $7 million, but for the record the deal wasn't even close to $7 million a year.

Here's a breakdown of what it really was: In addition to my salary, I'd get a $3.5 million signing bonus at the end of the '92 season.

In '93, '94, '95 and '96, the salary was $5.1 million. For '97, it was either a $2.5 million guaranteed buy-out or $5.9 million if I played.

Then there was another $500,000 a year in a personal services deal for four years after my career was over to do some promotional appearances for the Cubs. So that guaranteed $28.4 million was really spread out over 10 years. Now can you explain to me how that comes out to $7 million a year?

I can't, but people make what they want of things and you live with it. Regardless of the terms, I knew I'd retire as a Cub and I was overjoyed.

In the fall of '91, shortly after Larry Himes took over, he signed Mike Morgan, a veteran, free-agent pitcher who fit in nicely behind Greg Maddux in the starting rotation.

Morgan and Maddux were already good friends. They knew each other for years having grown up in Las Vegas together, and when Morgan signed, he'd been told they were close to signing Maddux to a long-term deal as well.

Morgan was thinking about a double-press conference for both of them, but the Maddux deal never materialized.

Cubs negotiator Dennis Homerin had come in with an offer of five years and $25 million in early December of 1991. Greg asked for a no-trade clause in the deal, but when the Cubs said no, Maddux called Homerin two days later and accepted the deal without the no-trade clause.

Homerin said fine, but he'd have to run it past Cook and Himes. Nine days later, on December 15, after getting the run-around and no official answer from the Cubs, Maddux sent them a letter stating that if he didn't hear from the Cubs by 5 p.m. on December 20, he would withdraw his acceptance of the deal and file for free agency after the '92 season.

At 5:05 p.m. on December 20, 14 days after Maddux had accepted the deal, Homerin called back and said the offer was no longer on the table.

In the months and years that followed, no one with the Cubs would admit that it had ever taken place. More importantly, from that day forward, Greg Maddux never felt quite the same way about the Cubs.

After I had signed my new deal in March of '92, my thinking was we've got to get Greg Maddux and Andre Dawson locked up, too. But Himes refused to even speak to Andre until the season was over, which angered Andre and I couldn't blame him at all. They were showing him no respect.

As for Maddux, he wasn't hearing anything, either. Greg was a friend and teammate of mine for six years, and when I signed, I just assumed they would re-sign Greg Maddux. How could you not, right?

Once the season started, Greg approached me a few times to ask me what I thought about his situation. I didn't really like to get involved in the business side of these things, but I listened to what he had to say.

I still didn't think it would be a problem getting it done. So I filed it away in the back of my mind for the moment, and figured it would all get worked out.

Well, Greg got off to another great start and was selected for the All-Star team. Not that he had anything to prove, but if he needed to send a message, his numbers were right there in black and white.

While we were in San Diego for the All-Star Game, the Cubs sat down with Greg again and tried to work out a deal. It didn't work out, and Greg and I sat together on the plane ride back to Chicago.

He was disappointed that they weren't any closer to a deal, and only a few months remained before he became a free agent.

He told me he wanted to stay with the Cubs, and I could relate to that since I went through it the year before. It's a struggle because you want to stay, but they never give you the feeling that they want you back.

Greg felt unwanted and unappreciated. Regardless of who you are or what your occupation is, if you're human you need to feel wanted and appreciated.

Well, here was probably the best pitcher in baseball, and you can't believe the things they were telling him on the day of the All-Star Game.

On the plane ride back to Chicago, Greg told me they pretty much hammered him for the entire negotiating session, telling him how worthless he was.

After pulling an offer from the table and watching him make the All-Star team, they came up with a whopping $500,000 raise per year, to $27.5 million for five years, and then belittled him.

"You're lucky we're even offering this," the Cubs negotiators told him. "You've never done anything. You've never won 20 games and never won the Cy Young. You're never going to get more than this. What have you ever done?" Mad Dog walked away wondering if they even thought he belonged in the big leagues, and here he was about to pitch in the All-Star Game.

Greg was a 26-year-old pitcher, not even in his prime yet, averaging 260 innings a year. But they even managed to turn that positive into a negative. The guy had never missed a start in his life, and they were murdering him in this meeting.

"You've pitched so many innings," one negotiator told him, "that it's only a matter of time before you get hurt. You're going to get hurt one of these days. Your arm's going to fall off."

They took the most positive stat a starting pitcher could possibly have — innings pitched — and made it a negative.

And this was a guy they wanted to keep?

Greg didn't want to negotiate during the season anyway. He had told them flat out in December that there would be no more talks. But like Al Pacino said in *The Godfather III*, "Every time I think I'm out, they pull me back in."

They have a way of dragging guys back into negotiations even when they don't want to be there. So now he was just more frustrated than when he got to San Diego.

They had succeeded in taking his mind off of baseball and then didn't do anything but tell him how lousy he was. All that combined with the fact that they had taken away an offer he agreed to in December, made me realize this was a really bad situation that was getting worse by the day. He was on his way to a big season, and his six-year numbers for wins, starts, innings, ERA and strikeouts were about the best in the business.

The Cubs were playing games and this was one I didn't want to lose.

Greg was our ace, the workhorse, and when he shared those things with me on the plane ride back to Chicago, I guess I shouldn't have been surprised, but I was.

I felt like I had to get involved.

"Is it OK if I go to them," I said, "and let them know how you feel?"

"That'd be great," Maddux said. "I don't know what's going to happen now."

I decided I'd make some calls. I spoke with Stanton Cook and he assured me that the Cubs would do everything they could to keep Greg. I didn't know if my voice meant anything there, but I figured that was the time to find out.

I told Cook that we couldn't afford to lose Maddux because his value to the club went far beyond his 36 or 37 starts per season. He was a leader and a teacher and he knew more about pitching than anyone I've ever met, including all the pitching coaches. It was like having another pitching coach right there on the staff.

Some of our pitchers might not know it, but in 1992 Greg called a lot of pitches from the bench. Sometimes Joe Girardi would look into the dugout and see what Maddux thought in certain situations, and Joe and Greg had their own set of signs. Greg would point to his chin for a changeup or his nose for a fastball or ear for a curveball. Girardi was a young catcher learning the game and he knew the value of Maddux's knowledge. He wasn't about to pass up the chance to learn from him and help out the other pitchers at the same time.

Greg knew more about what some pitchers should throw than the pitchers themselves.

His impact on the club was immense, but not everyone in the front office spent the time to find out what an important player he was.

Maybe they think of it as business, but I don't care what kind of business it is. If you play games with people's lives, bad things can happen.

Our pitching staff had a great year in '92, but our lineup was one bat short of producing, and we didn't score much that season.

One reason was a trade we made with four days left in spring training. Larry was reunited with his favorite player in baseball when he acquired Sammy Sosa from the White Sox in exchange for George Bell.

It obviously was not a deal that would help us in 1992, and I got the feeling that Larry had no intention of trying to win any time soon.

The Bell trade might've cost us the division title that year. We led the majors in ERA until the beginning of September, but we couldn't score all summer.

Larry never got us another No. 5 hitter to replace George and Sammy didn't do much for us because of injuries. We were shut out 20 times, while George drove in 112 runs for the White Sox.

Andre Dawson had no one hitting behind him in the No. 5 spot and he still drove in 90 runs. So what might he have done with George back there?

As soon as the trade was made, the guys were all over Hawk. "Better learn to hit that breaking ball again," Shawon Dunston yelled. "Cause you're never gonna see another fastball this year."

Shawon was right, too.

It was a feeling-out year for Jim Lefebvre and Tom Trebelhorn, who was the new bench coach. They had been American League managers and had to learn not just our club, but the other teams and the National League style.

We stayed in the race on the strength of our pitching until the end of August. But when Mike Harkey tore up his knee while doing a backflip in early September, that was the end of our run.

We finished six under and in fourth place, but it wasn't a bad year. Like the year before, I thought all we needed was a closer and we'd be darn close. Of course, now we needed someone to hit behind Andre, too.

The Hawk hit his 399th homer in his second at-bat on the final day of the season, and that also provided me with my 100th run scored.

When Andre came to bat with two outs in the bottom of the eighth, he got one of the loudest standing ovations I'd ever heard at Wrigley Field.

Everyone on the bench was standing and cheering, too, and we wanted Hawk to get No. 400 right there. But Expos pitcher Bill Krueger wasn't going to give him anything to hit, and he struck him out on a very high, 3-2 fastball.

"I wasn't going to walk," Hawk said with a smile. "But they weren't going to let me hit. It was just like 1987 when they pitched around me on the last day because they didn't want me to hit No. 50."

Hawk was awesome.

I thought he'd be back and he did, too, so they must've said something to him to make him feel that way.

And let's not forget Greg Maddux.

You know, the guy who couldn't win 20 games or the Cy Young?

He won 20 games and the Cy Young.

If we had scored any runs for him, he might've won 26 or 28 games, but we were shut out seven times when he started and the team collected a total of eight runs in his 11 losses.

Mark Grace also won his first Gold Glove, and he deserved it. I was happy he was with us and not Kansas City.

Those were the good things, but all kinds of bizarre moves took place that year.

Just one of them was the trade for Kal Daniels at the end of June. The Cubs could've waited one more day and signed him as a free agent at minimum wage because he'd been placed on waivers by the Dodgers. That cost the team about $400,000. Another was calling up Gary Scott and two other players from the minors on September 20. Scott had already been home for three weeks, enrolled in classes and hadn't touched a bat or a ball in a month.

They put him at shortstop for one game, even though he'd never played there before, and he almost fell over trying to field a ball.

Calling up three players that late cost the club about another $60,000 when you add up meal money, salary and the effect of service time on the next year's salary. None of them really played, so I don't know what the point was. The reason I bring up all the cash Himes was flushing down the toilet is because while he was doing that, he reneged on $10,000 bonuses he promised coaches Billy Connors and Chuck Cottier if their players met certain goals.

Billy had taken a staff that finished last the year before, and turned it into the best in the majors for five months. He met all the pitching goals, but Himes wouldn't come up with the money for him or Chuck Cottier.

If that wasn't strange enough, we used 41 different players in 1992, and in some weird combinations. At one point we might've had 12 pitchers and three catchers, or eight infielders and four outfielders. That must have been fun for Jim Lefebvre to manage.

Remember "scouts" Jim Frey and Jim Essian? Well, they traveled all summer and filed reports for six months, but apparently Larry Himes never read any of them.

We were no longer the professional organization Dallas Green had put in place in 1982.

Ten years later, it was pure Ringling Brothers.

I lost a string of nine straight Gold Gloves in 1992. That in itself didn't bother me. But the way I lost it did bother me.

There seemed to be a campaign going on for Pittsburgh's Jose Lind, which was fine because he was terrific that year. What bothered me were the shots being taken at me, because I didn't understand them.

That's when I began hearing I had lost some range. Well, who doesn't after 15 years as a pro? But how much could I have lost if I led the majors in assists and the NL in total chances?

It was just kind of strange. I played in 30 more games and had 100 more assists than Lind, and I played with seven different shortstops that year — Shawon Dunston, Rey Sanchez, Jose Vizcaino, Luis Salazar, Alex Arias, Jeff Kunkel and Gary Scott. (If you're surprised I can still name them, join the club.)

In any case, the new contract hadn't affected my performance, just like I had promised. I won my seventh Silver Slugger award, which goes to the top hitter at each position, and was second in the NL in total bases — which I considered one of the few worthwhile statistics.

I felt good about my season. Now if we could just keep our own players and sign a closer, I thought 1993 could be very interesting.

17 **The purge**

"Ryne Sandberg was a manager's dream. He was a great player, a Hall of Famer, who didn't want any special favors. You penciled his name in 160 times and never had to worry about him. What Ryno wanted was to be happy. He wanted to go to the park, be with his friends and have fun. Playing the game and winning was something special for him."
—*Former Cubs manager Jim Lefebvre*

During the final week of the '92 season, Larry Himes called me up to the front office and asked for my advice. He wanted my evaluation of the club and I thought that was pretty cool because that had never happened before.

Mike Morgan and I went together and I said our top priority had to be to sign Greg Maddux — the best pitcher in the league — and Andre Dawson — the best cleanup hitter in the league.

Other than that, I said we needed to keep the core of the team together and add a quality closer. Himes nodded as if he agreed with everything we said, and I felt good about our chances of keeping those guys when we left his office.

As it turns out, he wasn't interested in one word we had to say.

Weeks went by and nothing happened.

It wasn't until after the expansion draft in mid-November, that Larry had another conversation with Greg Maddux. Two days after the draft, Larry flew out to see Greg's agent.

After having no communication with his Cy Young Award winner for six weeks, he made the same offer he made at the All-Star break and said take it or leave it. That was on a Friday, and on Monday Himes said he was going to start signing pitchers.

Here was Greg Maddux, the best pitcher in baseball, and he had waited six years to become a free agent. The Cubs had pulled an offer from the table the year before, told him he was worthless in July, and now he was supposed to sign for the same money they offered him at the All-Star break when they told him he had never won a Cy Young or 20 games. Not only that, but it was a take-it-or-leave-it offer right then and there. Does that sound like the Cubs really wanted to keep Greg Maddux?

Not to me it didn't.

Maddux and his agent asked for one week to explore the market. Teams weren't talking before the expansion draft, so now they wanted seven days to talk to a few clubs that were interested.

But Himes would not discuss it. A few days later, Himes signed Jose Guzman and that was the end of Greg Maddux's career as a Chicago Cub.

Greg heard about it on the radio and rushed to a pay phone to call Himes. He said, "I heard you signed Guzman. Where do I stand? Is there enough to sign me?"

"We're not signing you," Larry said. "I couldn't wait for you. We had to move on. We had to sign someone and we don't have any money left."

Actually, he went on to spend another $20 million on free agents. Why didn't he just tell Greg Maddux that he didn't want him?

Maddux, Morgan and I all called Stan Cook to plead our case, but Himes must have convinced him that the Cubs didn't need Maddux.

That's when Greg realized he wasn't coming back. He was very disappointed, but he knew he had to start calling other teams.

The entire negotiating process since the All-Star break consisted of one meeting in November and an ultimatum with basically the same offer the Cubs made in July. With that in mind, I had serious doubts about whether the Cubs ever had any intention of keeping Greg Maddux. All Himes had to do was negotiate with him and Greg would've stayed in Chicago, but there was no negotiation.

His talk with Greg's agent after the expansion draft was just for publicity's sake, so that he could tell everyone he tried to keep Maddux. In fact, he held a press conference when he got back to Chicago to say that "nothing happened." It was like a *Seinfeld* episode.

"Ladies and gentlemen, I've called you all here to say that nothing happened."

It's the first press conference I'd ever heard of that announced nothing, but Larry was into damage control already and trying to make Maddux out to be the bad guy.

It worked on a lot of people, including me for a moment. When I heard Greg signed with Atlanta for just a little more than the Cubs had offered and I heard Greg say he wanted to play for a winner, I was mad.

Then I found out that what Greg really said was he had turned down $37 million from the Yankees and took the $28 million from Atlanta because he felt they had a better chance to win at that time, and his focus was on playing for a winner, once he realized the Cubs weren't interested.

I also realized that Greg just wanted to be wanted. The Cubs made it clear they didn't want him and my anger turned back to Himes.

He always thought he was smarter than everyone else and that he knew something the rest of us didn't. Himes thought he could do without a Greg Maddux, as if Maddux was just another pitcher.

It's not like he hadn't proven anything. It's not like he went to Atlanta and all of a sudden became a superstar. He already was.

He was a once-in-a-generation, born-in-the-organization superstar, and the Cubs told him to get lost.

When I was a young Cub I heard a lot about the Cubs' famous mistake of trading Lou Brock, and how it was the worst thing the Cubs ever did. Nothing against Lou Brock, but that's going to be a distant memory in Chicago by the time Maddux's career is over.

If the Maddux mess wasn't enough, the Cubs were hardly speaking to Andre Dawson, and his negotiation didn't start until the last minute either. They had given him assurances but were only stringing him along, I guess, for the sake of public perception.

By the time they made Dawson an offer, he had three days to take it or leave it. Larry had been on the job an entire year, and refused to talk about a contract with Andre. In fact, Hawk got on him in the press a few times that year and I think Larry was afraid of him. He'd walk through the clubhouse and wouldn't even say hello to Andre.

This was a guy with 16 years in the majors and 399 home runs, and with a three-day ultimatum, the Cubs offered him a $300,000 pay cut. Yes, a pay cut.

Once again I ask, what do you think he was going to say? It was just like the Maddux situation. Larry knew the answer would be "no" and it's what he wanted to hear.

It was a slap in the face to a guy who gave so much of himself to the club and to the fans and to the city. He was another guy who wanted to be a Cub forever, and the Cubs sent him packing.

Dawson wanted to play at Wrigley Field and retire there in front of the fans who loved and worshipped him. He signed a blank contract in '87. That's how bad he wanted to be a Cub. Over the last four years, he hit .279 and averaged 25 homers and 93 RBI, while I averaged .298 and 31 homers with 91 RBI. It was nice combination for the Cubs and a good situation for the team.

I'd spent six years with Andre and I knew what he meant to the club. Anyone who'd been around the clubhouse or even watched the games knew what he meant to the club. If you watched him go through the agony of preparing his knees for the games, you couldn't help but be inspired by him. The young players watched "the guy with 10 knee operations" give 100 percent and it made them want to go out and play hard, too.

But some people who make decisions never played in the big leagues. They can't understand what it means, or feel the emotion. Just like they don't understand chemistry.

If you sit in the front office, you don't have to deal with bad influences in the clubhouse. The manager, coaches, players and trainers have to, but the execs don't. And if they're not smart enough to see what it does to a team, then you wind up with a disaster.

The same goes for character players like the Hawk. But I don't know how you could miss seeing what Andre meant to everyone.

He was also one of the best cleanup hitters in the game, and if you think you can just plug anyone in there, you're wrong. It takes guts and smarts to hit there, not just an uppercut.

It's strange how some players had great timing and luck when it came to contracts, but Andre never got treated with the proper amount of respect.

The end result was another sad chapter because we had lost another Cub.

I realized then that if I hadn't gotten to Stan Cook in the middle of the night, I'd be gone just like Maddux and Dawson and all the rest. Larry didn't want any of us around.

Slowly but surely, everything the previous regimes had built up, Larry Himes was tearing down. Dallas Green had instilled pride and began a tradition, and during the '80s, players for the first time in decades wanted to be Cubs.

But not anymore.

Himes would be the one who decided what a Cub should or shouldn't be. He was making it clear that he didn't care what anyone thought or felt.

He was the boss — and he was making sure everyone knew it.

Before the '92 winter meetings ended, Andre Dawson found a team that saw what he had to offer.

While the Cubs had offered $3 million for one year, the Boston Red Sox gave Andre $9.4 million for two years. I was happy for him but sad for the Cubs. I couldn't believe he wasn't going to hit his 400th homer at Wrigley Field, retire as a Cub and go into the Hall of Fame wearing a Cubs hat. It was a thrill playing with Hawk, but now I was going to meet some new teammates — a lot of new teammates.

We ended the '92 season with three lefties in the bullpen: Paul Assenmacher, Chuck McElroy and Ken Patterson, but in one 15-minute span of the winter meetings we signed two more.

As long as I live I won't understand this one. The Cubs knew they were about to sign Randy Myers, which was great. We needed a closer, and Randy's one of the best.

But a few minutes before the Cubs signed him, and knowing they were going to sign him, they walked into another room and signed Dan Plesac.

Now this is nothing against Plesac, but what was the point of signing him? Dan will tell you himself he couldn't believe it happened and never would've signed with the Cubs had he known.

Plesac turned down more money from other clubs who wanted him to be a closer, but he thought he might as well be a closer or share the role in Chicago, which was where he made his home.

Can you explain to me why we needed Plesac if we were signing Myers? Now we had five, count 'em, five lefties in the bullpen. It's always nice to have a couple of lefties, but we had a whole team full of them.

Next, Himes went for Candy Maldonado and Willie Wilson.

Larry was like a kid in a candy store. He was spending money left and right and he was putting together a team based on stats, the way you put together a rotisserie team.

Now we needed a leadoff man, a cleanup hitter, a No. 5 hitter and a No. 1 starter. We got the closer, but Larry let so much get away that we had taken a step backward and created more holes.

We hadn't replaced Maddux with an ace, or Dawson with a right fielder or cleanup man, but we added two lefty relievers to the three we already had, and took on a part-time center fielder and a left fielder.

I'm sitting at home reading the transactions thinking, do we have a plan here? I couldn't figure it out if we did.

Maybe they figured they could take all the money they would've spent on Maddux and Dawson, and get a whole bunch of players.

Can you name one business in the world where you take quantity over quality? It doesn't work that way in baseball, either.

So he signed all those American League players, and only one National League guy, Randy Myers. Shortly after that the Cubs released Kenny Patterson, but we still had four lefties in the bullpen.

And the purge continued.

Himes released veteran Doug Dascenzo, another guy who wanted to be a Cub. Dougie's a great role player who didn't make a lot of money, but he wasn't a Himes guy so he was gone. In our meeting, I tried to stress to Himes the need for solid bench players who don't gripe when they don't play and can do the job when they do play. That's what Dascenzo did for us.

In the expansion draft we also lost Joe Girardi, a fine young catcher who — you guessed it — wanted to be a Cub forever. He grew up near Chicago and he loved the Cubs. But it was a good break for Joe because he got hooked up with a great organization in Colorado.

We had nearly enough talent to win when Himes took over, but the first thing he did was tear up the team.

He wanted his own people in place and winning with someone else's roster apparently didn't appeal to him.

In a year he had changed half the roster and we had no identity at all. Jimmy Lefebvre was doing everything he could to keep the team directed, but it's tough with a dozen new faces every year.

Chemistry meant nothing anymore. We'd bring in seven or eight new players a year and dump another six or seven, while paying no attention to the character of the guys we brought in.

Early in 1993, Jim Lefebvre told Himes several times that certain players didn't fit in or were causing trouble. Once in a meeting Lefebvre told Himes that one player "was poisoning the whole team. You have to get rid of him." Himes response was, "Get used to it. You've got him for another year and a half."

Himes often told coaches and managers that he didn't care about what players were like in the clubhouse. He cared only about what they did on the field. I guess he didn't realize the two go hand in hand.

He brought in veterans with baggage and they poisoned the clubhouse, especially the younger kids, making them difficult to manage and difficult to get along with. But what difference did that make to Larry? He didn't have to live with them. Apparently he didn't realize that it eventually destroys a team and would hurt him as well. But that's what happens when you put together a rotisserie team. You have to look inside the individual, not just at their stat sheets.

I went to camp in the spring of '93 needing a scorecard to figure out who was on the team. Mark Grace and I joked every day about needing a media guide to figure out if we were in the right clubhouse.

And for the first time in my career, I went to camp with no enthusiasm. I didn't like that feeling at all, because if you're not optimistic in spring training, you've got a problem.

I had a good year in '92, which surprised some people, who thought the pressure of the contract would affect me, but that's because they didn't know me. Contracts made me feel secure, not pressured.

I worked out hard as I always do over the winter, and came to camp in 1993 ready to play.

Aside from trying to learn everyone's name, it was a fairly normal camp, and we started the first game of the exhibition season March 5 at HoHoKam Park by pounding the Giants. We were up 7–0 and had two men on in the fourth when I walked to the plate for my third at-bat. Normally, you wouldn't get three at-bats that early in the exhibition season, but we scored a bunch of runs and batted around a couple times, so it was only the fourth inning.

I had spoken with Lefebvre and hitting coach Billy Williams and Jimmy said, "After this at-bat, get your work in on the other field with Billy and go home."

I was facing the Giants' Mike Jackson and I took a big swing at the first pitch and fouled it straight back. I was bearing down, trying to drive in some runs. As long as I was spending seven weeks there, I didn't waste my time and I used my spring training at-bats.

When I thought about it later, I realized Jackson might've sensed that I was getting into it.

After he threw me a breaking ball for a strike, it was 0–2, but his next pitch was way up and in, and I had to scramble to get my head, hands and body out of the way. It moved me way back and just missed my neck. That's what we call, appropriately enough, a neck-ball.

I didn't think too much about it, except for the fact that on the first day of games, you don't expect that pitch and don't have your timing down enough to get out of the way. It's very dangerous.

I'd faced Jackson a lot in the past and he's very tough to pick up from the right side because of the way he delivers the ball, and he's got real good stuff. He's got a big breaking ball and a fastball that rides in on you.

I was a little surprised and upset at that 0–2 pitch, and Jackson might've sensed that, too.

Well, the next pitch was the same one, only farther in. It was the same type of pitch and I just couldn't react in time. All I could do was get my head out of the way. But before the rest of my body could move, boom! The ball pinned my left hand against the bat, between the knuckle and wrist, right where all those little bones are. I went down in a heap.

My reaction time was off and his fastball rode right in at my face. The combination of the two resulted in a broken hand — the only major injury I had in 13 years.

I felt the deep pain right away and I could see the swelling through my batting glove. It was the first broken bone I'd ever had in my life and I knew the pain was different. Right away I thought, I'm going to be out of the lineup, missing a lot of games and I'm letting the team down. That was all racing through my mind in the split second after it happened.

So by the time I hit the ground and grabbed my hand, I was yelling out at Jackson. I used some choice words and when I stood up and looked at him, the benches emptied.

After one spring training game, I was looking at two months on the shelf. I'd never been faced with anything like that before.

I tried to find the positives in it. I had come to camp with one main goal: To get to the World Series. But now I had another one: To prove to everyone that I could come back from an injury at age 33.

I worked extra hard for two months. Near the end of April, I was feeling pretty strong and told the coaches I figured I could be ready for games in another three or four days.

Reporters were coming up to me and asking if I needed a rehabilitation stint in the minors, and I kept saying I didn't think so. At the same time, Larry was telling reporters he was working on an itinerary for me to go down to the minors.

But he never told me that, so I knew nothing about it. He never talked to the players about such things, but he'd tell everyone else.

There was no game plan as far as I knew. He never came to me to ask me how I felt or what I thought about it. He never asked if I needed a few games in the minors or any at-bats or what my thoughts were. No communication at all.

One day he just called me in and gave me an itinerary. He had it all planned out already. Two days in Daytona with a double-header and three days in Orlando with a double-header and so on and so forth.

It was all done already. I looked at it, looked at him, nodded my head and walked out of his office. I didn't say a word. I just took the itinerary and left. There was nothing to discuss. All the reservations were already made. I wasn't going to stand there and tell him what I thought because it didn't matter.

So I packed my gear and was out of the clubhouse in 20 minutes. See ya.

Himes said, "It's an organizational strategy. This is what we did with Sammy Sosa last year and we had a lot of success with it, so we'll do it with you."

Sammy hit a home run in his first at-bat back from a rehab stint so that was all Larry needed to know. There was never a plan, just hunches. His "strategies" were all guesswork and make-it-up-as-we-go-along.

As for his ability to communicate, he treated Lefebvre even worse than the players. Even when he pretended to let Jimmy in on things, he didn't.

When he was preparing to sign Willie Wilson, he asked Lefebvre to call Tony LaRussa and find out what he thought. Lefebvre tried for an entire day, but couldn't reach the Oakland manager.

When Lefebvre called Himes back to tell him he'd reach the LaRussa the next morning, Himes said, "Don't bother. I already signed Wilson."

Himes had already decided how much the manager would play him, too. As Himes went on the radio telling everyone that Wilson would start every day, Lefebvre — who had good reason to think he was actually the manager of the team — was telling everyone Wilson would be a "fine bench player for us."

But that wasn't as bad as the day Lefebvre got a call from a radio station, asking him for his reaction to the signing of Jose Guzman.

Lefebvre stuttered, put them on hold and called Himes because the GM had issued a press release without informing the manager of his move.

Now that's communication for you.

Most players hated the minor league stints. Even in spring training, there were sometimes too many pitchers so the club would find a minor league game to get them some work. Or if the manager wanted to see a fringe guy, he'd send a veteran to a minor league game because he didn't need to see him.

Every year, Maddux pitched in at least one of those games and always got hammered. Jose Bautista had one in '94 and the same thing happened to him.

"You can't set them up or anything. They don't think up at the plate," Bautista said laughing. "All they do is swing. It's a waste of time."

I knew it'd be the same thing for me down there. I was starting over from scratch. I missed a month of spring training and my spring training was going to take place during the season against pitchers who were two months ahead of me. So unless he wanted me to spend a month in the minors, there wasn't much point. Four days wasn't going to change anything.

The work down there was nothing I couldn't do with the club, but since that's what I felt, naturally Larry thought just the opposite.

I guess if I'd gotten hit in the face in Daytona by some kid who hadn't learned how to pitch yet, the point would've been made.

We always had pitchers complaining about those rehabs, too, because they wanted their major league trainers and coaches monitoring them.

But Larry always insisted. One time in '94 Larry wouldn't fly a pitcher back from Florida because it would've cost $1,000 and he wanted him to make another start there. But the pitcher wanted to see his trainers and doctors and he told him, "You spent all these millions on me and now you want to take a chance on ruining my arm? What's the matter with you?"

So the pitcher flew back anyway and sent Larry the bill.

But I wasn't going to discuss it, so I took the plane ticket and left.

My stint in the minors was short, but it was a different experience after 11 years in the big leagues. I always tried to find the positive in something, and in this case it brought back all the memories of being in the minors and it was actually fun being back — since it was only for a couple of days.

The kids at Class-A Daytona Beach were all directly out of high school or maybe one year removed. They were 18 or 19 years old and loving the game of baseball, playing on a terrible field, trying to catch the ball with bad hops and bad lights and never complaining about it.

They didn't even make enough money to eat three meals a day, but they didn't say anything about that, either.

There'd be a sell-out crowd of about 300, and I'd hear them making comments like, "Wow, big crowd tonight because you're here," and they were dead serious.

And the baseballs were so old and worn out that I sent them 1,000 new baseballs when I got back to Chicago. The minor league teams get the used balls passed down from the big league club, but by the time they go through Triple-A and Double-A, there's nothing left of them when they get to Class-A. It was like hitting a rosin bag, and I thought they deserved better than that.

It was a nice experience to see where I had come from and good to see kids enjoying the game again. It was a nice change for me, as it turns out.

I rejoined the major league club after about five days on April 30, but when I got back and looked around, I hardly knew anyone.

18 ◆ The summer of torture

"When it was the zaniest, that's when Ryno was the calmest. He's the soldier who, when guys are running in circles and confused, Ryno says, 'Guys, uh, I think we ought to go this way.' Whenever there was panic, you'd look over at Ryno sitting relaxed in front of his locker, and everyone else would relax, too."
—*Former Cubs manager Tom Trebelhorn*

There were a lot of adjustments to make in 1993, especially for the manager, Jim Lefebvre. It took time not only for the new players to feel comfortable with the team, but for the players that were already there to get used to the new guys — and for the manager to get used to everybody getting used to everybody.

Jimmy had to keep it all together while the new players learned a new league, and it took about half a season for them to adjust. That's very typical when you make major changes like we had done.

Jimmy still had no ace or cleanup hitter or leadoff man, but he was working hard and so were all the coaches. He rarely, however, got any support or praise from Larry Himes for it. Himes would call Jimmy's office before and after every game to tell him what he did wrong and how he wanted it done differently.

It was starting to wear on Jimmy, who was also

hearing how much players disliked Larry and all of his rules. Jimmy was caught in between. He didn't care for Himes either, but he didn't want his players focusing on the general manager.

On Opening Day of '93, Greg Maddux stuck it to Larry by beating us at Wrigley Field.

The next day, Jose Guzman was spectacular in throwing a one-hitter for us and beat the Braves. In the clubhouse after the game, Larry brought in Stanton Cook, the acting team president, to meet Guzman and show off his prized possession.

It was embarrassing for everyone, most of all Jose Guzman. Guzman is no Greg Maddux, and Jose will tell you that himself. He didn't want to be compared to the best pitcher in baseball, and it's not even fair to compare the two. But there was Larry showing off Jose. You know he was thinking, "See how smart I am? I don't need Greg Maddux."

He would find out later how wrong he was.

We were starting to get our act together and had won six of eight by May 19. We were in St. Louis and three over .500, six-and-a-half out at 20–17. It wasn't bad considering the Phillies were on fire and trying to run away from everyone in the NL East.

We were having fun and playing good ball and there was a lot of energy coming from Jimmy.

And that's when it happened.

Himes made a comment on the radio in Chicago that he expected us to be 10 games over the .500 mark by the All-Star break.

And that's when the stuff really hit the fan.

That was all anyone talked about for the next two months. We couldn't figure out why he would say that.

What did it mean? What if we didn't get there? Was everybody gone?

There was a lot of speculation and the guys thought maybe Jimmy would be fired immediately.

The manager, coaches, players and trainers sat around wondering what the guy upstairs was thinking.

And we had a game to play!

I just never understood why every time it seemed like we were getting on track he would rip the team in the papers or on a radio show. It was never anything positive. And all that did was anger the players and turn them against Larry. I don't know what his purpose was but that was the moment the players really turned against him for good.

We went to Florida after St. Louis and it was talked about so much that it became a distraction and we didn't play well.

The last thing you'd expect was for the GM to keep you from playing well. Didn't he want us to play well? Or did he want us to play bad so he could fire Jimmy? And what sense does that make, since he hired Jimmy? You try to figure it out. We couldn't.

If it was meant to be a morale boost or light a fire under us, it didn't do that at all. It hurt Jimmy and it hurt the team.

After that Florida series, we got home and Jimmy called a meeting and had us regroup.

"We have to pull together and pull for each other and be positive," Lefebvre said. "Let's knock off the negative attitude and let's concentrate on baseball."

It was a very positive meeting and we seemed to turn it around again.

But Jimmy was really suffering inside. He'd been left shorthanded to begin with, and then he lost me for two months and Shawon Dunston for the entire year. He had all those new players and he was doing the best he could to keep us motivated.

But all of Himes' remarks throughout the season really got to the club, and by mid-season it was all of us — the manager, players, coaches, trainers — on one side and him on the other side.

We were hanging in there and playing some good baseball and the fans were enjoying it. We were having some fun and it seemed like we were on the verge of doing something good — until Larry opened his mouth.

Jimmy felt like his job was on the line. The players were on Jimmy's side as if it was an Army unit; we rallied around our wounded commander. We went to war for him and tried to save his job.

But the tension was getting worse every day and there were some arguments in the clubhouse.

It got to the point where I don't even know why Jimmy wanted to come back. Larry was torturing him. Phone calls every day. Mounds of silly paperwork. Constant questions.

Why did Larry hire a manager if he wanted to manage the team himself? I couldn't figure it out.

Shortly after the furor began with the "10 games over" comment, Larry and Jimmy discussed the situation.

"Do you want a vote of confidence?" Larry asked. "I can do that."

"No," Jimmy replied. "That'd be the worst thing you could do. The media will pick up on that and this will never die."

"Well, then you have to diffuse this situation," Larry said.

"I have to?" Jimmy said. "You did this. You diffuse it. The team is very angry. I'll try to keep the team together but you have to diffuse it in the media."

"Fine," Larry told him.

But he never did it.

Larry Himes could never say he was wrong. He just couldn't do it. If just once he'd said, "I'm wrong," he could've reaped great benefits from that, especially with the players. Especially with me. We all make mistakes and we all admit them. But he couldn't.

He'd sign a guy who was terrible and blame someone else for the guy's failure, or blame someone else for the signing. As the year passed after Maddux left, he'd say something like, "I'd love to have a No. 1 pitcher. I wish we had a guy like a Greg Maddux or a Roger Clemens."

He'd forgotten the whole thing. In his mind he wasn't the one who blew it with Maddux. Like it was an out of body experience or something. Or maybe selective memory loss, I don't know.

But the loss of Maddux was devastating.

As our No. 1 guy, he had faced the other team's No. 1 starter almost every time out, which means the other pitchers on the staff didn't have to face the best pitcher.

If you think that doesn't matter, take a look at our 1993 pitching staff and you'll see the difference. Some guys can't take the pressure of facing that No. 1 pitcher all the time. That's usually a tough, 1–0 or 3–1 type game, and every pitch you make is important.

Your No. 1 guy also starts winning streaks and stops losing streaks, and when you walk out on the field, the position players are confident that he's going to give you eight or nine solid innings.

Our staff in '93 fell apart at the seams without Maddux. All the guys who had career years in '92 went in the tank. Billy Connors did everything he could do, but he was given several American League pitchers and some who simply didn't have the talent.

So many of the young guys would say they missed Maddux, not just for his innings and the pressure he took off the bullpen, but for his knowledge of the hitters and the strike zone.

A lot of the kids fell apart, not the least of whom was Frank Castillo, who'd had a terrific year in 1992.

Poor Frankie would be sitting in a meeting and Larry would say, "Didn't you learn anything from Maddux? Didn't he teach you anything?"

And Frankie would say, "Yeah, but where the heck is he? Why isn't he still here to help me now?"

That's what we were all wondering.

The week after the great "10 games" debate, we faced the Giants at home and the tension was brutal. Himes' comments were hanging over us like a dark cloud. Guys were starting to snipe at each other.

We'd had problems with the Giants in the first game of the series with brushback pitches, and there was tension between the two clubs because of Jackson breaking my hand in spring training.

By the second game, we were ready to fight someone. Between Himes and the Giants and some locker room jabbering, it was on the verge of getting nasty.

In the second game of the series, it did.

In the third inning, Mark Grace took a called third strike that was about a foot outside, and while he argued Jimmy Lefebvre came out of the dugout and wound up getting thrown out himself.

It was a very emotional game and we fought back to take a 3-2 lead in the bottom of the fifth, when I came to bat with the bases loaded and two outs.

I hit a grounder to short and beat the throw by three feet. It wasn't much of a hit, but as I crossed the bag I thought, at least we got a run out of it and the inning was alive. I was safe and I knew it, but first base umpire Charlie Williams called me out. Coach Jose Martinez went nuts at first and Chuck Cottier, subbing for Lefebvre as manager, came flying out of the dugout to argue.

"What were you looking at?" I asked Williams, while Cottier and Martinez screamed at him.

"What were you looking at?" I asked again. "What were you looking at?"

I must've said it 20 times. Before I could say it the 21st time, Williams threw me out and tossed Cottier as well.

My first, and only, game ejection. I'd been thrown out of a sporting event for the first time in my life.

I had to get one in the books, I guess. You know, "Career High Ejections: 1993 — One."

I'm not sure what I was thinking, but I guess I wanted to know what he was looking at.

I was usually very good to the umpires. If I said something to them at home plate, no one in the park would know but the umpire and the catcher. I'd do it with my head down, talking to the ground.

Early in my career I was intimidated by the umpires because I didn't want to make them mad. If a young player gets a veteran umpire mad, many of them take it out on you the rest of the year with bad calls.

I learned at a young age. I got some advice from guys like Larry Bowa and Bill Buckner, who said, "Don't worry about the umpires. Just do your job."

Over the years, I got to know them personally and talked to them out at second base or at home plate. If I felt that a call wasn't right I'd let them know how I saw it, but I'd leave it at that.

I'd do it talking to the ground or walking away. If they believed the whole stadium could see a player questioning the call, they'd get uptight about that.

It's a matter of respect. You have to show them respect because they're professionals and most of them are very good at what they do. At the same time, I'd let them know if they blew a call, because my team deserved respect, too.

We were 20–17, six-and-a-half out and had won six of eight before the "10 games" debacle, but we immediately lost 14 of 22 after Larry made his comments and fell to 14 games out of first by the time we got swept in San Francisco in mid-June. Jim Lefebvre, the embattled general, was doing the best he could to keep the troops fighting, but injuries were taking a toll.

In three days in San Francisco we lost third baseman Steve Buechele and starting pitchers Mike Morgan, Greg Hibbard and Mike Harkey to the disabled list.

The Giants series was filled with brushbacks, hit batters and ejections like the week before in Chicago, so I felt like I had to do something.

After the final game at Candlestick Park, I stopped my old teammate Davey Martinez in the tunnel between the two clubhouses, and asked him to get Mike Jackson for me. I figured that someone was going to get hurt if the two teams didn't stop throwing at each other, and I felt sure that the spring training incident with Jackson had something to do with it.

When Jackson came out of the clubhouse, we shook hands right away and he apologized for hitting me before I could even say anything. It wasn't what I was looking for, but it was nice of him.

"I didn't mean to hit you," he said. "I tried to find you during spring training a few times so we could talk about it, but I couldn't find you."

We spoke for a minute or two and agreed that our teams should put it behind us. We shook hands again, wished each other luck and that was the end of it.

I just didn't want to be responsible for someone getting hurt, so I was glad to be done with it.

The bullpen situation had developed into a full-blown disaster by the middle of the '93 season. We had four lefties, two righties and it was having a terrible effect on the entire pitching staff.

Chuck McElroy had one of the best young arms in the game and had been a solid reliever the past two years. But with four left-handers in the bullpen, there wasn't enough work for him and he was struggling.

Dan Plesac had the same problem. He was pitching poorly, but that was because Lefebvre couldn't find enough work for him. There was no room at the inn, and our $1.6-million-a-year free agent was doing mop-up work in 10-0 games.

Himes asked Plesac to accept a rehab stint in the minors so he could get some work in, but Plesac told him to forget it. I don't blame him, either. Dan was furious that he had been put in this spot and all he wanted was a trade. He begged for it. The White Sox wanted him, too, but Himes wouldn't pull the trigger. That would be admitting a mistake.

It was killing the staff, so Larry's solution was to send down McElroy, and that only made his confidence problem worse.

The most bizarre scene might have been before a game in Houston, when Himes was down in the bullpen showing McElroy and Billy Connors what Chuck was doing wrong.

Now Himes was a pitching coach, too. He already wanted to be manager, so I guess the next step was leadoff man.

Paul Assenmacher always took the ball, which means he would pitch every day if you asked him to, and he was effective. So he set up for the closer, Randy Myers.

Jimmy was going with Assenmacher, who was getting people out. It's a Catch-22. You can't give the ball to a guy who can't get anyone out, but if he doesn't pitch, he'll never get his stuff together and he'll definitely never get anyone out.

The two righties were also affected. Bob Scanlan had to pitch virtually every day in the important situations, because Jimmy didn't know anything about the other righty, Jose Bautista. So Scanlan got worn out and Bautista was ineffective from lack of work.

As you can see, the entire bullpen was screwed up for two reasons.

First of all, Larry put Jimmy in a position of having to win immediately, and that affects a manager's decision-making process.

And secondly, the unnecessary signing of Plesac created a disastrous situation.

It affected every pitcher on the staff. Scanlan was worn out by pitching too much and ineffective by July. Bautista didn't pitch enough. McElroy had his confidence shattered. And Plesac was ready to quit entirely.

But the worst was yet to come, and the next guy to get it was Paul Assenmacher.

One consistent thing during the Larry Himes regime was that when we had a player who was loyal, wanted to remain a Cub and said so publicly, it was almost automatic that he would be traded or released.

It was happening so much that it started to get very frustrating and disappointing for me. I'd always get the feedback and the phone calls from the players who said they were sorry it happened or that it couldn't be worked out even though they wanted to stay.

I always heard that from the players who were leaving. One after another. Those guys were friends of mine and teammates and players I went to war with. That's what being a team is all about.

Himes was removing guys who wanted to be Cubs, and replacing them with guys who didn't seem to want to be anywhere, least of all in a Cubs uniform. The uniform meant nothing to them, and that hurt me, too.

I spent my whole career in that uniform and we worked so hard to get people to respect it and take pride in it. It seemed like we were regressing in that department.

So I began speaking out for the first time in my career during the 1992 and '93 seasons. I was so tired of seeing all the good players and good guys sent packing, and I didn't want to start all over again. I didn't have time for another five-year plan.

I guess Himes wanted a whole new team, and I had to watch as I saw a lot of good players and friends leave the ball club. By mid-1993, after 18 months under Himes, I was one of the few players left from before Larry got there and I figured he'd want me gone, too. I wasn't one of his guys so I didn't feel I was a part of the future of the Cubs.

That point was driven home on July 3 in Colorado, when I recorded career hit no. 2,000. I didn't think too much about it, until Rockies GM Bob Gebhard sent a bottle of champagne down to the clubhouse in honor of the occasion.

Chicago Cubs GM Larry Himes, who was on the trip, never even came down to shake my hand.

All year long it'd been rumored that Paul Assenmacher would be traded. It heated up in the middle of July and it was rough on Paul and his family. They'd bought a house in Chicago and enjoyed being a part of the Cubs family.

But it became obvious he was a goner because there were rumors in the papers for a month. After weeks of wondering every day if the trade would be made, Himes finally pulled the trigger on July 30 and sent Assenmacher to the Yankees. It sent a big message from Himes to the team: "The season is over, fellas."

Things had been going pretty well for the club, but when you trade a veteran reliever who you need to have in a pennant race, the GM is telling you the pennant race is over.

At the time, Assie was maybe the best lefty in baseball at coming in to get the tough lefty out in the seventh or eighth inning. Ask Barry Bonds or Will Clark or Fred McGriff. Paul was always called on to get the best hitters with guys in scoring position and he usually beat them. His curveball, when he's on, is unhittable and probably the best around.

The worst part about the deal was the Cubs had to pay at least half of his contract for the next two years, so the Cubs didn't even dump his salary in the process. The trade just made the rift between Himes and the players grow even wider.

A couple of weeks after the deal, Assie blasted Himes in the papers, calling him a minor-league guy who didn't have a clue about how to run a major league team. A few days later, Assie made it to Wrigley Field for a Sunday night game as the Yankees were arriving in town to face the White Sox. He watched the game from the first row behind the bullpen, yucking it up with his old pals down there, and visited the clubhouse after the game. As he sat in the trainer's room, the guys filed by, one by one, high-fiving him because of what he said in the paper about Himes.

The strange thing is if Larry could've just admitted his mistake and traded Plesac, everyone would've been happy, most of all Plesac. There were so many times Himes could've scored big points with the people he had to work with and work for had he just shown a little humility, but he couldn't see it because he was too interested in making people believe he was right.

As for 1993, we saw the Assenmacher trade as a sign that the season was over and Jimmy had to pull us together again. We'd won 11 of 16 before the deal, but after the trade we lost eight of the next 12.

Once again, Larry had squashed our enthusiasm.

19 ♦ Beginning of the end

> "I think he's a Hall of Famer. He has the credentials with an MVP and 10 All-Star Games and nine Gold Gloves. He was the best at his position for a decade. He did a lot for the game of baseball on and off the field. Ryne Sandberg was good for baseball."
> —*Hall of Famer Billy Williams*

I came back from my broken hand in spring training and felt pretty good in '93, but I never recovered the hand strength completely, and my power was down.

My season ended the same way it began: With another freak injury occurring against the Giants.

On September 13, I slid home feet first to score a run, but as I hooked the plate with my left foot, my right hand hit the steel toe in the shoe of home plate umpire Charlie Reliford. I'd been hot, hitting safely in 24 of 25 games, but now the season was over for me because of a dislocated right ring finger.

For the rest of the club, it was a much better ending.

Jimmy Lefebvre still didn't have a contract for the 1994 season, and the team fought like heck for him.

After September 3 we went 20–8, and our September/October record of 20–10 was the best by a Cubs team since 1945. At 84–78, it was one of only three Cubs teams to finish over .500 in 22 years.

But instead of patting anyone on the back, Larry Himes managed to find the negative as always and told the media, "I don't know why they didn't do it all year."

He failed to mention the rotating roster and the 38 players Jimmy had to use during the course of the year.

He failed to mention the fact that it took time to get all those new players acclimated to their new surroundings.

He didn't mention the fact that Greg Maddux was winning his second straight Cy Young Award in Atlanta instead of in Chicago.

He didn't mention the fact that during September when we were playing teams with 30 or 35 guys on their roster, Jimmy had to manage with 25 players, some injured, because the organization wanted our veteran Triple-A club to win a championship.

Himes moved players up from Double-A to Triple-A to help Iowa win, but he wouldn't call up any players to the majors until Iowa's season was over.

I guess he was trying to prove to his bosses that his farm system was producing, but he wasn't fooling anyone. That Iowa team had an average age of about 30 and a payroll that was incredibly high for a Triple-A team.

In the meantime, while Steve Trachsel spent half of September helping Iowa win the coveted minor league crown, Jim Lefebvre was suffering in Chicago.

One of Larry's favorite tricks was to take a player who'd never played a position before and plug him in that spot. He'd find a player somewhere and say, "Well, let's see. You can run fast, throw the ball and bunt. OK, you're a center fielder and leadoff man."

Even though a player may have never done it in the past, all of a sudden in major league baseball, with the best 700 players in the world, he was going to be whatever Larry wanted him to be.

Hoping and wishing was our chief philosophy. "I hope this works," and "I wish this would happen."

Himes made life all but impossible for Lefebvre, but somehow Jimmy kept us together and kept us fighting, and we finished up strong in spite of Larry's interference.

For the last three months of the 1993 season, whenever I was asked — which was almost every day — I gave my opinion and let everyone know I wanted Jimmy Lefebvre back. And almost all of the players said the same thing. It's very rare these days to have a team back a manager the way we did in 1993 and play the way we did for him, because there are so many individual agendas in a club.

In 1993, though, the team backed Jim Lefebvre and I don't know how you could see that as anything but positive.

But it didn't matter what the players thought. It certainly didn't matter what I thought.

What's hard for me to understand is why it bothered Larry so much. Was he jealous that Lefebvre was popular? That doesn't make sense. He hired Lefebvre and Lefebvre did well, so that's a positive reflection on Himes. But for some reason, that seemed to rub Himes the wrong way.

When he was asked about the support of the players for the manager, Larry would make some kind of remark like, "The players are entitled to their opinion," or something like that — as if what we thought was completely irrelevant.

But we were behind Jimmy and we let everyone know it. The really amazing thing is that everyone was behind Jimmy. The players were behind him, the fans were behind him, the media was in favor of him returning and the front office staff at Wrigley Field loved him.

Jimmy was big into being a Cub and promoting that idea. He wanted the uniform to mean something and wanted the people who wore it to be proud of it. That was something front office employees took notice of.

Everyone was in a group on one side of the fence making positive comments, but Himes was still on the other side of the fence, negative as ever.

Every time I got the chance publicly, I begged Himes to keep Jim Lefebvre and sign Mark Grace to a long-term deal. Grace is another guy who said repeatedly that he wanted to be Cub, but Larry couldn't wait to get Grace out of town, either. Larry didn't like Grace, probably because he was popular, too. Larry didn't seem to like anyone who was popular, especially if he wasn't responsible for the person being there.

All Larry could find to talk about was Sammy Sosa and his magical "30-30 season." He didn't talk about the job Jimmy Lefebvre did. Not about Mark Grace, who hit .325 with 98 RBI and another Gold Glove.

No, all he talked about was Sammy.

He took credit for Myers, naturally, though he didn't mention all the free agents he signed that were busts. The fact is, signing Myers was a great idea and I was glad he did it. Myers was nearly perfect in '93, setting the National League record with 53 saves, and it was a great confidence factor for us. Myers gave all the credit to his set-up men, mainly Assenmacher and Scanlan, but Randy was amazing any way you look at it.

If Himes had kept the team together and simply signed Myers, we might've been drinking champagne when the 1993 season ended.

As for Lefebvre's fate, well, Larry didn't like the fact that Jimmy had stopped listening to all of Himes' nonsense. Jimmy decided to manage the team the way he wanted to manage it, not the way Larry wanted him to.

He decided the hours and hours he spent doing idiotic paperwork could be better spent helping the players or spending time with his coaches.

He decided that if he was going to get fired — and the "10 games over .500" quote certainly made it sound that way — then he might as well do things the way he wanted to do them. It worked because the team responded and we had a great second half of the season.

So Himes couldn't fire him now because he'd done such a great job. There's no way he'd fire Lefebvre because Tribune Co. does not look kindly on its people who hire and fire at the alarming pace Himes had been on.

And the company doesn't like to see its executives fire employees they've hired because it looks as though you have no idea what you're doing. In the case of Lefebvre, the employee also happened to have been successful.

I had a lot of opinions about Larry, but I never once thought he was stupid. In fact, I've heard he has great baseball skills when it comes to scouting and developing players, and he pays great attention to detail.

But I didn't think in a million years he'd fire Lefebvre, because if he did that, he'd be pointing the gun at himself, too.

He'd be telling Tribune Co. that the circus is in town and the animals are running loose all over the city.

After finishing so well and fighting to save Jimmy's job for him, the scene in San Diego on the final day of the season was pretty amazing. We were all hugging each other and high-fiving one another and the chemistry because of Lefebvre had improved dramatically. He'd taken this hodgepodge and made something out of it, and it was one of the best feelings I've ever had at the end of a season.

There was a positive feeling looking ahead to 1994 and Jimmy gave a wonderful season-ending speech about coming back prepared to win.

We knew we'd saved Jimmy's job, and we had some direction and some good things to take into 1994. It was really fun.

That Sunday night when the season ended, Jimmy and I took the same flight back to Phoenix and we sat next to each other.

Jimmy was excited and he talked about how proud he was of the team and how he really appreciated the hustle and energy we had in the second half. He knew it was all for him. We started talking about who we could get to improve the team for '94 and what guys we'd have out to Mesa during the winter for mini-camps.

Jimmy had a winter program that'd been very successful for guys like Mark Grace and Derrick May and Rick Wilkins the year before, and those players all had their best years in '93.

Jimmy was a great hitting coach and the work he put in during the winter was a big reason why a lot of guys had big years.

I talked about how I could defer some salary or do whatever it took to make sure we could sign Mark Grace and a free agent or two, and Jimmy had a lot of good ideas about what to do for '94.

"I feel like I learned a lot this year," Lefebvre said on the plane. "Overall it was a good year and it's something to build on."

Jimmy was sure he was coming back because he'd spent hours and hours with Larry talking about 1994. Himes asked him every question you could imagine and got all the information he could from Lefebvre.

Jimmy thought there was no way he'd be fired because Larry kept asking, "What should we do about this next year?" and "Who would you like to see at this position next year?" And on the last day in San Diego, Larry sat in the visiting manager's office and listened to Jimmy's year-ending talk before the game. It was very emotional and extremely positive. It was all geared toward the next season.

"When you get to spring training in 1994," Jimmy said, "I want you guys to be prepared to win a title, because that's what we're going to do."

It was a great speech, and when it ended, the guys cheered Jimmy as he walked into the manager's office. Larry said, "Very nicely done. Great talk."

So it seemed like only a formality that Jimmy would be back. Larry had one year left on his contract and it only made sense that he'd extend Jimmy for a year.

The two of them met again two days after the season ended, on a Tuesday in Phoenix, but Larry didn't give Jimmy a decision. He again grilled Jimmy for hours on the team and what to do for next year, but then he sent him home.

I talked to Lefebvre that night and Jimmy was all fired up. "We talked about the team a lot," Lefebvre said. "We're going to try to improve several things and I told him what we needed to win."

Jimmy was excited. He was talking a mile a minute. "We're meeting tomorrow morning again," Lefebvre said. "But everything looks great."

If things always look darkest before the dawn, then it must be true that things always seem brightest right before the sun falls out of the sky.

When they met Wednesday morning, Jimmy walked into the room and sat down all smiles.

Larry said only one sentence: "I'm going to make a change so I'm not bringing you back."

And that was it.

Jimmy sat in stunned silence. He didn't know what to say.

"Why, Larry?" Lefebvre asked. "What is your decision based on?"

"I'll tell you in a month," Himes answered. "I'll tell you then."

He gave him no reason at all. Maybe because he didn't have one.

I was absolutely shocked when I heard the news.

I didn't talk to anybody. The phones kept ringing, and I just unplugged them all. I had nothing to say. I'd said it all for four months, and obviously my opinion didn't mean a thing to the Chicago Cubs. Every suggestion I'd given over the past two years had been dismissed or ignored by management. People asked for my opinion and I gave it to them, and there were many times I gave it unsolicited.

As a veteran on the team, I became more open about my feelings and about the direction. I figured I was near the end of my career and I had a stake in things. I didn't want to regret later on that I hadn't spoken up.

Being a 12-year veteran, I spoke for the players in a lot of areas but Larry never listened. Everything I said or suggested, he did the opposite. That made me feel like an outsider.

It was a nightmare. I was totally frustrated and disappointed.

I didn't talk to Jimmy that day. I waited until two nights later and it was rough. He suffered so much that year and what he accomplished was amazing. I felt terrible for him. There was nothing for me to say to anyone. I felt like there was nothing to look forward to. There was no reason to be optimistic and it sucked all the enthusiasm right out of me. I didn't want to take part in any of their winter activities at Fitch Park as Lefebvre had planned. I was just sick about it.

And how was I supposed to think about spring training?

Another new manager, another new direction. Starting all over again. Going into my 13th year with the Cubs, I was getting my 11th manager.

Even more than usual, I was at a loss for words.

Within about a week of Lefebvre being fired, one of my friends in Chicago called and told me Himes was quoted in the papers as saying, "Everyone's available. We'll talk about anyone with any club that wants to talk."

So in essence, Himes was saying he thought nobody on the club was worth keeping. He didn't care if anyone left, including me. I was feeling very unappreciated. Tossing out '93 for a minute because of my hand, I'd hit .302 over the last three years, while averaging 31 homers, 96 RBI, 107 runs scored and 604 at-bats.

To say there were no mainstays on the ball club, no one to build around, no one worth keeping, that hurt. How is that supposed to make me feel? How is that supposed to make Mark Grace feel? Or Randy Myers or Rick Wilkins or Steve Trachsel or Steve Buechele?

Everyone was available. That was Larry's upbeat message to the club after we had the third best record the Cubs had had in 22 years.

I took it to mean he was mad we had a good year. He was mad that we did so well and made it difficult for him. Does that make sense?

To take a shot at all 25 players like that and make them all feel like garbage, I felt like he was mad that we did so well.

Were we trying to win? What was our goal? What was our plan? There was no answer because there was no plan.

We were a rudderless ship drifting through time, wasting the prime years of my career.

I had worked so hard for so long to get to a World Series, but when Jimmy Lefebvre was fired I realized we were a long way away again. We might've been lacking some talent in 1993, but Jimmy got to a lot of us and made us into a team again.

Under Jimmy, we had a direction and a purpose. Most of all, Jimmy always made us believe there was hope.

Larry Himes threw that all away with one bizarre and inexplicable decision when he fired Jim Lefebvre.

A few days after Lefebvre was fired, my old pal Billy Connors left the Cubs for the second time during my career. Even though he's one of the best pitching coaches in baseball, Larry couldn't stand him and was just waiting for the right opportunity to fire him. So Billy took a job as pitching coach of the Yankees.

Billy called me and said he wasn't going to sit around and wait for Himes to fire him, and he wasn't the first person to see it that way.

Peter Durso was our traveling secretary for seven years. His wife Barb worked for the Cubs, too, and they loved Chicago and the Cubs more than life itself.

But after the '92 season, Peter bolted for Colorado because he wasn't going to give Himes the satisfaction of firing him. Himes treated Peter like a dog and he knew he was on the way out.

Himes would make trades and Peter would read about it in the paper the next day, even though the traveling secretary is supposed to know first so he can make the arrangements. Players would just appear in the clubhouse, having made their own travel plans, because Himes rarely told Durso what was happening.

In August of '92, Himes fired minor league director Bill Harford and scouting director Dick Balderson, just two weeks after the Rockies had asked permission to speak with Balderson.

The Rockies wanted to hire Balderson and Himes could've just said, "OK, take him." But instead, Himes had to fire him so it wouldn't look like everyone was abandoning ship.

In the year they worked together, Balderson said Himes never even spoke to him, and to top it off he had to humiliate him by firing him when another team wanted to hire him.

The good news for Balderson was the Cubs had to pay him his full salary for the rest of the year, costing the Cubs a lot of money. Now you can see why sticking to a budget was a problem at Wrigley Field during the Himes regime.

Larry would never just fire someone or tell them they weren't wanted anymore. He tried to make them miserable first and hoped they'd quit or leave, and a lot of people did. If they didn't, though, he'd get around to firing them eventually.

But with people like Maddux and Dawson, he never told them he didn't want them. He made it look as if he'd tried to keep them for the sake of public appearances. Eventually they'd all leave and public opinion would be askew. Himes would confuse the situation enough to make it look like it wasn't his fault.

In the meantime, he systematically forced out or fired every-one he didn't like or didn't want to be a part of his world, even if they did their jobs perfectly well.

Billy Connors had watched all that and by the end of 1993, he wasn't going to wait any longer.

Losing Billy was tough for me because he was a good friend and a great coach. At least a couple of pitchers a year would say they owed their careers to Billy Connors.

I didn't like seeing coaches go anymore than I liked seeing managers or good players leave. To me, coaches are a big part of the team and I always treated them the same as players.

I was close to the coaches, and it bothered me when they were left hanging every year. Every time we switched managers, the coaches had to wonder if they'd be out of work, too.

It seemed as if I was getting more and more of those calls every winter. Coaches and players and executives were leaving and the guys would call and tell me they really wanted to stay, but just weren't wanted anymore.

I was getting used to the calls in October, November and December, but I didn't like it at all. I was saying good-bye to friends constantly and it was a habit I didn't enjoy.

For some reason, Himes seemed to hate Billy Connors more than anyone.

When Larry took over in '92, the first thing he did was take Billy off the pension plan. Only four coaches can be on the pen-sion plan, so Larry took Billy off and put his own coaches on it. Here was the pitching coach, maybe the most important coach, and Larry left him off.

He was obviously trying to drive him out of town.

The next thing he did was renege on the $10,000 bonuses he promised Connors and Chuck Cottier.

He spent, literally, millions of dollars on the most ridiculous stuff you've ever seen, but he wouldn't pay his coaches what he owed them.

He spent about $750,000 on a new video room, three times as much as any other team in baseball. It was more like a motion picture studio than a video room and I kept expecting Steven Spielberg to walk out of that room any minute. He spent $75,000 on a new weight room and would only buy the most expensive equipment he could find no matter what the project.

He flew first class everywhere he went on a moment's notice, and he did it frequently.

On one trip to Cincinnati and Houston in July of '93, the team flew out to Cincinnati on Sunday night, but he flew first class on his own on Monday morning. We left Wednesday night for Houston, but again he went on his own the next morning. And before the team flew home Sunday night, he left in the afternoon.

That's three first-class, one-way trips on short notice that cost the club plenty when he could've flown with the team. This went on all the time.

When he first took over the Cubs, Himes didn't like the fact that the fans could stand outside the fence in the outfield and look in at the players during spring training at Fitch Park, so he spent $25,000 to put up tarps all the way around the fence.

One thing we all laughed at were these goofy eye-test contraptions that the Cubs rented for $500 a month. All they did was sit in boxes and collect dust.

Everyone who had a gimmick came calling on the Cubs, because we were sure to buy into it.

Got a pitching machine that breeds Cy Young Award winners? Call the Cubs.

Got a batting machine that makes singles hitters into home run kings? Call the Cubs.

Got a computer program that teaches you how to win the World Series? Call the Cubs.

We even had a team psychiatrist who would join us on the road at times. You could see him sitting in the dugout near the manager or lying on the dugout steps in street clothes.

That was a joke.

And food was a big deal, too.

Himes eliminated the sandwiches and chili we used to eat during spring training, and Diet Coke and doughnuts, too, just for good measure. Those things obviously hurt us in '84 and '89.

It was bizarre.

Himes also overloaded all the coaches and managers with paperwork. There were meetings every day at every level of the organization.

Himes tried to re-invent the game, but the game was fine for 120 years before he got to it.

He was so busy spending money that he went over budget at the major and minor league levels in 1993. He blew the minor league budget by $500,000, and had to cancel some important programs, like the fall instructional league.

He blew the major league budget and failed to plan ahead. So by the middle of '93 he was telling the world he'd have to cut $7 million from the payroll for '94.

That wasn't even accurate. Actually, he had to keep the payroll the same, at around $36 million. What he did have to do was cut was $7 million in *projected* payroll for the 1994 season, because he hadn't thought ahead to escalating salaries and arbitration.

But he made it sound as if Tribune Co. was forcing him to cut back, and that probably wasn't the best move he could've made, either.

Lots of people took note when he blamed his financial woes on the company that hired him.

The budget was so badly botched that by the time the deadline arrived for offering contracts in December, Himes had no choice but to give away Bob Scanlan and Chuck McElroy in minor trades that netted the Cubs very little. He tried to do the same with Mike Harkey, Greg Hibbard and Dwight Smith, but he couldn't swing deals and they were all released.

Just like that, 20 percent of the big league club was gone because of poor planning.

It was disappointing to hear what happened with all those guys, and Smitty was an especially tough loss for me.

I'd spent five years with him and he was one of the main guys from the '89 team. He was a great guy to have around and great for the chemistry of the team.

He always wanted to play, but hardly ever said a word when he wasn't playing. That's a tough line for a bench guy to walk. He wants to play every day and wants everyone to know that, but at the same time he doesn't want to irritate everybody. Some guys can't do that, but Smitty could.

Smitty, like Billy Connors, could always make me laugh, too. He's a buddy of mine and I was sorry to see him go. The thing is, there really was a place for him on the Cubs. His role was still there but it was filled by someone new. The year before he set the all-time Cubs pinch-hit mark, which says what type of player he is and what kind of job he does.

It went on and on, and by the time Jose Vizcaino was traded in the spring of '94, we had only three players remaining from the day Larry Himes took over only two years before.

Grace, Dunston and I were the only ones left, and he tried all spring to trade Shawon and all winter to trade Grace.

From what I hear, someone at Tribune Co. stepped in during the winter of '93-'94 and told Larry he couldn't trade Grace, because all of a sudden he was pulled from the trading block.

If not for that, Grace probably would've joined a list of players Himes got rid of that included Rick Sutcliffe, George Bell, Danny Jackson, Greg Maddux, Andre Dawson, Jose Vizcaino, Paul Assenmacher, Dwight Smith, Bob Scanlan, Chuck McElroy, Mike Harkey, Joe Girardi, Jerome Walton, Luis Salazar, Chico Walker, Gary Scott, Greg Hibbard, Jeff Robinson, Doug Dascenzo, Doug Strange, Heath Slocumb, Matt Walbeck, Steve Lake, Dave Stevens and Shawn Boskie.

Larry had taken the 1991 team, which still had a young core from '89, and torn it apart.

When Himes took over we didn't need to rebuild. We needed a couple of players and we could've been right in the hunt. But not anymore.

The list of coaches, managers and front office personnel that Himes went through is far too long to list, but it's in the scores.

Perhaps his most inhumane personnel decision came two days after Christmas in 1993, when he fired baseball administration director Ned Colletti, who had worked for the club since 1982, first in media relations and then in the business side.

Ned and I joined the Cubs at the same time. He used to tell me how he'd seen every game of my career in person, with very few exceptions.

Larry never told him why he fired him, just like with Lefebvre. He never told anyone why it was necessary. Colletti was known throughout the National League as a Chicago Cub. He went from being a Bleacher Bum to getting a front-office job. It was a dream come true for a guy who grew up a Cub fan.

Now his dream was shattered, and a man with a wife and two kids and a mortgage had no job two days after Christmas. Himes knew there were no jobs to be had that time of year. If he knew he was going to fire him, couldn't he have done it in September when jobs were available?

The part I couldn't understand was that while all this was happening, while people were being fired or forced out and lives changed forever, there was no one there to stop it. Himes apparently had free rein to do what he pleased, and no one was there to say, "No."

The Colletti firing was another in a very long line of terrible things I saw happen to people, and it was getting very difficult to stomach.

The night Jimmy Lefebvre was fired, Greg Maddux was winning a playoff game for the Braves after his second straight Cy Young season.

Whenever I spoke to Greg or saw him on TV, I'd hear him talk about how great the Braves organization is and how great the future is there.

The thing he likes most is the lack of rules and regulations, the laid-back atmosphere. The Braves treat their players with respect and like adults. All they ask of the players is that they be ready when it's time to play.

They can have golf clubs in the locker room and they even have holes in the clubhouse floor so the guys can putt whenever they want.

I was glad for Greg and happy he was having success and pitching in the playoffs.

I've never had any regrets about re-signing with the Cubs, because being a Cub was important to me.

But, quite obviously, I was misled about the direction we were going, and until December of 1993 I never accepted the cold, hard fact that we had no chance to win.

I could see now that we were farther away from a championship than at any time since Tribune Co. bought the team in the summer of 1981. Now in late December of 1993, we were in terrible shape again and going nowhere.

I also knew that every time a manager was fired it meant another year of adjustment and another year of losing. The hopelessness, surprisingly enough, didn't affect my winter workouts. I guess I was on auto-pilot that time of year. I was so regimented that I continued my routine of lifting weights four or five days a week and running two or three miles a day.

In January, like always, I'd add bats and balls to my workouts, and before pitchers and catchers reported I'd get over to Fitch Park and start taking ground balls.

The winter of '93–'94 wasn't any different in that sense. But the one thing that always kept me going, winter after winter, was the hope of getting to a World Series. That winter, however, I didn't think about it. Deep down, I knew what our chances were.

For the first time in my professional career, I went into spring training knowing my team had no chance to win.

20 ◆ The flame burns out

"You can fool other people, but you can't fool yourself when the desire is gone. Some players hang on for the money, some walk away with their dignity. Ryne Sandberg walked away with his dignity."
—*Nine-time All-Star Ron Santo*

During the winter of 1993-94, probably around New Year's, as I was running up hills and lifting weights and swinging a bat, the thought was gradually occurring to me that I had been doing that routine for 17 years, and I was enjoying it even less than usual.

At first, it was just occasionally, but soon it was every day. And then one day I was running up a hill back toward our house, when it dawned on me.

A constant thought had been running through my mind and I didn't even realize it until then.

In my head, over and over again, I was asking myself this question: How many more years do I want to do this?

When that hits you, it's a shock. At least for me it was, because I thought for sure I'd play another three or four or five years. But once it hits you, it's real and you can't get rid of it.

What you're not even aware of is that once the doubt enters your mind — at that precise moment — you're done. You've already given in to the feeling. I fought it for a while, but then I had no choice but to accept it, and the next step was putting a time frame on it.

In mid-January, I sat down with my family and said it out loud for the first time. I told Cindy and the kids that the thought of retiring had crossed my mind.

I said I didn't know when, but I didn't think I'd be able to play out my contract, which ran through 1997. In fact, I said, I think I might even retire at the end of the 1994 season.

The funny part is that they didn't even seem surprised. I thought they'd really react to it, but they weren't shocked at all.

I guess sometimes you can't see the forest for the trees, and maybe those closest to you see it before you do.

That time of the year was really tough. As I was getting older, I'd be incredibly sore from the lifting and there were days I'd be running and feel like throwing up. At 34, you don't get out of bed the same way you did at 24, and the workouts get tougher and tougher. I was tough on myself because I knew each year I'd bat 600 times and play 155 games in the field. My off-season work had to carry me through a long summer.

I went through the pain every year and pushed myself hard and never had a problem doing it. It's OK as long as you have a goal. It's OK as long as you have hope. It's OK as long as you want to do it.

But now there was no hope. I wasn't sure I wanted to put myself through it anymore.

The firing of Jim Lefebvre and all the other nonsense that had taken place the previous couple years left me void of any desire to play the game. And as I sat with my kids at dinner each night in January and February, it made me angry that I'd be leaving them soon, and I wondered how I was going to make it through the '94 season.

I was working very hard because I felt like I had something to prove coming off the 1993 season, during which I had the broken hand and dislocated finger.

I hit .309 with nine homers and 45 RBI with 67 runs scored in three-quarters of a season, and at least a month of that was my own personal spring training in the majors. So even though I wasn't satisfied, I didn't consider it a disaster. But my left arm didn't have the strength in '93. They say that's normal after a break and a long, inactive period. Mentally I had to adjust my game a little because I was so far behind the pitchers when I came back. I couldn't be as aggressive as I normally was and I had to take base hits to right and up the middle, instead of pulling the ball.

By the spring of '94, I felt normal physically and my effort was there, but thoughts of retiring were starting to weigh on me.

A big part of it was being around the kids all winter. When I started working out again I knew it was the first step in the process that always wound up with me leaving the kids behind in Arizona while I went to Chicago.

My yearly dilemma had returned. I was trying to look forward to the season and get mentally prepared, but I knew it also meant something bad for me — leaving the kids.

One day I just forced myself to admit it.

That's it, I thought, I can't do this anymore. By the time I got to Fitch Park for the beginning of camp on February 21, I knew it was going to be my last spring training.

When spring training started, I was always optimistic.

That's one thing about baseball that touches everyone. It's a fresh start and a new season and everyone starts from scratch.

But in 1994, there wasn't much to feel good about or be optimistic about.

It was good to get back on the field because I loved the game. It just felt right to be back out there.

So I tried to find the good things, but then again, we had another new manager, new pitching coach and half a dozen new players again.

It was another new direction and a new spring training program with new drills and a new style of play. Another year of adjustments.

I tried to remain positive and hold off on judgements until I saw a couple of months of baseball, but I looked around the room and I didn't know a lot of the players. It didn't even feel like a team because nobody knew each other. We were all in the same clubhouse but we hadn't been around each other long enough to know how the chemistry would be. We didn't have that close-knit feeling of being a team. We knew at least one more trade had to be made, because we were carrying four shortstops.

It didn't happen until the last possible minute, when it was the most difficult on everyone. Larry Himes had all winter and all spring to make a deal, but he didn't pull the trigger until March 30, two days before we broke camp.

That's when Jose Vizcaino was dealt to the Mets for Anthony Young. Jose was one of the nicest guys I ever played with, and a brilliant player on the field. He could play second, third or short as well defensively as just about anyone, and he never said a word if he wasn't in the lineup.

Sometimes a player like Vizcaino is more valuable than a starter, because he can fill in for a day or a month or a year at all three positions if something happened to a starter. Those kinds of players don't grow on trees. But his most valuable asset is his personality. He never gets upset and he never complains no matter what his situation. When you talk about good chemistry, you start with players like Jose Vizcaino.

So, naturally, the Cubs traded him to the Mets, where he became an immediate starter, and Young wound up on the operating table with the "Tommy John" elbow surgery.

I was happy for Jose because he was getting a chance to play every day, but I'd lost another good teammate.

And it happened at a tough time for Vizcaino.

Every year a truck packed with all the Cubs' equipment and supplies leaves Mesa for Chicago with about five days left in spring training.

Players and team personnel put as much of their personal belongings as they can on the truck because it facilitates the move back to Chicago after two months of living in Arizona.

If players aren't told whether they've made the team by then, they have to hold onto their possessions. At the last minute, sometimes with only hours to go before the plane leaves, they have to find a way to get all of their belongings sent somewhere.

And if a player who'd made the team, like Vizcaino, is traded at the last minute, it means all of his luggage is already en route to Chicago on the truck, while he's off to another destination.

It may not seem like much but it terribly disrupts a person's life, and when that happens all the players on the team take notice.

I know I've said this, but it all goes back to treating people with respect and doing what you can to make life simpler. If you do that and make players happy in that regard, it stands to reason that you're going to get a better performance out of them.

Players have families to move from city to city, and personal things to attend to, and those things affect them mentally. The truck is just one thing that makes the move a little easier.

On top of all that, Jose had rented a apartment in Chicago, where his wife was already moved in, and she was due with their second child at any minute.

It just got to the point where half the team was in a state of flux at all times.

For example, Mark Parent came to camp with us in '94 as the backup catcher and had the team made from the minute he got to Arizona. Everyone knew it, including Himes. But he never told Parent, and with two days left in camp, Parent still hadn't been told. Himes told the reporters, but he never told Parent he was on the club. When people complained about communication, that's what they were talking about.

As if an afterthought, Himes finally told Parent four days after the truck left for Chicago, the day before we left Arizona, that he had made the club.

The day we left Arizona, a writer asked me if this season felt in any way like the spring of 1989.

"No," I said with a chuckle. "No, it doesn't feel anything like that. That was exciting and the team was young and there was optimism."

Now our game plan seemed to be mostly hoping and wishing. "I wish this guy could stay healthy," and "I hope this guy can suddenly become a star," and "I wish this guy could win games for the first time in his life."

There aren't many times in baseball when wishing gets you a pennant, and as much as I had tried to be optimistic, I had been around long enough to see what was coming.

What we had was a hopeless situation, and there were no miracles waiting for us at Wrigley Field.

I felt bad for Tom Trebelhorn, who was named as the new manager when Jim Lefebvre was fired in October. Treb's a good guy and a very hard worker, and as a coach I considered him a part of what we had accomplished the season before.

But the 1994 season was set up for failure from the beginning. Treb's hands were tied by Larry Himes and he did the best he could under the circumstances.

He took all the heat and never blamed Himes or the players Himes had assembled, but he easily could have.

It was a circus. Every day there was some bizarre new twist and something that didn't make any sense at all.

It was misery, pure misery.

And there was so much tension. The gap between Larry and everyone down on the field was like the Grand Canyon, and Larry was getting into it verbally in the press with some of the players.

As if we weren't down enough already, Himes used his weekly radio show to blast the players and blame us for everything short of the Kennedy assassination.

Randy Myers, who almost always took the lead on such matters, blasted Larry right back, saying, "It's easy for him to point fingers when things are going bad, but it's never as easy to point the finger at yourself. Maybe Larry needs to look in the mirror."

I'm still at a loss to explain why Himes felt the need to make enemies with almost everyone he came in contact with. I don't think I've ever met another person quite like him.

As if we weren't struggling enough, our daily pre-game meetings were becoming longer and more tiresome. No one else in baseball did this—that I knew of—but don't forget we were re-inventing baseball.

In Lefebvre's two years under Himes, we had very brief, but unnecessary meetings every day. In the second half of '93, Jimmy had them whittled down to about a minute, something I'm sure Larry was upset about.

But now in '94 we had major meetings before every game. We were getting all this computerized information and going out to play after the meetings was really confusing some of the guys. It was too complicated. I didn't think it was helping us at all. They were over-analyzing a kid's game.

And computers don't win games in the majors, people do, but the people were confused by the computer read-outs.

In our meetings on how to pitch to the hitters, they'd say "don't throw this pitch and don't throw that pitch, and if you throw this pitch, throw it right there on the outside corner at the knees."

The pitchers listened to all that and by the time they got out to the mound they were afraid to throw any pitch.

Instead of pitching to their own strengths, which is how they got to the majors, the Cubs were teaching them to stay away from the hitters' strengths. In the process they couldn't throw anything right.

Instead of letting them use their ability and their brains, we were telling them how the computer would do it, but I've yet to see a computer get anyone out.

Do you think Greg Maddux needs a computer to tell him where to throw a pitch? And how come we didn't have meetings in '84 and '89?

In those days we'd have two or three meetings a year when things weren't going well, just to get the guys together and regroup.

Before the Himes regime, when I got to the park I'd be prepared mentally to face the pitcher of the day, and knew what I'd try to do. All I had to do then was relax before the game, take batting practice and some grounders and I'd be ready to play.

But now we were having 20-minute or half-an-hour meetings on pitching and defense and hitting and we were given handout sheets with all this writing on it and information.

It was like Nintendo baseball.

I didn't need it before, so why did I need it now? We'd go out on the field and have all this information going through our minds and we were tired mentally by the time the game started.

Instead of just playing the game and reacting like athletes, they wanted us to be robots, doing what the sheet said. It obviously didn't work and it made the game more difficult to play.

And it didn't last too long. About a month into the season, we were in Houston when a reporter asked me how I felt about the meetings. Within a minute, Mike Morgan, Steve Buechele and Mark Grace were climbing all over each other trying to get to the reporter so they could say how they felt. Randy Myers almost pulled a hamstring running over to get involved.

Morgan might've had the best line when he said, "We may be in last place, but we've already clinched the division in number of meetings."

Added Buechele, "We've had more meetings this year than the president has during a term."

And Grace summed it up perfectly when he said, "It seems like someone from outside the clubhouse is trying to manage the team."

After that hit the newspaper, the meetings were cut down to just once at the beginning of every series, and they weren't nearly as long.

I felt bad for Treb, because he was just doing what Larry told him to do, but it was getting out of hand and Treb knew that. He tried to help us as much as he could.

But now the system had changed again. Were we guinea pigs? Was there a plan? Or was it all experimental?

Like, "Let's try having 20-minute meetings this year before the games and see if that works."

All of the silly ideas and rules had finally gotten to the players and the meetings were the last straw. We didn't feel like baseball players. We felt like all they cared about was the paperwork and schedules and rules, and all of it had to be followed. It didn't help us win any games, of course, but that was how the Cubs were doing business in the '90s.

And while it wasn't quite a full-blown mutiny yet, it was total rebellion.

◆21◆ Free at last

"I don't play for the money. I play for the opportunity to make a great play or get the hit that wins a game. I respect Ryne for doing what he did. I'm sure it was a tough decision. But in my opinion, when the game stops being fun, it's time to get out."
—Giants slugger Matt Williams

One thing the Cubs always did was win at home — until 1994. We lost the first 12 at home to start the season and set a club mark for the 20th century.

It was brutal.

I never would've believed a time would come that I'd dread going to Wrigley Field, but in '94 it was a nightmare every day and it was no fun being there.

Even the circus feeling became a reality when Ernie Banks led a goat around Wrigley Field on May 4 in an attempt to break the curse.

I don't think it was the goat as much as the pitching of rookie Steve Trachsel, but we finally beat the Reds 5–2 for our first home win of 1994.

After the game, there was Himes basking in the glow of the victory, shaking Sammy Sosa's hand. Steve Buechele, Randy Myers and I were all standing there watching him since our lockers were right across the aisle from Sammy's.

We couldn't believe it. We knew Sammy was his guy, but I went 2-for-3, Boo had a big RBI in the fourth inning to make it 3–1, and Myers struck out the side in the ninth to get the save. But Himes didn't say a word to any of us.

We all watched as Larry patted Sammy on the back, and then Boo looked over at me and said, "Ryno, did you play today?"

"I think I played nine innings," I said. "How about you Randy? Did you pitch today?"

"I did pitch today," Randy said real loud. "How about you, Boo, did you play today?"

"Yes, Randy," Boo said as loud as he could. "I played the whole game."

And then we all shook each other's hands and said, "Nice job," and made a joke of it, but it wasn't really funny.

It was the same thing every day. Himes had decided we were the enemy long before that, and on this day it would be no different.

It was getting nastier by the minute.

About a week later, after we returned from a trip to St. Louis, Himes got into an argument with Mike Morgan in the locker room about whether he should be on the disabled list. It got so heated that Morgan actually had Himes by the shirt and was picking him up. "Go ahead and hit me," Himes yelled. "Come on, hit me." But Mo realized it was a lost cause and let him go.

While the Cubs were the laughingstock of baseball, Greg Maddux was on his way to his third straight Cy Young Award in Atlanta.

In New York, Billy Connors and the Yankees had the best record in the American League.

In Boston, Andre Dawson was moving up to 22nd on the all-time home run list.

All over baseball, ex-Cubs were flourishing, and a few of them — like Rick Sutcliffe, Danny Jackson, Shawn Boskie and Maddux — even found the time to beat the Cubs in '94. Jim Lefebvre, one of the best hitting coaches in baseball, was in Oakland while we fell from fifth to 11th in the league in offense, and several of the guys who had career years in '93 struggled.

We released Willie Wilson on May 16, which was strange, since he wanted to stay. The year before when he wanted to be released and Jim Lefebvre begged Himes to let him go, Himes insisted Wilson stay.

Pitchers were having surgery left and right and we made roster moves by the dozen.

Yes, all over baseball ex-Cubs were surviving just fine — and laughing at our expense.

Not that we ever really had one, but the relationship between Himes and me deteriorated to the point where he wouldn't even talk to me.

He ignored me and anyone who had supported Lefebvre the year before, and anyone who ever questioned his tactics.

I wasn't a part of the Cubs anymore. I wasn't wanted and the man in charge made sure I knew it.

The Chicago Cubs were in last place and it was really worse than it looked — and believe me it looked pretty bad. We played lousy baseball and I was tired of seeing it. It's one thing to go out and play hard and play good baseball and do everything you can to win, but it's another thing to play terrible baseball and lose the way we were losing.

It was embarrassing. I don't think there was another time in my career that I was embarrassed to be on the field wearing a Cubs uniform.

Our fundamentals were so bad that it was unusual if we hit a cut-off man or successfully laid down a bunt. It was pathetic.

And contrary to popular belief, that is not the coaches' or manager's fault. This wasn't a team full of 20-year-old rookies. It was a veteran team. So if players didn't know how to play by then, they weren't going to learn and maybe shouldn't have been there in the first place.

In the clubhouse, it wasn't any better. It wasn't any fun and there was little professionalism.

Guys were coming to the park at the last minute they had to be there and you rarely saw anyone come in early to talk about baseball or get in extra work.

As soon as the game was over, it was a race to see who could get out of the clubhouse the fastest. In baseball the way I knew it, we'd sit around for hours before and after games just talking about baseball.

Maybe it's not just the Cubs. Maybe that's the way baseball is today. I came up in a time when the guys really cared about the game, and I liked it a whole lot more.

Maybe other teams still have it, but the 1994 Cubs had no camaraderie or togetherness.

It was the worst chemistry I've ever seen in my life and the whole team was miserable because of it.

That wasn't Tom Trebelhorn's fault, either. He had a mishmash of players from all over the world. Hardly any of the guys had ever played together before, didn't know each other and a lot of them didn't like each other.

In the past what I had always enjoyed about the game, maybe more than anything, was coming to the park and having fun with the guys. That environment didn't exist anymore. It was just miserable.

All these things were going through my mind and it was building and getting a little worse every day. It was to the point where I didn't want to go to the park anymore, and there was something very, very wrong with that.

During one game against the Mets, I looked over at Dallas Green in the other dugout and I wondered what he must have been thinking.

I wondered if he felt as sick about what had happened to the Cubs as I did.

Around the middle of May, I got a great phone call from my daughter Lindsey. She told me she missed me and said, "Dad, when are you going to retire, because I'm 11-and-a-half and in a few years I'll be going to college."

I was blown away by that. Stunned. I don't think I answered it very well, but I couldn't get that out of my mind. I thought about it every single day. I realized it was summer and the kids were out of school.

I was depriving them of being with their dad at the most important times of their life, and I was depriving myself, too.

On Friday, June 10, 1994, I played the final game of my career, but I don't remember much about it because I didn't know it was going to be the last time I ever walked on the field as an active player.

I know I went 0-for-4 against the Dodgers' Kevin Gross because I looked at the box score the next morning, but I don't recall anything else about it.

And nothing special happened to me on that Friday that clinched it. When I left the park I didn't know it was the last game I'd ever play.

But I was so unhappy and so confused that I couldn't sleep that night. I tossed and turned and couldn't get Lindsey's words out of my head.

I missed my kids desperately, and for the first time in my life I hated baseball.

I might've slept a few minutes, but when I got up Saturday morning, I sat at the end of the bed for a minute. I rubbed my eyes and tried to wake up.

Then I just took a deep breath and it hit me, like a cold slap in the face: I was done. I was absolutely done with baseball. I couldn't play one more day.

It all came together so clearly in my mind and I decided there was no time like the present.

It was so obvious that I couldn't believe it took me that long to figure it out.

But thank God I finally did.

What was the final straw? That's difficult to say.

It was a lot of different things over the years, but when Jimmy Lefebvre was fired after the '93 season it was a big blow to all of us.

That team came together so well and so strong in '93 and everybody did it to bring Jim Lefebvre back. That means the players felt that with Jimmy we had a chance to win in '94. We thought we had to go out and prove that and we did for a good two or three months in '93. In August and September, we beat all the best teams, like the Braves, Phillies and Giants, winning three of four or sweeping.

But when Jimmy was fired it meant starting over again. It meant another year of adjustment and almost certain defeat. And poor Treb, he was doomed from the beginning. If I stayed through '94, I knew I'd have another new manager in '95, and another year of losing, too.

I wanted to give it one more shot in '94 to try to win, but with the chemistry and the attitude, I could see we weren't going to win this year or any time soon.

There were people who felt I abandoned the team, but they didn't know what I was feeling or what was happening in my mind. I wasn't having fun and I wasn't happy, and I felt that for the sake of my family and my health, I needed to leave the game and go on with my life.

I couldn't be physically ready if I wasn't emotionally ready, and if I wasn't physically ready then I wasn't doing anyone any favors out there. I didn't do the team any good going out there the way I was the few weeks before I retired.

I tried to get it going like I always did and physically there's no doubt I could've still played another three or four years.

There's no question in my mind that athletically I could still do the things I did in '92, when I hit .304 with 26 homers. In '93, I was hurt, but I still hit .309 in 117 games.

In '94, I started off well, but went into a slump as I became more and more unhappy. I was in a 1-for-28 streak when I retired, but it's not like I couldn't get out of a slump. It wasn't inability. It was a shocking indifference. You have to be mentally tough and have that desire to get it going, but I didn't have it anymore. I'd always fight my way through two or three slumps a year, but this time there was no fight.

There were times in '94 that I wouldn't be hitting the ball and the team wasn't doing well, and I'd go home and shrug it off and say, "Well, I'm done after the season anyway." I always fell back on that because it was in the back of my mind, and I knew there was something totally wrong with that. That wasn't me at all.

In the past, I would've gone to park early and taken extra hitting. I would've looked at some films and worked on some things.

I always wanted positives to take into the next year and it was my job to help the team win, so I would've fought with everything I had to break the slump. But in 1994 there was no next year for me and the team was helpless.

The fire was already out and I hadn't realized it.

Mentally I had given up, and the physical part is just a matter of time after that.

I knew it in my heart probably two months before, but it took some time to dig up those feelings and bring them to the surface.

But on that Saturday morning, it all came together quickly and really made a lot of sense.

The relief I felt was monumental.

The next three days took a long time, so I was ready to get the press conference over with and I couldn't wait to start living my life again.

Now it was just the process that I didn't know about and I'd be remiss if I didn't say that one guy who was helpful on Sunday when I told him was Himes. He was respectful and dignified. If he was happy about it, he didn't make it obvious and he was professional about it.

Both Treb and Stanton Cook were very supportive and that helped because I wasn't sure how people would react to my decision.

On Sunday, I sat back and watched the game and felt very relaxed. I looked around Wrigley Field and it was beautiful. The vines were in full bloom and the sun was out and the stands were full. But it looked different to me from the bench.

At the press conference on Monday, June 13, when I announced my retirement, the majority of the people accepted what I said, but you're not going to please everyone. I felt very good about what I said, because it came from the heart. There are always some who will start rumors and look for other reasons, because like I said, you're never going to please everyone.

On the way out, I made a quick stop in the clubhouse and about a third of the team was there getting ready to leave for San Diego on the off-day. A lot of them had seen the press conference on TV and most said they were happy for me. It felt pretty strange not driving with them to the airport, knowing the team was leaving without me for the first time in 13 years, but I was relieved and at peace for the first time since the thought of retiring popped into my mind so many months before.

It had been a big burden keeping that to myself for so long. When I left Wrigley Field, it was almost like I was leaving the park after a game. There were quite a few fans outside, so I stopped and signed autographs like I always did after a game. That was a ritual for me.

I never had a farewell tour, but I never would've wanted it. I didn't want any special attention or to be in the spotlight or under a microscope any more than usual. And besides, every game I ever played in every stadium was special for me. I didn't need any ceremonies to feel that.

I never really did address the team and explain things in any detail. I never could've walked away from the '89 team because I had so many friends and felt so close to them. But the only guys on the '94 team even left from '89 were Shawon Dunston and Mark Grace.

When it was time to leave, the only guys I told were a few coaches, Chuck Cottier, Tony Muser and Garrett Giemont, and catcher Mark Parent.

I needed to see their reactions. They were guys I felt comfortable with and they could see where I was coming from. But there weren't many guys left that I knew well, and with all the people who had come and gone over the last few years, I was to the point where I was ready for Himes to get rid of me, too. I didn't feel like a part of the Cubs anymore. It wasn't as if I had been there 13 years at all. I didn't feel important to the Cubs anymore, whereas in the past the Cubs made me feel like they needed me 12 months a year.

I didn't fit into Larry's plans and I didn't feel comfortable about that situation.

On top of all of that, I was a player caught between two generations: The one I came up with and the one I left behind.

The one I came up with was gone, and I didn't fit in with the one I left behind.

It was time to go.

Saying good-bye

> "If you talk to anybody who plays this game, the time they say to walk away from it is the time that they've lost the love for it. Obviously, Ryne Sandberg lost that love. And it gets very tiring losing all the time, you know?"
>
> *—All-Star first baseman Mark McGwire*

Let's play "Jeopardy." I'll give you the answers before I even hear your next two questions.

The first answer is, "No."

The first question, of course, was: "Will you ever play professional baseball again?"

A lot of people thought that because Larry Himes was fired and that maybe the Cubs were turning things in the right direction, I might come back. But the Cubs were only half the problem.

The other part was I wanted to be with my kids, and that'll never change. I want to be a professional dad now.

The second answer is also, "No."

And the question was: "Would you have left if the Cubs were in first place?"

I hate to speculate on that because it's hypothetical and all I know is what was happening at the time and for the past several years. The lack of fun played a big part in my decision. But if we were winning and in first place, I guarantee you I wouldn't have retired because winning is fun and my performance would've been a lot different.

But by now you understand that the morass we were in took years to develop and changed my outlook on the game, so I don't think the hypothetical is even applicable here.

And there will be no comeback. Period. I'll never play the game again on the pro level, despite media speculation to the contrary.

About two weeks after I retired one newspaper said I was planning to come back and play for the Phoenix franchise.

Now that makes sense. I was 34 when I retired in '94, and I'd be about 38 by the time we have a team in the Valley, so I'd be in perfect playing condition after four years off from baseball.

How do people dream that stuff up?

And then there was the reporter who asked Ed Lynch in December of '94 if he had plans to talk to me. When Lynch said, "Yes," there were headlines suggesting a possible return. Poor Ed just wanted to have dinner.

Oh, and then there was the report in Chicago that I was coming back as a Cubs coach. The funny thing is I was there when the reporters asked questions about 1995, and never did I say I'd come back as a Cubs coach.

Hadn't I just spent the summer telling everyone that I didn't want to travel anymore and that I wanted to stay home with the kids?

I don't know, maybe I need to speak more slowly.

It just disappoints me because I thought I had a pretty good relationship with the media, and during the summer after I retired there were a lot of things reported that were hurtful or simply inaccurate.

I never thought I'd have my personal life dragged through the mud in the press. I know I'm naive when I say this, but I don't understand why my personal life is important enough to end up in the papers.

When I retired, I thought I'd seen the last of my troubles with Larry Himes, but even 1,440 miles away in Phoenix, Himes managed to irritate me.

You see, as part of that last contract I signed, I had a four-year personal services deal worth $500,000 a year. The idea was that at the end of my career, I would get together with the Cubs and agree on ways for me to be involved with the organization.

It was a nice thing for both sides because they were finding a way to put some extra money in the package, and at the time I signed the deal I thought it would be nice to stay involved with the Cubs after my career ended. I would stay around and attend some Cubs Conventions or Cubs Care benefits and maybe host a golf tournament to raise money for charity.

The point is, it would be simple for me, beneficial to the team and to charities, and easily agreed upon.

Well, after I walked away from $16 million and made it clear I didn't want to be away from my children any longer, Himes still didn't get it. The guy just plain didn't get it. He told the newspapers that he was thinking about having me travel around to the minors and coach the young guys on how to play second base. He didn't say it to me, mind you, just to the reporters. (Why does that sound familiar?)

OK, let me get this straight. I left behind four years on my contract because I wanted to go home, and now he wants me to travel around the minor leagues, ride buses with the kids and show them how to turn the double play?

You see what I'm saying about the communication thing? The guy doesn't listen and he just doesn't get it.

Obviously, I told him to take his personal services deal and file that wherever he deemed appropriate.

Since the day I made the decision to retire, I haven't had a moment of second thoughts or regrets.

I do miss being a member of a team and the camaraderie that goes along with it. That was always the best part of baseball for me. But in 1994, those things were gone, and it wasn't as if I was missing something.

I miss the things that took place in the other years of my career. I've reflected a little bit on my whole career and all the teams I played and all the good times and great friends I made.

I feel bad that everything we worked so hard to create slipped away. Dallas Green did such a magnificent job of changing the Cubs into winners from losers and brought respect to the uniform. When I retired the Cubs did not command that respect. For that, I feel bad and somewhat empty.

There were so many who tried so hard and cared so much over the years, and anyone who wanted the Cubs to be respected was probably affected by what happened.

What surprised me about Larry Himes' firing was that he managed to stay on as a scout, and that showed a lot of compassion on the part of the new Cubs organization, led by Andy MacPhail.

The organization got Himes a two-year deal as a scout, and with two more years of service, Himes would be at five years and fully vested in the Tribune Co. pension plan.

It just strikes me as odd considering all the people that Himes fired. He didn't seem interested in finding any of them jobs and wasn't too worried about their financial future.

I also wondered if they really thought he would mind his own business and not try to get involved. I knew better than that.

As soon as he got to Arizona to start his new job in November, he called Cubs trainer John Fierro and gave him an order. He wanted injured pitcher Jessie Hollins brought out to Mesa to work on some things and get checked out.

"Excuse me," Fierro said. "You're not the general manager anymore. I don't answer to you."

So Fierro called new GM Ed Lynch, who told him Himes "is a scout, not a GM. Don't listen to anything he says."

That could wind up being a very strange situation if Himes continues to meddle in Cubs affairs when he's supposed to be scouting the minor leagues.

It also didn't stop him from taking another shot at Mark Grace in the papers in early December. But that's Himes.

I didn't have any real personal feelings at all when I heard about Himes being ousted, but as an interested observer I was anxious to see who'd be hired in his place.

Really, the changes began back in July of '94, when Tribune Co. executive Jim Dowdle took over the Cubs operation. I don't know Jim well, but I try to get a lot of different people's opinions, and I heard nothing but good things about him.

When I saw his first move, I knew Dowdle was very bright. He hired Andy MacPhail away from Minnesota and made him the president, so he could run the Cubs from top to bottom.

MacPhail's reputation is spotless and his record of success speaks for itself. I hear MacPhail is a nice man, too, and compassion is certainly something that's been lacking at Wrigley Field.

With Dowdle and MacPhail in charge, the Cubs can look forward to some very productive and happy years.

I was also very pleased to hear that Ed Lynch would be the general manager.

I played against Ed for several years when he was with the Mets and then played with him on the Cubs in 1986 and '87. He's a great guy, but very tough. I'll never forget when he drilled Keith Moreland in 1984 during the pennant race in August, starting a bench-clearing brawl.

But when Ed Lynch was on your team, you never had to worry about a pitcher protecting you. If someone hit a Cub, Lynch was right there sending a message back to the other team. He's a very competitive guy with a lot of heart and baseball savvy, and that's why Dallas Green brought him over in 1986. He's definitely a Dallas-type guy.

I saw Ed occasionally over the last few years of my career, while he was working for the Padres and Mets, and after I retired I saw him quoted in the newspapers sticking up for me.

Joe Morgan always made it pretty clear that he wasn't a big Ryne Sandberg fan. I don't know why, but you couldn't miss the tone if you ever heard him talk about me.

Anyway, after I retired Morgan made some derogatory re-marks about my career and my decision, and Ed Lynch — someone

I hadn't had much contact with for seven years — came to my defense.

Morgan was asked about whether I should be in the Hall of Fame, and apparently his answer wasn't very flattering. The same writer asked Ed Lynch about Morgan's comments, and Ed said, "It sounds to me like Joe Morgan is jealous and wants to be the only second baseman who ever made it to the Hall of Fame. Morgan was a great player. A Hall of Famer. But offensively, Ryno was as good and he didn't have the benefit of the Big Red Machine and its supporting cast. Defensively, Ryno's the greatest who ever lived, so I don't know what Joe Morgan's talking about."

I'm not sure what Joe had against me, because I respected the heck out of him. Oh, well.

In any case, I feel good about what the Cubs did in the fall of '94. Maybe all the new hirings are a signal that the Cubs are back on track and headed back toward the Dallas Green way of doing things. I sure hope so.

I did feel terrible seeing Tom Trebelhorn get fired. Treb got labeled as "Larry's guy," but what was he supposed to do, turn down the job when it was offered to him after Lefebvre was fired? There was also talk that he did things to hurt Jimmy Lefebvre the year before, and that simply wasn't true. Treb's a good man and a stand-up guy who was stuck in a bad situation.

I'm also sorry that Tony Muser didn't get the Cubs' managing job, because he's going to make a terrific manager when he gets the chance. Tony comes from a different era of players, and he wouldn't put up with a lot of the stuff you see players get away with today. Muser is tough and mean, but also compassionate and has solid baseball intelligence.

I don't know the new manager, Jim Riggleman, very well, but I've heard good things about him and his discipline. I wish him the best. Maybe he'll get more of a chance than the 11 managers I played for.

I was really glad also to find out that Fergie Jenkins was added as a pitching coach, because he deserves the opportunity.

For years I said the Cubs were missing the boat on Gary Matthews, but finally in January of '95, the Cubs hired him as a minor league hitting instructor. I hope that's just the beginning for him and that it's not long before he's back in the majors — whether it's on the field or in the front office.

The Cubs have a chance now to right a lot of wrongs and I think they're moving in that direction, but only time will tell.

It's sad when I look back on all the mistakes that were made and all of the people who suffered because of it.

I hope that with Jim Dowdle and Andy MacPhail in charge, the Cubs will become a professional and compassionate organization again. From what I hear about those two men, they fit the bill nicely.

Hopefully, the nonsense is over.

The day I retired I sort of half-jokingly said that one thing I wouldn't have to do is go on strike, but I never really imagined that a season would be wiped out because of a work stoppage.

I've never been comfortable talking about business matters, so I was glad I didn't have to be a part of it for that reason.

I felt bad for the fans because there are so many people who rely on baseball to get them through a day. If you think that sounds corny, walk through a hospital sometime while the Cubs are on, especially during a day game, and you'll see what I mean. I feel bad about that.

At the same time, I feel a kinship with all the players and an obligation to stick up for the next generation of players, the way all the players before me did so that I could make a nice living for my family.

This is still America and I hope people always have a chance in this country to do the best they can for themselves and their families in a free market situation.

But it was a tough spot for the players to be in and all I could think of was I was glad I was gone and didn't have to answer all of the questions.

In early February 1995, there was a lot of talk about the owners hiring replacement players. That's nothing short of an insult to the intelligence of the fans — not to mention the tradition of baseball.

I can't imagine replacement players wearing Cubs or Yankees or Dodgers uniforms.

The owners started the war because some small-market teams couldn't run their business and wanted big-market clubs to give them some help.

So when the owners couldn't agree among themselves, they let a minority run the show and they turned their guns on the players.

What a mess they made of a good thing.

I didn't miss that in the summer of '94, but I did miss some of the people I'd grown fond of over the years.

I miss my buddy Yosh Kawano, who's been the Cubs' clubhouse man since 1943. He's been there so long I can't believe no one ever offered him the manager's job. On second thought, he's probably better off.

Yosh was one of my closest friends the last few years of my career, and I really enjoyed my dinners with him and Arlene Gill, who's been the executive secretary for the Cubs since I broke in with the team.

She's been through a lot of general managers and presidents, and most people probably aren't aware of it, but Arlene is the person everyone goes to when they need to know about all the complicated rules governing the game today.

Come to think of it, Arlene and Yosh probably have more baseball knowledge between them than any other two people in the game.

I miss Jimmy Farrell, too. Jimmy's the umpire's room attendant and always sat on the bench during the game. We had a lot of good laughs and good times together in the dugout. Jimmy had the unenviable job of coming up to me every day before games and asking me for autographed balls for the umpires.

The umpires are just like everyone else. They don't like to do it, but they've got every relative and friend under the sun wanting players' autographs, so they have to get them. Jimmy's the guy at Wrigley Field who runs the errands for them.

I miss the umpires and the ushers and the security people and all the workers I came in contact with every day. I miss going to

Philadelphia, where the broadcasters would come up to me every series and say they still couldn't believe the Phillies traded me.

One thing I'd always heard retired athletes talk about was missing the camaraderie of the locker room. I felt some of that after I retired, but I also felt that during the last year or two of my career. I think I missed it more then than I do now.

Being a part of a team was one of the best parts about being in baseball, but that feeling was long gone by the time I retired.

I miss leaving Wrigley Field with Rick Sutcliffe after a day game. We'd stand outside and sign autographs for about 15 minutes, and on our drive home, kids would stop us at every corner on the sidestreets and ask for our signatures.

I guess it's always the little things you miss the most.

There are so many people I'll never forget, like Bill Harper, the scout who followed me for two years in high school and convinced the Phillies to draft me.

And Ruben Amaro, an infield instructor in the Phillies' organization when I was a minor leaguer, and then a Cubs coach from 1983-86.

And Larry Rojas, my very first professional manager at Helena, Montana. After 1978, he was a roving infield instructor in the Phillies' system and worked with me a lot during minor league spring trainings and seasons. Rojas used to stand up at the Phillies' organizational meetings and tell the others that I could play, and sometimes he was the only guy who believed in me.

And Pete Rose, who predicted I'd be an All-Star second baseman.

I'll never forget the winter ball team I couldn't even make, and the bus wreck I was just happy to survive.

And I'll miss all of the Cubs trainers, who were great to me. I never really knew Tony Garofalo, because I was afraid to walk in the trainer's room my first five years.

Unfortunately, when I hurt my ankle in 1987 I spent a lot of time with John Fierro and Dave Cilladi. Cilladi and I worked very hard together and he was shocked by how quickly I recovered.

Dave got a special boot for me that I wore inside my shoe and in my first at-bat back from the injury I homered.

When I broke my hand in '93, Fierro, Brett Fischer and strength coach Garrett Giemont got me back on the field quickly again.

Those were the only two times I suffered serious injuries, but those guys were there for me when I needed them. All throughout my career, the doctors and trainers in Chicago were the best medical guys in the game.

So many players, coaches, managers and executives influenced me that I couldn't name them all, but I really owe a lot to Dallas Green, Jim Frey, John Vukovich, Billy Connors, Larry Bowa, Bill Buckner, Scott Sanderson, Junior Kennedy, Rick Sutcliffe and Gary Matthews, among many others.

Chris Speier is another good friend who helped show me the ropes early in my career and I was glad to hear the news in December of '94 that the Cubs had hired him as a minor league instructor. It shouldn't be long before he's back in the majors.

It wouldn't be right if I didn't mention Bruce Sutter. I played golf with him on an off-day in Atlanta in 1993.

Until then, I'd never talked to him about the "Sandberg Game," and he's the one who brought it up. He's a Hall of Famer and maybe the most dominating relief pitcher over an eight-year span there ever was.

But that day in 1984, he threw me two pitches that changed my life.

One thing baseball allowed me to do was help out the less fortunate and at the same time give something back to the community after I was given so much.

Each year, Cindy and I looked for different ways to help out, both financially or with our time.

Whether it was the American Red Cross after the Bay Area quake in 1989, or the Juvenile Diabetes Foundation after Cindy's brother passed away in 1990, or something else, we always looked for ways to do something for those who couldn't do for themselves.

Since 1984, I bought 25 season tickets to every home game for a season and gave them to underprivileged or handicapped kids, and during most seasons I donated a certain amount per hit, home run, RBI, etc., to specific charities. But while the financial part of it helped others, I was more gratified when I spent some time with people who needed it. The Make-A-Wish Foundation is an extremely important group and the people there do tremendous work. I always tried to help them, or visit the hospitals when I could.

One thing I learned early on was that 10 or 15 minutes with someone who cherished the time could mean all the difference in the world to that person.

I thank baseball for allowing me to brighten someone else's world for just a few minutes by simply being me.

Looking back on my career, I feel very fortunate to have been given the opportunity to be a major league baseball player.

It's every boy's dream and it was certainly mine.

I got a chance to play for 17 years as a pro and 13 in the big leagues and that was my fill.

I accomplished a lot that I'm proud of, like the MVP and the Gold Gloves and the All-Star Games and hitting 40 home runs and stealing 54 bases.

The one regret I have is not being able to play in the World Series. I wish I could've felt what it was like to be there and the feeling of winning it. That's my biggest regret. I loved the feeling of winning as a team and the World Series has to be the ultimate in that.

But I was on some teams that had a chance to get there, and I guess that's all you can ask. Not everybody makes it to a World Series. Not everyone ever plays in the playoffs, and I was there twice.

Those two years, 1984 and 1989, were very special and gave me a taste of what it was like to be on a winning team.

I guess 1989 was the most fun because it was such a surprise and so emotional. It was one of the few times I really allowed myself to get swept up in the day-to-day emotion and I probably played with more fire than at any other time in my career.

One thing I heard a lot about during my career was the Hall of Fame. I heard comments about it constantly, but I always looked at it as something that was way down the road because I was still playing. I was just trying to play baseball and enjoy myself and enjoy the game. I didn't want to think about it, because I didn't want my career to ever end.

I played the game because I enjoyed it. I looked at the Hall of Fame the way I viewed all the awards and the All-Star Games. That was something extra, like icing on the cake, and all of that is in other people's hands.

Now that I'm retired and have allowed myself a chance to think about it, it'd be the greatest honor of all, because it would say something about my career. To be there with all of the greatest players who ever played would be incredible. It sends a shiver up my spine when I think about it.

But I had so much fun playing the game and enjoyed it so thoroughly, that no matter what happens, no one can take that away from me.

23 ◆ You can go home again

"I always said I would walk away from basketball on my terms, when my desire to play the game was gone. I think every athlete knows when it's time to go, but some stay longer. I'm fortunate that I could leave when I wanted to."
—*Michael Jordan*

I was happy for Michael Jordan when he walked away from basketball at a time he felt was right for him, even though it was a disappointment to everyone who loved watching him play the game.

And some tried to draw comparisons between the two of us because we both wore No. 23 in Chicago, both walked away from our jobs at such a young age, and both of us shocked a lot of people when we did it.

I guess there are some very reasonable comparisons, especially when it comes to losing that competitive edge. I remember hearing Michael say that he was mentally exhausted from having to get himself to a certain competitive level for every game of every year.

People who are immensely competitive can understand what he means by that. Michael wouldn't go out on the court at anything less than 100 percent emotionally. He would never play at anything less than that level, which physically and mentally destroyed his opponents.

His competitive desire was ferocious and he wouldn't give in to anyone, even in an exhibition game. And when he decided he was mentally tired of getting to that level every time out, he walked away.

In that sense, so did I.

When you lose the drive and the edge at the levels of competition that we're talking about, and you're making that kind of money doing it, you can't go out there and play without those things inside of you.

I certainly wouldn't do it for the money. That would be stealing from the Cubs organization and the Cub fans.

So be happy for M.J. that he left on his own terms, and please be happy for me, even if I disappointed you by leaving.

Because I'm happy. I'm happier than I've been in a very long time and I'm enjoying life again. I hope that helps you understand why I did what I did.

From the moment I left Wrigley Field on June 13, 1994, I've felt nothing but relief. I remember driving back to Lake Point Tower that day, watching all the people playing in and around Lake Michigan, and being excited about the opportunity to do the same myself.

And that's pretty much what I've done.

A lot of my fun in the summer of '94 was related to activities I did as a kid and haven't had an opportunity to do for a very long time.

All the things I loved to do and grew up doing had been put on the back burner since the Phillies took me out of Spokane and dropped me in Helena in 1978.

Since then, I put everything aside because I wanted to give everything I had to the game of baseball for 12 months a year. I didn't have as much fun as some guys away from the game during the season, because I wanted to save my energy for baseball.

I put all my concentration, all my time and all my off-seasons into baseball. It was total dedication. That's the way I did it and nobody forced me to do that.

I could've gone snow skiing or water skiing or lots of things, and risked ending my career, but I didn't.

All of those things were appealing to me again in 1994, and baseball wasn't. I had a 17-year interruption in my life, and now I'm picking up where I left off.

Spending a lot of time with my kids also reminds me of when I was a kid spending time with my parents.

It was getting to the point where I was feeling guilty that the kids weren't going camping as much as the other kids or didn't know how to water ski. They didn't get to have fun with their dad doing a lot of things that their friends got to do with their dads.

I can give them that now.

When I got home after I retired, I immediately started thinking about all the things I wanted to do and started making plans. It was my first summer vacation in 17 years, since I was 17 years old, so I had some catching up to do.

The first thing I did was call my brother and sister to find out when they were heading over to Thomas Lake near Spokane. They still live up there with their families, and every year they take their kids to the lake.

That's a tradition that started when we were young. My parents used to take the whole family on a two-week camping trip to Thomas Lake, and everyone but me continued to make that trip even after they had their own families. They never missed a year.

But I haven't been able to do it since I was 17 so that's the first thing I wanted to do. I put that on the calendar and I took the kids up there in July and did all the things we used to do when I was a kid.

We did a lot of fishing and hiking and swimming and it brought back a lot of memories for me. We took a lot of pictures that look quite similar to the pictures my mom has of me as a kid at Thomas Lake.

It also brought home even more the realization that I missed so much of my kids' childhood. In the past they had taken camping trips without me, or didn't get to go at all. And if I had played another three or four years, they would've been nearly off to college and I never would've had the chance. It's almost by magic that I got an extra four years with my children. I'm so thankful that it all came together in my mind when it did, before it was too late.

I really like being a dad and I like raising my kids, and I never had a chance to do it full-time before.

A lot of the values that I received from my parents, I try to instill in my kids. Things like, "Eat everything on your plate," and "Be thankful for what you have because not everyone has it." I know I didn't have a lot when I was a kid, but I've tried to teach my kids that you always have each other, and that's the most important thing.

These are things that are important to me and I think I can stress them more often by being with them instead of 2,000 miles away.

I made it back to Chicago on July 22, 1994, to be inducted into the Cubs' Walk of Fame. That was quite an honor, considering that already inducted were Ernie Banks, Billy Williams, Fergie Jenkins, Ron Santo, Phil Cavarretta, Hack Wilson, Harry Caray and Jack Brickhouse.

The Cubs wanted me to wear a suit that day but I declined and wore shorts. I haven't been in a suit since the day I announced my retirement.

The Cubs also asked me to throw out the first pitch to my old teammate Mark Grace, but just as I was about to release the pitch from the mound, Gracie put his hands up and said, "Not here."

He motioned that we run over to the right side of the infield and do what we'd done thousands of times before. I went to my old spot at Wrigley Field between first and second, and Gracie rolled me an easy grounder. I didn't want to boot it at a time like that, so I followed all my old rules and watched it all the way into my hands (I had no glove on), set myself, planted and made a good, strong throw to first.

That got us a standing ovation from the crowd and it felt good to be back in front of the fans at Wrigley Field again. Except this day, I wasn't going into the dugout after I made the play. I was going to enjoy Wrigley Field — and I did.

In my 13 years there, I'd never been in the stands before, so I sat in several different places. The bleachers were the most fun, and I had a great time with the fans out there. The Cubs were worried that I'd need security, but I talked them into just one security guard, even though I didn't want any. One thing I've tried to explain is that if you make a big deal out of it, it gets out of hand. But if you relax and let people come to you and sign some autographs, then everything's fine. I've been doing it for years that way.

So I watched the game from all the different locations and the Cubs players were waving to me everywhere I went. I think a few of them were jealous that they couldn't come out to the bleachers and have a little fun.

The fans were great and the park looked wonderful and I'm sure I'll do it again sometime soon.

I made a second trip up to Washington in September to see my mom, because she had hip-replacement surgery and it gave me more time to spend with my family up there, too.

I went back again for Thanksgiving, and I drove around for a while and looked at everything I hadn't had much of a chance to see for almost two decades.

It was fun seeing my old high school baseball field, which is now named after me. That took place in a ceremony after the '84 season, and I look at it as one of my greatest honors. I think no matter how old you are you still want the people you grew up with and the coaches you played for to be proud of you, and that told me the people of Spokane and the community around North Central High were proud of me.

I also saw some of the local spots where I spent the summers camping and fishing and swimming at the pool and playing every sport we could find to play.

Little did I know that when I signed my first pro contract, that I wouldn't be able to do those things again for 17 years.

I spent the summer of '94 playing catch-up. I went to the water slide park with the kids and went down all the slides, and went fishing and camping and sailing and whatever else you can do outside during the summer.

Maybe the best thing I did was buy a ski boat, which I never could've done during my career.

It's something I wanted to do for about five years, but it wasn't practical because of baseball. It would've just sat in the garage and collected dust.

We really took advantage of the boat. We went tubing and I learned how to knee-board, and most importantly I learned how to water ski. I never would've done that during my career for fear of injury.

Along with all the activities was just the enjoyment of waking up with the kids and making plans every day. What do we do today? The water park or the driving range or the tennis court or the mountain or the lake?

It was fun just making up my own itinerary, instead of the Cubs' itinerary that we always had.

During my first winter out of baseball, I went with friends on a trip to Utah right after Christmas for a week of snow skiing, and that was a riot. I can't believe I missed out on that all this time.

One thing that always scared me about leaving baseball was leaving behind the every-day athletic challenge and the joy of success. But I want to be good at all of these activities and enjoy them, so there are still athletic challenges in my life, and I need that.

I didn't get up the very first time I water skied, but I did get up my second time out and now I love it and want to excel at it. It's demanding physically, too, which is important to me. I'll still lift weights and run and stay in shape, but for fun, not at a pace to be ready for the grind of 162-game schedule.

Golf is another sport where I think I can get to a higher level. I'm about a six-handicap, but I've shot as well as two-over in the Phoenix pro-am and two-over at Kapalua in Maui.

It's too late for the pro tour, but maybe I can be ready for the senior tour. But that's a long way off, when the kids have gone out on their own.

I want to get better at tennis, too. The bottom line is I like competition and I like exercise. I can combine that with all of the things I've wanted to do but never had the time or freedom to do.

The truth is I'm busy as can be and having the time of my life.

The extent of my employment during my first summer off was a trip I made to Chicago so I could caddy for my next-door neighbor, professional golfer Mark Calcavecchia.

That's something we talked about for years but put off until 1994 when I finally got the opportunity. It was a lot of fun and I learned a lot.

The first couple of days I just watched the other caddies and stayed out of the way. I wanted to do things right and I didn't want to distract him or the other golfers. By on the final day, he was asking me my opinion on a couple of putts and help with the wind direction on a few approach shots. I was pretty comfortable with it.

Mark was tied for the lead after nine holes on Sunday and got a huge ovation on the ninth green and the 10th tee box. The gallery was cheering for me and cheering for Mark at the same time and it turned into a home course for him because of all the Cub fans.

He finished third and he said it gave him a boost, not just for that tourney, but for a good two or three months after that.

Other than that job, I was captain of the boat and assistant coach of Justin's flag football team. I plan on watching all of Justin's baseball games and all of Lindsey's gymnastics meets from now on. Aside from that, we'll make it up as we go along.

Don't get me wrong, because I'm not closing any doors right now. I'm still in a transition from playing to a normal life and working is not on my mind. I think after a few years I may want to do something.

Early in '95, the personal services deal with the Cubs was worked out and that will keep me in contact with the team for four years. So that's something there.

But I'm not eliminating any opportunities or closing any doors on anything that might come my way later.

I might work for a baseball team in some front office capacity. I'm close with Jerry Colangelo and when he gets a team in Phoenix, there might be something there for me. But right now I'm not looking for a job and I can't honestly tell you when I'll be ready for that.

Quite obviously, my life has changed dramatically and is full of new challenges. I left baseball, which occupied a huge part of my life for 17 years, and the divorce also changed one of the longest relationships of my life. Things are much different now and the adjustments are many, but the opportunities for myself and my family are varied and exciting.

Physically, I feel better than I have in years. I feel so much healthier without the stress and the strain and the grind of the baseball season, and I feel reborn. There were times during the baseball season that I'd get my back or my neck worked on every day just so I could play. Those were nagging problems that would occur from sitting on planes or from hotel air conditioning or playing on Astroturf — or just eight months of baseball.

Today, I get up out of bed and feel great. I don't need as much sleep, either. I can go real well now on five or six hours, compared to eight or nine during a baseball season.

I just feel wonderful. My health is better and my mind is a lot clearer — and I'm very glad about that.

I feel almost as good now as I did when I left Spokane in 1978.

I'm sorry if anyone felt cheated or abandoned when I left baseball, but I felt it was time to get my life back. I gave 17 years to baseball and the rest is now for my family. I'm grateful to every teammate and coach and manager for allowing me to play the game with them, and I thank my opponents for every pitch and ground ball they ever sent my way.

Most of all, I thank you, the fan. In every park I ever played in you treated me with respect, and I appreciate that.

And in Chicago, words couldn't aptly describe how I feel about Cub fans, who treated me like one of the family. From the start of my career to the finish, I never stopped being amazed by Cub fans, who are absolutely the most patient and forgiving fans in the world. They never ask their team for anything but an honest effort, and I hope they believe I gave them that.

They kept me going for 17 years of professional baseball. They gave me a reason to fight the fight even when the standings didn't suggest there was a reason to. They may not realize how much they meant to me, but I know what Cub fans did for my career.

During that time, however, my dedication to the game cost me time with my children, and it's now time for my total dedication to them. So if you'll excuse me, it's time for me to get on with my life.

I truly thank Cub fans for everything, because I know in my heart that without them, there never would've been a Ryne Sandberg.

I'll miss you all, but I promise I'll never forget you, and you'll be with me forever.

I give you my word on it.

The Sandberg File:
Career Stats

Batting Highlights

◆ finished his career in the Cubs' all-time Top 10 in 10 major offensive categories.

◆ scored 100 runs in a season seven times, joining Stan Hack as the only Cubs to record seven 100-run seasons.

◆ had 100 RBI during the 1990 and 1991 campaigns...became the first second baseman in Cubs history to record back-to-back 100-RBI seasons and the first major league second baseman to achieve that mark since Boston's Bobby Doerr in 1949 (109 RBI) and 1950 (120 RBI).

◆ had at least 60 extra-base hits during the 1989-1992 campaigns, becoming only the second second baseman to record 60 extra-base hits in four consecutive seasons (Juan Samuel, 1984-1987).

◆ had at least 4 hits in a game 34 times during his career.

All stats courtesy of the Chicago Cubs.

◆ stole 30-plus bases during the 1982-1986 campaigns, equalling the club mark for consecutive 30-steal seasons (Frank Chance, 1906-1910).

◆ in 1985, he became the third player in major league history to have 25 or more homers and 50 or more steals in one season (Cesar Cedeno, Joe Morgan)...hit 26 home runs and stole a career-high 54 bases.

◆ scored 103 runs in his rookie season of 1982, a club record for runs by a rookie...Billy Herman had held the rookie mark, scoring 102 runs in 1932.

◆ his 32 stolen bases in 1982 were a record for a Cubs third baseman, breaking Harry Steinfeldt's mark of 29, set in 1906.

◆ his first major league hit came with the Phillies, a single off the Cubs' Mike Krukow on September 27, 1981, at Wrigley Field...his first Cubs hit was a single off St. Louis' Joaquin Andujar on April 13, 1982, at Wrigley Field.

◆ recorded his 1,000th career hit on August 7, 1987, in New York off Ron Darling.

◆ reached the 1,500-hit mark on June 29, 1990, off San Diego's Greg Harris.

◆ recorded his 2,000th career hit on July 3, 1993, at Colorado off Curt Leskanic.

◆ his final major league hit was a single off Philadelphia's Heathcliff Slocumb on June 7, 1994.

Home Run Highlights

◆ of his 245 homers, 240 came as a second baseman, the fourth-highest total in major league history at that position behind Joe Morgan (266), Rogers Hornsby (263) and Joe Gordon (246).

◆ had 2 homers in a game 20 times...hit 3 grand slams.

◆ hit a National League-high 40 homers in 1990 after hitting 30 roundtrippers in 1989...was the first second baseman to lead the N.L. in homers since St. Louis' Rogers Hornsby hit 39 in 1925 and the first second baseman in major league history to reach the 30-homer mark in consecutive seasons.

◆ his 40 homers in 1990 was the third highest single-season total for a second baseman...Hornsby hit 42 in 1922 and Atlanta's Davey Johnson equalled that total in 1973.

◆ became the first player in history to have a 40-homer season and a 50-steal season during his career...stole 54 bases in 1985.

◆ homered in five straight games between August 7-August 11, 1989 (6 homers), tying the club record established by Hack Wilson in 1928.

◆ hit his first career home run on April 23, 1982, off Pittsburgh's Eddie Solomon.

◆ hit the 100th homer of his career on June 19, 1988, off Montreal's Neal Heaton.

◆ recorded his 150th career homer on June 2, 1990, off St. Louis' Greg Mathews to become the first player to hit 150 homers and steal 150 bases as a Cub.

◆ hit his 200th career homer on August 18, 1991, off Philadelphia's Danny Cox.

◆ hit his final home run on June 1, 1994, off Philadelphia's Shawn Boskie.

All-Star Facts

◆ made 10 All-Star appearances and 9 starts, including 8 consecutive starts between 1986–1993.

◆ became the first major league second baseman to make 9 starts (Rod Carew and Nellie Fox made 8) and the first second baseman to make 8 consecutive starts (Joe Morgan made 7).

◆ his 8 consecutive All-Star starts are the most ever by a Cub...his 10 appearances rank 2nd in club history behind Ernie Banks (14).

◆ was the N.L.'s leading votegetter for the All-Star Game during the 1990-1992 campaigns.

Fielding Highlights

♦ finished his career with a .990 fielding percentage at second base, the highest fielding average at that position in major league history.

♦ is the only second baseman in major league history to win nine Rawlings Gold Glove awards.

♦ led National League second basemen in assists seven times...the only second baseman to lead the N.L. in more than seven seasons was Bill Mazeroski (nine times).

♦ joined Charlie Gehringer as the only second basemen in major league history to reach the 500-assists mark in six different seasons.

♦ went through a season without committing a throwing error four times.

♦ had five errorless stretches of at least 50 games, 10 streaks of at least 40 games and 17 streaks of at least 30 games.

♦ played in 123 consecutive games without committing an error from June 21, 1989-May 17, 1990...handled 584 chances between errors.

♦ set major league records for consecutive errorless games by an infielder (excluding first basemen), breaking Joe Morgan's record of 91 straight errorless games at second base on April 12 and Jim Davenport's record of 97 consecutive errorless games by an infielder on April 18.

♦ did not commit an error in his final 90 games of 1989, the longest single-season errorless stretch for a major league second baseman...had 432 total chances in the 90 games.

♦ did not commit a throwing error from July 4, 1990–May 5, 1993...went 393 games and 1,298 assists between throwing miscues.

♦ earned the first Rawlings Gold Glove of his career in 1983 in his first full season at second base...became the first player in N.L. history to win a Gold Glove in his first full season at a new position.

◆ on June 12, 1983, against St. Louis, he tied a major league record for most assists by a second baseman in a nine-inning game (12).

◆ committed 2 errors in a game only four times.

Other Awards and Notes

◆ received numerous postseason honors in 1984, including the National League Most Valuable Player Award.

◆ became the first Cub to win the MVP Award since Ernie Banks in 1959.

◆ also was chosen by *The Sporting News* as the major league Player of the Year in 1984.

◆ was the National League's Player of the Week seven times.

◆ was named to *The Sporting News'* Silver Slugger team seven times.

◆ in the 1989 N.L. Championship Series against San Francisco, he was 8-for-20 (.400) with 3 doubles, a triple, a homer, 4 RBI and 6 runs scored...hit safely in all 10 NLC games in which he played.

Professional Record

Year Club	AVG.	G	AB	R	H	2B	3B	HR	RBI	BB	SO	SB	E
1978—Helena	.311	56	190	34	59	6	6	1	23	26	42	15	24
1979—Spartanburg	.247	*138	*539	83	133	21	7	4	47	64	95	21	35
1980—Reading	.310	129	490	95	152	21	12	11	79	73	72	32	20
1981—Oklahoma City	.293	133	519	78	152	17	5	9	62	48	94	32	21
Philadelphia	.167	13	6	2	1	0	0	0	0	0	1	0	0
1982—CUBS	.271	156	635	103	172	33	5	7	54	36	90	32	12
1983—CUBS	.261	158	633	94	165	25	4	8	48	51	79	37	13
1984—CUBS	.314	156	636	*114	200	36	+19	19	84	52	101	32	6
1985—CUBS	.305	153	609	113	186	31	6	26	83	57	97	54	12
1986—CUBS	.284	154	627	68	178	28	5	14	76	46	79	34	5
1987—CUBS	.294	132	523	81	154	25	2	16	59	59	79	21	10
1988—CUBS	.264	155	618	77	163	23	8	19	69	54	91	25	11
1989—CUBS	.290	157	606	+104	176	25	5	30	76	59	85	15	6
1990—CUBS	.306	155	615	*116	188	30	3	*40	100	50	84	25	8
1991—CUBS	.291	158	585	104	170	32	2	26	100	87	89	22	4
1992—CUBS	.304	158	612	100	186	32	8	26	87	68	73	17	8
1993—Daytona#	.200	2	5	2	1	0	0	1	2	1	0	0	0
Orlando#	.222	4	9	0	2	0	0	0	1	3	1	0	0
CUBS	.309	117	456	67	141	20	0	9	45	37	62	9	7
1994—CUBS	.238	57	223	36	53	9	5	5	24	23	40	2	4
M.L. TOTALS	.289	1879	7384	1179	2133	349	72	245	905	679	1050	325	106
CUBS TOTALS	.289	1866	7378	1177	2132	349	72	245	905	679	1049	325	106

\# Injury Rehabilitation Assignment
* Led League
+ Tied for League Lead

Career Statistical Breakdown

	AVG.	AB	H	HR	RBI
Totals	.289	7384	2133	245	905
Day	.303	4433	1341	150	569
Night	.268	2951	792	95	336
Vs. Left-handers	.299	2078	621	57	215
Vs. Right-handers	.285	5306	1512	188	690
Grass	.298	5240	1562	191	700
Artificial	.266	2144	571	54	205
Home	.306	3678	1126	144	523
Road	.272	3706	1007	101	382
Before ASG	.285	3944	1126	132	486
After ASG	.293	3440	1007	113	419
Chicago	.333	3	1	0	0
Florida	.214	42	9	0	3
Montreal	.278	789	219	24	74
New York	.283	828	234	24	115
Philadelphia	.290	792	230	27	101
Pittsburgh	.288	792	228	28	87
St. Louis	.290	786	228	31	111
Atlanta	.310	546	169	23	70
Cincinnati	.297	575	171	16	63
Colorado	.317	63	20	2	12
Houston	.293	508	149	21	74
Los Angeles	.266	571	152	15	61
San Diego	.248	541	134	19	75
San Francisco	.345	548	189	15	59
April	.235	959	225	20	92
May	.306	1348	413	48	173
June	.304	1235	375	54	173
July	.282	1200	338	33	132
August	.299	1354	405	47	158
September	.291	1192	347	39	161
October	.313	96	30	4	16

League Championship Series Record

Year Club	AVG.	G	AB	R	H	2B	3B	HR	RBI	BB	SO	SB	E
1984—CUBS vs. SD	.368	5	19	3	7	2	0	0	2	3	2	3	1
1989—CUBS vs. SF	.400	5	20	6	8	3	1	1	4	3	4	0	0
LCS TOTALS	.385	10	39	9	15	5	1	1	6	6	6	3	1

All-Star Game Record

Year Club/Site	AVG.	G	AB	R	H	2B	3B	HR	RBI	BB	SO	SB	E
1984—N.L./SF	.250	1	4	0	1	0	0	0	0	0	0	1	0
1985—N.L./Min	.000	1	1	1	0	0	0	0	0	1	0	0	0
1986—N.L./Hou	.000	1	3	0	0	0	0	0	0	0	0	0	1
1987—N.L./Oak	.000	1	2	0	0	0	0	0	0	0	0	0	0
1988—N.L./Cin	.250	1	4	0	1	0	0	0	0	0	2	0	0
1989—N.L./Cal	.000	1	3	0	0	0	0	0	0	0	2	0	0
1990—N.L./CUBS	.000	1	3	0	0	0	0	0	0	0	0	0	0
1991—N.L./Tor	.333	1	3	0	1	1	0	0	0	0	0	0	0
1992—N.L./SD	.000	1	2	0	0	0	0	0	0	0	1	0	0
1993—N.L./Bal	.000	1	1	0	0	0	0	0	0	1	0	0	0
ASG TOTALS	.115	10	26	1	3	1	0	0	0	2	5	1	1

Sandberg at Second Base

Year	PCT.	G	PO	A	E	TC	DP
1981	1.000	1	2	0	0	2	0
1982	.993	24	57	95	1	153	9
1983	*.986	*157	330	#571	13	#914	*126
1984	#.993	156	314	#550	6	#870	102
1985	.986	153	353	500	12	865	99
1986	#.994	153	309	#492	5	806	86
1987	.985	131	294	375	10	679	84
1988	.987	153	291	#522	11	#824	79
1989	.992	155	294	466	6	766	80
1990	.989	*154	278	*469	8	755	81
1991	#.995	*157	267	#515	4	786	66
1992	.990	157	283	#539	8	*830	94
1993	.988	115	209	347	7	563	76
1994	.987	57	96	202	4	302	35
TOTALS	.990	1723	3377	5643	95	9115	1017

* League Leader
# Major League Leader

Sandberg's 30-Plus Club

Ryne Sandberg's Errorless Streaks of 30 or More Games:

123	June 21, 1989-May 17, 1990
61	June 30-September 7, 1984
60	May 26-August 1, 1992
58	August 21, 1991-April 27, 1992
52	August 25, 1990-April 27, 1991
48	September 22, 1983-May 20, 1984
48	August 3-September 24, 1985
47	June 25-August 19, 1991
45	September 26, 1985-May 18, 1986
42	August 5, 1993-April 12, 1994
38	May 21-June 29, 1983
36	May 22-June 30, 1986
36	July 25-September 2, 1986
36	April 30-June 10, 1991
32	September 5, 1986-April 13, 1987
32	May 19-June 20, 1990
30	August 22-September 26, 1987

Sandberg and the Cubs' All-Time Top 10 List

CATEGORY	RANK	TOTAL
Stolen Bases	2nd	325
Home Runs	4th	245
Total Bases	5th	3,360
At-Bats	5th	7,378
Extra-Base Hits	6th	666
Runs Scored	6th	1,177
Hits	6th	2,132
Runs Batted In	7th	905
Games Played	8th	1,866
Doubles	8th	349

Career and Game Highlights

Most hits: 5 (twice), most recently 6/29/85 in Pittsburgh

Most RBI: 7, 6/23/84 vs. St. Louis

2-homer games: 20, most recently 9/1/92 vs. Los Angeles

Career grand slams: 5/31/83 vs. Houston (LaCorte)
9/2/91 in San Diego (Lewis)
9/9/92 in Pittsburgh (Cox)

Inside-the-park home runs: 2, most recently 7/27/91 vs. Atlanta (Smoltz)

Steals of home: 4, most recently 5/20/85 vs. Cincinnati

Longest hitting streak: 18 games (twice), most recently 6/18-7/6/85

The 200 20–20–20–20 Club

No player in baseball history has ever had a season when he had 200 or more hits plus 20 or more doubles, triples, homers and stolen bases. Ryne Sandberg came the closest to achieving that plateau, falling short by one homer and one triple in 1984. Here are a few of the players who have come the closest in baseball history:

PLAYER	YEAR	TEAM	HITS	2B	3B	HR	SB
RYNE SANDBERG	1984	CUBS	200	36	19	19	32
Willie Mays	1957	N.Y. Giants	195	26	20	35	38
George Brett	1980	Kansas City	212	42	20	23	17
Jeff Heath	1941	Cleveland	199	32	20	24	18
Jim Bottomley	1925	St. Louis (NL)	227	42	20	31	10
Frank Schulte	1911	CUBS	173	30	21	21	23

1994 Season in Review and Career Overview

On June 13, Ryne Sandberg, a 10-time National League All-Star and the winner of nine Rawlings Gold Glove awards, announced his retirement...he appeared in 57 games and batted .238 with 5 homers and 24 RBI.

◆ Sandberg joined the Cubs on January 27, 1982, coming to the club from Philadelphia along with shortstop Larry Bowa for shortstop Ivan DeJesus...began his Cubs career as a third baseman and batted .271 during his rookie season.

◆ moved to second base late in 1982 campaign...the following year, he earned his first Rawlings Gold Glove Award, becoming the first player in National League history to win a Gold Glove in his first full season at a new position.

◆ went on to win the Gold Glove every season through 1991...is the only second baseman in major league history to win nine Rawlings Gold Gloves.

◆ led league second basemen in assists seven times and in fielding percentage four times...is the only National League second baseman to have six 500-assist campaigns...retired with the highest fielding percentage for a major league second baseman, ending his career with a .990 fielding average.

◆ reached the national spotlight in 1984, a season in which he won the N.L.'s Most Valuable Player Award...batted a career-high .314 with a league-high 114 runs scored and 200 hits.

◆ had one of the best all-around seasons ever for a second baseman in 1990, leading the league with 40 home runs while winning yet another Gold Glove...became only the third second baseman to reach the 40-homers mark...also became the first player in major league history to have a 40-homer season and a 50-steal season during his career.

◆ hit 240 of his homers as a second baseman, the fourth-highest
   total in major league history at that position behind Joe Morgan (266), Rogers Hornsby (263) and Joe Gordon (246).

◆ Ryne Dee Sandberg was born September 18, 1959, in
   Spokane, WA. He began his professional career in 1978 after
   being drafted by the Phillies' organization in the 20th round
   of the June draft.

1993 Season in Review

Despite suffering through his most injury-plagued campaign, Sandberg finished the season with a .309 batting average, his highest mark since 1984 (.314).

◆ sustained a fractured fifth metacarpal in his left hand in the Cubs' spring training opener on March 5 when he was hit by a pitch thrown by San Francisco's Mike Jackson.

◆ was on the disabled list until April 30…saw injury rehabilitation action with Daytona (A) and Orlando (AA).

◆ on May 5 vs. Colorado, he made his first throwing error since July 4, 1990…went 393 games and 1,298 assists between throwing miscues.

◆ on May 26 at Wrigley Field, he was ejected by first base umpire Charlie Williams during the Cubs' victory over San Francisco…it was the first ejection of his major league career.

◆ recorded his 2,000th career hit on July 3 at Colorado off Curt Leskanic.

◆ dislocated the fourth finger of his right hand sliding into home plate on September 13 at San Francisco and missed the remainder of the season.

◆ at the time of his season-ending injury, he had hit safely in 24 of 25 games (35-101, .347).

◆ made his 10th All-Star appearance, his 9th start and his 8th straight start…became the first major league second baseman to make 9 starts (Rod Carew and Nellie Fox made 8) and the first second baseman to make 8 consecutive starts (Joe Morgan made 7).

1992 Season in Review

Ryne hit .304 with 100 runs scored, 26 home runs and 87 RBI...finished the season over the .300 mark for the fourth time during his career.

◆ ranked second in the National League in total bases (312), third in hits (186), fourth in runs scored, fifth in slugging percentage (.510), sixth in homers and seventh in at-bats (612)...tied for fifth in extra-base hits (66) and for sixth in triples (8), multi-hit games (53) and games played (158).

◆ reached the 100-runs mark for the seventh time, joining Stan Hack as the only Cub to record seven 100-run seasons.

◆ with his 66 extra-base hits, he became only the second second baseman to record 60 extra-base hits in four consecutive seasons (Juan Samuel, 1984-1987).

◆ averaged 1 homer every 23.5 at-bats, the ninth-best ratio in the league.

◆ had a club record-tying 8 consecutive hits July 29-August 1, becoming the seventh Cub to accomplish the feat.

◆ reached the combined 200 mark in hits and walks in a season for the 11th consecutive season.

◆ batted .332 after the All-Star break (96-289)...opened the second half by hitting safely in 17 of his first 18 games (29-77, .377).

◆ was the N.L. Player of the Week for September 14-September 20, winning the weekly honor for the seventh time...batted .500 during the week (11-22) with 10 runs scored, 3 doubles, 4 homers and 8 RBI.

◆ despite failing to win the Rawlings Gold Glove Award, he led major league second basemen in assists (539) and N.L. second basemen in total chances (830), recording a .990 fielding percentage.

◆ led N.L. second basemen in assists for the seventh time...the only second baseman to lead the N.L. in more than seven seasons was Bill Mazeroski (nine times).

- committed 8 errors, marking the sixth time in 10 seasons as a second baseman that he committed fewer than 10 errors.
- went through the season without committing a throwing error for the second consecutive year and for the fourth time during his career...has not committed a throwing error since July 4, 1990, a span of 389 games and 1,279 assists (225 in 1990; 515 in 1991; 539 in 1992).
- joined Charlie Gehringer as the only second basemen in major league history to reach the 500-assists mark in six different seasons.
- committed 2 errors on August 15 vs. Houston, only the fourth time in his career that he has had 2 miscues in a game...the first error was his first at Wrigley Field since June 11, 1991 (106 games).
- was the N.L.'s leading votegetter for the All-Star Game for the third straight year...received 2,434,660 votes in earning his 8th All-Star start (7th consecutive).
- was named to *The Sporting News'* Silver Slugger team for the seventh time...also was selected to that publication's N.L. all-star team.
- became the third member of the 40-homer, 25-steal club, joining the Milwaukee Braves' Hank Aaron (44 HR, 31 SB in 1963) and Oakland's Jose Canseco (42 HR, 40 SB in 1988).
- reached the 1,500-hit mark on June 29 off San Diego's Greg Harris.

1991 Season in Review

Ryne became the first second baseman in major league history to win nine Rawlings Gold Glove awards, winning the award in each of his nine seasons at second base.

♦ led major league second basemen with a .995 fielding percentage (4 E/786 TC) and 515 assists, 52 more than any other second baseman (Seattle's Harold Reynolds, 463).

♦ committed a career-low 4 errors, marking the fifth time in his career that he committed fewer than 10 errors in a campaign.

♦ improved his career fielding percentage at second to .990, the highest percentage in major league history at that position.

♦ played errorless ball in his last 40 games.

♦ did not commit a throwing error...it marked the third time in his career that he did not have a throwing error in a season (1985, 1988).

♦ has appeared in 1,393 games at second base with the Cubs, the highest total in club history...surpassed Johnny Evers (1,368) for the top spot during the season.

♦ offensively, he hit a team-high .291 with 26 homers and 100 RBI.

♦ reached the 100-RBI mark for the second straight year...drove in his 100th run in his final at-bat of the season on October 6 against St. Louis—a run-scoring double in the seventh inning.

♦ became the first second baseman in Cubs history to record back-to-back 100-RBI seasons and the first major league second baseman to achieve that mark since Boston's Bobby Doerr in 1949 (109 RBI) and 1950 (120 RBI).

♦ scored 104 runs to record his third consecutive 100-run season and the sixth 100-run season of his career...the last Cub to score at least 100 runs in three consecutive seasons was Billy Williams (1964-1966).

◆ became only the fourth Cub to have consecutive 100-run/100-RBI campaigns.

◆ drew a career-high 87 walks and reached base by hit or walk a career-high 257 times...on base via hit or walk at least 200 times in each of his 10 major league seasons.

◆ ranked 3rd in the league in runs scored, 4th in games played (158), 6th in walks, 7th in on-base percentage (.379), 8th in at-bats (585) and 9th in extra-base hits (60)...tied for 6th in hits (170) and total bases (284), for 7th in RBI and sacrifice flies (9), for 8th in multi-hit games (47) and for 10th in homers.

◆ hit his 200th career homer on August 18 off Philadelphia's Danny Cox.

◆ was hit by a thrown ball on July 2 against Pittsburgh during a stolen base attempt and missed 2 games, the only contests he missed all season.

◆ made his 8th straight All-Star appearance, his 7th start and his 6th consecutive start—the most ever by a member of the Cubs.

◆ was the major league's leading votegetter for the All-Star Game, receiving 2,526,747 votes...it was the highest vote total since Montreal's Gary Carter received 2,785,407 votes in 1982.

◆ after the season, he was named to *The Sporting News'* Silver Slugger team for the sixth time...also was selected to that publication's N.L. all-star team.

1990 Season in Review

Ryne had one of the best all-around seasons ever for a second baseman, hitting a National League-high 40 homers and winning his eighth consecutive Rawlings Gold Glove Award.

◆ led the majors with 344 total bases and led the N.L. with 116 runs scored.

◆ ranked second in the league in slugging percentage (.559) and extra-base hits (73), third in hits (188) and multi-hit games (57), sixth in at-bats (615) and 10th in batting (.306)...tied for sixth in RBI (100).

◆ was the first second baseman to lead the N.L. in homers since St. Louis' Rogers Hornsby hit 39 in 1925.

◆ his 40 homers was the third-highest single-season total for a second baseman...Hornsby hit 42 in 1922 and Atlanta's Davey Johnson equalled that total in 1973.

◆ is the first second baseman in major league history to reach the 30-homer mark in consecutive seasons.

◆ stole 25 bases...became the first second baseman and the first Cub ever to hit 30 homers and steal 20 bases in one season.

◆ became the first player in history to have a 40-homer season and a 50-steal season during his career...stole 54 bases in 1985.

◆ became the third member of the 40-homer, 25-steal club, joining the Milwaukee Braves' Hank Aaron (44 HR, 31 SB in 1963) and Oakland's Jose Canseco (42 HR, 40 SB in 1988).

◆ had a career-high 100 RBI, becoming just the second Cubs second baseman to reach that mark (Hornsby, 149 RBI in 1929).

◆ reached the 1,500-hit mark on June 29 off San Diego's Greg Harris.

◆ recorded his 150th career homer on June 2 to become the first player to hit 150 homers and steal 150 bases as a Cub.

◆ became the first second baseman in N.L. history to win eight straight Gold Glove Awards...Pittsburgh's Bill Mazeroski also won eight Gold Gloves, five consecutively...besides Mazeroski, the only other second baseman to win eight Gold Gloves was Kansas City's Frank White.

◆ played in 123 consecutive games without committing an error June 21, 1989-May 17, 1990…handled 584 total chances between errors.

◆ set major league records for consecutive errorless games by an infielder (excluding first basemen), breaking Joe Morgan's record of 91 consecutive errorless games at second base April 12 and Jim Davenport's record of 97 consecutive errorless games by an infielder April 18.

◆ broke Manny Trillo's record of 479 consecutive errorless chances April 22.

◆ led N.L. second basemen in games (154) and assists (469).

◆ made his 7th consecutive All-Star Game appearance and his 5th straight start…was the N.L.'s leading votegetter.

◆ in All-Star Workout Day festivities, he was the winner in the Gatorade Home Run Derby, hitting 3 home runs.

◆ after the season, he was the leading votegetter on the Associated Press major league all-star team…also selected to *The Sporting News'* N.L. all-star team.

◆ named to *The Sporting News'* Silver Slugger team for the fifth time.

1989 Season in Review

◆ did not commit an error in his final 90 games, the longest single-season errorless stretch for a major league second baseman...had 432 total chances in the 90 games (4.8 per game).

◆ in the season's final game he broke the single-season record of 89 consecutive errorless games, set by Philadelphia's Manny Trillo in 1982...the two-season record for consecutive errorless games is 91, set by Cincinnati's Joe Morgan from July 6, 1977-April 22, 1978.

◆ became the first second baseman in National League history to win seven straight Rawlings Gold Glove Awards.

◆ hit a career-high 30 homers, the second-highest total for a Cubs second baseman (Rogers Hornsby, 39 in 1929)...the last major league second baseman to reach the 30-homer mark was California's Bobby Grich in 1979.

◆ hit 6 homers in 5 straight games from August 7-August 11, tying the club record established by Hack Wilson in 1928... Wilson hit 5 homers in 5 games.

◆ on August 20, he became only the fourth Cub to homer twice in a game at the Astrodome...the others were Jody Davis, Brian Dayett and Mark Grace, who accomplished the feat the day before.

◆ at the All-Star break, he was batting .262 with 44 runs scored, 11 homers and 34 RBI...after the break, he hit .321 with 60 runs scored, 19 homers and 42 RBI.

◆ after July 28, when the Cubs trailed Montreal by 3.5 games, he batted .346 (81-234) with 18 homers and 38 RBI.

◆ tied for the league lead in runs scored (104) with San Francisco's Will Clark and New York's Howard Johnson.

◆ finished 10th in the league with a .290 batting average.

◆ ranked fifth in the league in homers, at-bats (606), hits (176), total bases (301) and multi-hit games (49)...was sixth in slugging percentage (.497).

◆ played in his 6th straight All-Star Game...started at second base for the 4th time.

◆ in the N.L. Championship Series against San Francisco, he
    had 8 hits in 20 at-bats (.400) with 3 doubles, a triple, a
    homer, 4 RBI and 6 runs scored…has hit safely in all 10
    NLCS games in which he has played.
◆ after the season, he was selected to *The Sporting News'* N.L.
    all-star team and to the publication's Silver Slugger team…re-
    ceived the Silver Slugger Award for the fourth time.

1988 Season in Review

Ryne became the first second baseman in National League history to win six straight Rawlings Gold Glove Awards.

◆ the only other player in Cubs history to win as many as five straight Gold Gloves is former third baseman Ron Santo (1964-1968).

◆ did not commit a throwing error all season...his last throwing error was June 10, 1987 (227 games).

◆ led major league second basemen in assists (522) and total chances.

◆ hit the 100th homer of his major league career on June 19 off Montreal's Neal Heaton...went into the 1989 season with 109 homers, 13 shy of 10th place on the Cub's all-time list.

◆ batted .198 in April after an 0-for-15 start...has a career average of .222 in April...beginning May 1, Sandberg's lifetime average is .294.

◆ batted .405 from April 30-May 8 (15-37).

◆ was third in the N.L. with 618 at-bats.

◆ voted to the N.L. All-Star team as the starting second baseman and went to the game for the 5th straight year...was the first Cub to go to five straight games since Don Kessinger (1968-1972) and the first to start three straight since Ernie Banks (1958-1960).

◆ after the season, he was selected to the Associated Press major league all-star team and to *The Sporting News'* N.L. all-star team.

1987 Season in Review

Despite missing 26 games because of a severely sprained right ankle, Ryne won his fifth consecutive Gold Glove at second base...he became the first N.L. second baseman since Pittsburgh's Bill Mazeroski (1963-1967) to win a Gold Glove in five straight seasons.

◆ on May 17 in Houston, he committed his first error on artificial turf since July 2, 1985 (75 games).

◆ Ryne suffered the ankle injury on June 13 in St. Louis while trying to avoid a first-base collision with St. Louis's Jack Clark...was on the disabled list until July 11.

◆ homered vs. Los Angeles on July 11 in first at-bat following his return.

◆ returned to the lineup in time to make his third start and fourth All-Star Game appearance.

◆ in his 872nd game, Ryne recorded his 1,000th hit on August 7 in New York off Ron Darling.

◆ had a team-high 52 multi-hit games.

◆ his ankle injury cost him a chance to become the first player in Cubs history to steal 30 bases in six consecutive seasons...stole 21 bases in 23 attempts (91%).

1986 Season in Review

Ryne won his fourth consecutive Gold Glove Award at second base while establishing N.L. records for fewest errors (minimum 800 chances) in a season (5) and highest fielding average (.9938).

◆ Ryne had three errorless streaks during the 1986 season of 35 games or more (35, 36 and 36).

◆ he opened the season with a 10-game errorless streak and extended it to 45 games.

◆ his 492 assists was the top total among major league second basemen.

◆ offensively, Sandberg had a club-high 53 multi-hit games, including 11 in May.

◆ from April 26-May 8 he had a 13-game hitting streak (19-50, .380).

◆ was N.L. Player of the Week for May 26-June 1 by hitting .522 (12-23) with 2 homers, 8 RBI, 6 runs scored and 4 multi-hit games.

◆ he stole 34 bases, giving him five straight 30-steal seasons.

◆ Ryne hit .404 with runners on third base, driving in 32 of 64 runners.

◆ he batted .286 in the second spot in the lineup and .275 in the third slot.

◆ Ryne participated in baseball's All-Star tour of Japan during November.

1985 Season in Review

1985 season followed Ryne's third straight Gold Glove.

◆ established career highs in homers (26) and stolen bases (54) to become only the third player in major league history to have 25 or more homers and 50 or more stolen bases in a single season.

◆ his 26 homers were the most by a Cub second baseman since Rogers Hornsby hit 39 in 1929.

◆ his 54 steals were the most by a Cub since Frank Chance stole 57 in 1906 and represented the club record for steals by a 2nd baseman.

◆ stole home for the fourth time in his career on May 20 against Cincinnati.

◆ was 11-for-11 in SB vs. Montreal.

◆ made his second All-Star Game appearance.

◆ batted just .192 in April (14-for-73) with 2 homers and 3 RBI.

◆ had only 4 extra-base hits and 2 RBI in first 17 games covering 69 at-bats.

◆ in his first 17 games in May he raised his average to .257.

◆ hit safely in 24 of 26 games in May batting .308 with 11 steals.

◆ was named National League Player of the Week for the period June 24-June 30.

◆ during that week he batted .500 (13-for-26) with 2 homers, 4 RBI.

◆ July was his best month offensively, batted .355 with 6 homers and 20 RBI and added 10 stolen bases.

◆ hit safely in 22 of the 27 July games.

◆ was moved from the No. 2 spot in the batting order into the No. 3 position on a daily basis beginning August 12.

◆ prior to that date he appeared in 101 games and was batting .293 with 15 homers and 41 RBI.

◆ in the final 52 games of the season he hit .332 with 11 homers and 42 RBI.

◆ had his only 2-homer game of the season on August 21 at Atlanta...also had a season-high 6 RBI in that game.

◆ went over the .300 mark for the first time on August 30 (.302) and never dipped below .300 after that point.

◆ Ryne also hit very well in September, batting .347 with 5 homers and 20 RBI along with 13 stolen bases.

◆ had 10 multi-hit games and hit safely in 21 of 27 games in September.

◆ led the club in at-bats (609), runs scored (113), hits (186), total bases (307), triples (6), homers (26) and steals (54).

◆ was second in doubles with 31 and in average among regulars at .305.

◆ after May 1 Ryne hit .321 (172-for-536) with 24 homers and 80 RBI in 140 games.

◆ Ryne batted .281 with runners in scoring position.

◆ with the Cubs either tied or trailing by 3 or less runs after the fifth inning, Ryne hit .347.

◆ he hit .450 in the same game situation with runners in scoring position.

◆ besides 10 game-winning hits, contributed 14 game-tying hits.

◆ six of the game-tying hits came in the seventh inning or later.

◆ defensively, Ryne had a fielding percentage of .986.

◆ committed 12 errors in 865 total chances.

◆ he had a 48-game errorless streak from August 3 through September 25.

1984 Season in Review

Ryne received numerous postseason awards including the league's Most Valuable Player Award and *The Sporting News*' Player of the Year award...became the fifth Cub and the first since Ernie Banks in 1959 to win the MVP...earned a Gold Glove at second base for the second straight season, becoming the first Cub to repeat at one position since shortstop Don Kessinger was honored in 1969 and 1970.

◆ batted .314 in 156 games in 1984, the fourth highest average in the league.
◆ his 200 hits were second in the league to San Diego's Tony Gwynn and the most by a Cub since Bill Buckner collected 201 in 1982.
◆ led the league in runs scored with 114 and tied Philadelphia's Juan Samuel for the league lead in triples with 19.
◆ also tied Samuel for third in doubles with 36.
◆ his .520 slugging percentage was third in the league behind Dale Murphy of Atlanta (.547) and Philadelphia's Mike Schmidt (.536).
◆ Sandberg had 331 total bases, one behind league-leader Murphy. The last second baseman to lead the league in total bases was Rogers Hornsby (409) in 1929.
◆ had a career-high 19 homers, the most by a Cubs second baseman since Hornsby had 40 in 1929.
◆ also set career highs in runs scored, hits, doubles, triples, average and at-bats.
◆ Ryne narrowly missed becoming the first player in baseball history to have 200 or more hits plus 20 or more doubles, triples, homers and stolen bases in the same season. He finished 1 homer and 1 triple shy.
◆ became the first Cub second baseman since Billy Herman in 1935 to have more than 70 extra-base hits in a season.
◆ he was second in the club in stolen bases to Bobby Dernier (45).
◆ swiped 32 in 39 attempts (82%).

- committed 6 errors in 870 chances for a league-leading fielding percentage among second basemen of .9932.
- led the majors in total chances (870) and assists (550) for the second straight season.
- he also had the longest errorless streak for a N.L. second baseman—61 games from June 29 to September 6.
- had an 18-game hitting streak (.421, 32-76) from April 24 through May 16, the longest streak of his major league career...had 10 multi-hit games in the streak, including 6 straight and three straight 3-hit games.
- collected his 100th hit June 27 to become the second player in the league to reach that level.
- was the first to score 100 runs on September 1 at Atlanta.
- had one of the greatest single games in baseball history on June 23 at Wrigley Field in leading the Cubs back from a 7-1 deficit against the St. Louis Cardinals. The Cubs rallied to beat the Cards 12-11 before a national television audience...went 5-for-6 with 2 homers and 7 RBI...with the Cubs trailing 9-8, Sandberg led off the ninth inning with a homer off Bruce Sutter...after the Cardinals scored a pair of runs in the 10th inning, Sandberg hit a two-out, two-run homer off Sutter to tie the game again.
- earned first All-Star start...singled in the game at Candlestick Park in San Francisco...hit the All-Star break with a major league high 118 hits.
- had his most productive month just prior to the break when he was named the National League's Player of the Month for June by hitting .376 with 8 homers and 21 RBI.
- hit .366 in August...batted .368 in the NLCS against San Diego, second in the club to Jody Davis' .389.

1983 Season in Review

Ryne earned the first Gold Glove of his career and became the first player in National League history to win a Gold Glove in his first season at a new position. He was the first Cub to win a Gold Glove since 1970 when shortstop Don Kessinger was honored.

◆ led all National League second basemen in fielding percentage (.986), games played at the position (157), assists (571), double plays (126) and total chances (914).

◆ Ryne did play shortstop for an inning as a defensive replacement.

◆ he was second in the club in hits (165) and games played (158).

◆ led the club in runs scored (94) for the second straight year...also led in stolen bases with 37 and official at-bats (633)...the 37 steals represented the most stolen bases by a Cubs second baseman since Johnny Evers stole 46 in 1907.

◆ hit the first grand slam of his career on May 31 when he connected off Houston's Frank LaCorte.

◆ batted .312 with runners in scoring position, second among regulars to Leon Durham (.313)...with runners in scoring position and less than two outs he batted .367...Ryne scored runners from third with less than two outs 71 percent of the time (17 of 24).

1982 Season in Review

Ryne was selected Chicago Rookie of the Year by Chicago Baseball Writers Association of America.

◆ after a 1-for-32 start, he finished with a .271 average, reaching a season high on August 12 (.276).

◆ was second on the team with 33 doubles and 32 stolen bases.

◆ led the team with 103 runs scored, becoming the first Cub since 1978 to score more than 100 runs (DeJesus, 104)…103 runs scored also established a team record for runs scored by a rookie, breaking the 50-year mark set by Hall of Famer Billy Herman in 1932.

◆ Ryne's 32 stolen bases also broke the team mark for steals by a third baseman. Harry Steinfelt's record of 29 had stood since 1906.

◆ from May 7 to September 1, Ryne played in 105 games and failed to hit safely in two straight games only twice during that stretch.

◆ during a 43-game stretch dating from July 16 to September 1, Ryne batted .298 and scored 33 runs…had a 10-game hitting streak during that period, his longest hitting streak of the season.

◆ began season as a third baseman and committed 11 errors in 140 games. He moved to second base on September 3, playing there most of the month.

◆ became the first Cub to steal home since Rodney Scott (June 6, 1978) on July 17 against the Braves and pitcher Bob Walk.

◆ connected for two homers in one game against Pittsburgh on April 23. Both homers came off Eddie Solomon…the homers were his first two in the major leagues.

◆ was the best Cub at advancing runners in scoring position with less than two outs, being successful on 43 of 76 opportunities…was also the best at advancing runners on first with one or less outs (33-for-74)…had one stretch when he stole 15 bases in 17 attempts.

Index